UNDERSTANDING THE BIBLE

A Basic Introduction to Biblical Interpretation

REVISED & EXPANDED EDITION

George T. Montague, SM

PAULIST PRESS
New York/Mahwah, NJ

Cover and book design by Lynn Else

Library of Congress Cataloging-in-Publication Data

Montague, George T.
    Understanding the Bible : a basic introduction to biblical interpretation / George T. Montague. — Rev. & expanded ed.
        p.   cm.
    Includes bibliographical references (p.   ).
    ISBN 978-0-8091-4344-3 (alk. paper)
    1. Bible—Hermeneutics. 2. Bible—Criticism, interpretation, etc.—History. I. Title.
    BS476.M58 2007
    220.601—dc22
                                                            2007000047

Published by Paulist Press
997 Macarthur Boulevard
Mahwah, New Jersey 07430

www.paulistpress.com

Printed and bound in the
United States of America

Contents

Introduction

Welcome to the fascinating world of hermeneutics—the science or the art (which is it?) of interpretation. In Greek mythology Hermes was the god who served as herald and messenger of other gods. Usually depicted with winged shoes and hat, he had the mission of telling the listener what the other gods had to say and, implicitly, what they *meant* to say. Hermes was believed to have invented speech and language, hence the skill of communication, a broad term for hermeneutics, which in more congenial terms we call *interpretation*. Without knowing the name, we have as human beings been engaged in hermeneutics virtually from birth. Without adverting to the process, we quickly learned the meaning of a smile. If we got a role in a school play, we became a hermeneut when we offered our own interpretation of the character we were playing. When someone said something we didn't understand, we asked, "What do you mean?" We were asking for an interpretation.

When we began to read, we often wondered what a text meant. Perhaps it was an unfamiliar word in the text that stumped us. Or a sentence that seemed misplaced. Or a reference to a story that we had never heard. We needed an interpreter—or, if we had the tools at hand, like a dictionary or an encyclopedia, we could get into the process ourselves.

This book deals with the more restricted field of biblical hermeneutics. The process of interpreting the Bible is not unlike the general process of hermeneutics—we begin by wondering what a text means and then we pursue the avenues that will lead us to understand it. But the Bible is also in a class by itself, because not only is it making statements—it is also addressing us as readers with the expectation of a response that changes our lives. So in the Bible more than any other literature the question is not only "What is the text saying?" but "What is it saying *to me?* What claim is it making upon my life?" And, although the next question really goes beyond interpretation, we ask, "Do I want to accept what it says? Do I want to let it convert me or not?"

I once heard a priest begin his sermon this way: "I have two problems in giving a sermon. The first problem is getting into it." Then, after a dramatic pause: "The second problem is getting out of it." The problem that faces many persons, especially students, for whom hermeneutics is an uncharted universe, is how to get into it. The literature is vast, and bibliographies abound. But often beginning students find themselves plopped into a head-spinning conversation without a clue even to the language that is being spoken. What they need is a tool that will make hermeneutics "learner-friendly." I offer this book to fulfill that need.

This book is an introduction. The philosophical and theological questions that underlie much of contemporary hermeneutics are hardly understandable without knowing how we got to where we are. For we are not the first ones to have grappled with the question of meaning or the process of discovering it in texts that are removed from our time and culture. To paraphrase Chesterton, if we can see farther than those who went before us, it's because we are standing on the shoulders of giants. Thus, by leading the student through the major stages and the principal theorists and practitioners of biblical hermeneutics, we hope to give him or her an experience not unlike the climbing of a mountain. From the humble horizon at the foot of the mountain we gain an ever broader vista as we climb, and when we reach the crest we see our earlier discoveries balanced by the perspective of the whole. We also see perhaps where false paths led, from which we had to retrace our steps or find another way out. And even as we stand surveying the past we realize we are not at the end, for the path leads on.

In the first chapter of this book we begin with a biblical text as an example, noting the questions that arise as we read it. Then in succeeding chapters we see how the biblical authors themselves grappled with some of those questions and then how the postbiblical interpreters and theorists did so right up to our day. Our penultimate chapter is a study of the most authoritative church document of the twentieth century on biblical interpretation, the Constitution on Divine Revelation of Vatican Council II *(Dei Verbum)*. Finally, we conclude with discussion questions on *The Interpretation of the Bible in the Church*, published by the Pontifical Biblical Commission in 1993, a document we assume the reader will have in hand.

Pertinent bibliographical references are provided in the notes for those students who wish to pursue questions further (or professors who want their students to do so!). Also, should the professor or the student wish to pursue an exercise using the various hermeneutical methods, an outline for such a project is provided in the appendix.

In writing this book I was helped not only by the authors I read but by several colleagues at St. Mary's University who reviewed the manuscript: Rev. Charles Miller, SM, Dr. Glen Hughes, Professor Michael Ariens of the School of Law, and especially Dr. James Sauer, Professor of Philosophy, whose comments, especially on the philosophical sections and the Reformation were very helpful. For their help I am deeply grateful. However, I accept full responsibility for the final text.

Welcome to the journey!

A Note on the Revised and Expanded Edition

This edition contains notable changes and additions. Bearing in mind that the book may have two audiences, the general reader on the one hand, and students on the other, I have organized the book in a way I believe more helpful to both by dividing it into two parts: the road already traveled, which discusses how our predecessors have struggled with the question of biblical interpretation, and the road ahead, the challenges that lie before us. In this second part I have organized the various hermeneutical methods used today. Ideally, the road already traveled should be taken first, as written, but in the academic time constraints of a semester, a professor may wish to get the students started earlier on a paper applying the different methods to a gospel passage. I suggest an outline for such a project in the appendix. I have found that taking a gospel passage myself first and illustrating how each method could be used to interpret the text helps the students understand better what is expected of them.

I have added a section on Jewish methods of interpretation in chapter 2, a section on historical criticism in chapter 10, a complete revision and expansion of the chapter on "Community and Canon" (chapter 12), and a totally new chapter on the spiritual senses (chapter 13). A comparison with legal hermeneutics, formerly in a note, has been expanded and moved into the text of chapter 11. In the first edition the references to De Lubac's work on medieval exegesis were given from the French original, his four-volume *Exégèse Médiévale*. Since two of these volumes have now appeared in English, I have referenced the English version where it was available; otherwise references are to the French original. Bibliography has been updated in the notes.

ONE

Questions

Nearly everything this book deals with can be illustrated by examining a single scripture passage, the story of Philip encountering the Ethiopian on the road to Gaza (Acts 8:26–38):

²⁶*Then the angel of the Lord spoke to Philip, "Get up and head south on the road that goes down from Jerusalem to Gaza, the desert route." So he got up and set out.* ²⁷*Now there was an Ethiopian eunuch, a court official of the Candace, that is, the queen of the Ethiopians, in charge of her entire treasury, who had come to Jerusalem to worship,* ²⁸*and was returning home. Seated in his chariot, he was reading the prophet Isaiah.* ²⁹*The Spirit said to Philip, "Go and join up with that chariot."* ³⁰*Philip ran up and heard him reading Isaiah the prophet and said, "Do you understand what you are reading?"* ³¹*He replied, "How can I, unless someone instructs me?" So he invited Philip to get in and sit with him.* ³²*This was the scripture passage he was reading:*

"Like a sheep he was led to the slaughter,
 and as a lamb before its shearer is silent,
 so he opened not his mouth.
³³ *In [his] humiliation justice was denied him.*
 Who will tell of his posterity?
 For his life is taken from the earth."

³⁴*Then the eunuch said to Philip in reply, "I beg you, about whom is the prophet saying this? About himself or about someone else?"* ³⁵*Then Philip opened his mouth and, beginning with this scripture passage, he*

1

proclaimed Jesus to him. ³⁶*As they traveled along the road they came to some water, and the eunuch said, "Look, there is water. What is to prevent my being baptized?"* [37] ³⁸*Then he ordered the chariot to stop, and Philip and the eunuch both went down into the water, and he baptized him.*

This well-known story is an illustration of biblical interpretation. "Do you *understand* what you are reading?" is the fundamental hermeneutical question. "How can I unless someone instructs me?" is the admission of the reader's need of help. The Ethiopian obviously understands the words but not to what or to whom they refer (what is called the *referent*). More than that, he does not yet understand what the text means *for him*. As the story unfolds, we see that it will become for the official the source of a life-changing experience. But that is the climax of a process. From this story we learn several of the dynamics any reader experiences in trying to understand a passage of scripture.

1. The royal official is reading a text. He is not listening to someone preach or teach, nor is he engaged in conversation with a living person. If such were the case, he could understand much of the speaker's meaning immediately, or he could ask questions of clarification, as the scribe did of Jesus in Luke 10:25–37. And the speaker could check the accuracy of the listener's understanding.

The official is not even listening to a text being read. He is reading it himself. Had someone been reading it to him, he might have caught some clues at least to the *reader's* understanding of the text by the reader's inflection, his facial expressions, his pauses, and so on. In some cases of oral reading these helps are sufficient to make clear the meaning. But in the official's case the meaning remains obscure.

The first thing we can note about interpretation is that the context of one's encounter with the word differs considerably depending on whether the communication is oral or written.

2. The fact that he is reading from a copy of the scriptures is extraordinary, because every text of the scriptures in those days was handwritten, on papyrus or parchment. While copies were kept in synagogues, only the wealthy would have sufficient means

to have their own copies. The eunuch's possession of a copy testifies to his access to wealth. Why not? He was a chief official of the queen. But such personal copies were rare indeed. We are centuries away from the printing press and even farther from electronic media.

3. The fact that he can read at all puts him in the educated minority of the ancient world—a very small minority. Most people depended on scribes and other learned people to read for them and to read to them. Or to write their letters, for that matter. Even in some underdeveloped countries today you will find persons sitting in the street with a pen or typewriter ready to write a letter for those who cannot read or write. They make their living as scribes. Such a situation was everyday fare in biblical times. This means that the culture of those days was much more oral than ours. What writing there was, aside perhaps from merchants' records, was a help to oral communication. The meaning of life, especially its religious meaning, was found in ways other than writing. There were pilgrimages and festivals, like the one from which the official is now returning. There were processions, music, songs, dancing, dramatic reenacting of the mysteries of salvation. The liturgies were thus a primary interpreter of meaning. Later Christians would add sacred art and drama to the instruments of interpretation.

Every participant, every dancer, every artist no doubt had his or her own interpretation of the event. But there were also recognized authoritative interpreters. The Jewish people, like other peoples of those times, depended on scribes and priests to interpret the meaning of the rituals, the festivals, and the traditions that they celebrated. The Ethiopian official appears to recognize in Philip one such authoritative interpreter. The authoritative interpreters, however, did not feel free to interpret arbitrarily. They felt bound by a tradition preceding them.

4. The official assumes that in the text there is a meaning intended by the writer, and he wants to find it. He does not just paste any personal interpretation on the text. This text probably had special significance for him because of the words, "Who will tell of his posterity?" As a eunuch the official was incapable of posterity. Belonging to a culture that prized progeny, he longed to

find what this deprivation might mean for his life. Thus we see in this reader both a concern for the original author's intention but also a very great concern for meaning in the historical circumstances of his own life. Is the reader capable of finding more meaning in the text than the author put there? The author was probably not referring to a eunuch at all, but this eunuch sees an application of the text to his own considerably different situation. Is finding such a "surplus of meaning" in the text (to borrow a term we discuss later) justified? This is an intriguing question to which we return in detail later in this book.

5. The official needs help in interpreting this particular passage. Had the passage been less obscure the task might have been easier. If he were reading, "Thou shalt not kill," he would hardly have needed an interpreter to know that the Bible here is forbidding murder. Or if he had read, "You shall love the Lord your God with your whole heart," the meaning would have been rather clear. But this is one of many scripture passages that remain obscure, and thus the Ethiopian asks, "How can I know what I'm reading unless someone shows me?"

6. The help comes from a Hellenistic Jewish Christian. Philip actually belongs to three worlds. First, he is a *Jew*. The whole Jewish tradition has fashioned his outlook on the world. That tradition includes the Law, the Prophets, and the Writings, as well as other elements of his culture and tradition that form his "world." Hence, he is familiar with the text of Isaiah that the official has been reading. But he is a *Hellenistic* Jew, a Greek-speaking Jew, and that means that the primary channel through which he has received the Jewish tradition was not Hebrew but Greek. His was the Septuagint Bible, a Greek translation begun some 250 years earlier and part of a broader phenomenon of Jewish Hellenization with its greater openness to the gentile world than was the case in the Aramaic-speaking communities of Jerusalem. But most significant of all, Philip is a *Christian,* and that means he has come to believe that Jesus Christ is the fulfillment of all that the Old Testament pointed to. Jesus, in his teaching, his life, his death and resurrection, and in his sending of the Holy Spirit, "crystallized" the diverse elements of Philip's world that until then were floating around in his consciousness. Hence, Philip's interpretation is distinct. He stands

apart from the non-Christian Jewish community who do not see Jesus as the fulfillment of the Isaian passage. He is convinced, of course, that his interpretation is the right one—an interpretation with which Christians today would likewise agree.

7. This points to another question: Is interpretation a "given" or is it a "choice"? In the Ethiopian's story we just noted that Philip's interpretation was not the only *possible* interpretation of the text. And if we look back from where Christians stand today to the earliest beginnings of religious interpretation, we can see that we stand in a stream that is the result of hundreds of choices made earlier by our interpretive forebears. Abraham chose to follow the interpretation of his life given him by the Lord rather than remain in the polytheism of the Chaldeans. After leading the people into the promised land, Joshua urged the people to choose the Lord rather than the Canaanite gods that surrounded them. Jeremiah's interpretation of the events of his day differed radically from the king's sycophant counselors. The voices of the prophets ultimately prevailed over the attractions that the sensuous Canaanite cult had on the masses. Jesus' interpretation of the Old Testament differed in many ways from that of the scribes of his day. And church councils have made interpretative choices about the meaning of the scriptures right down to our day. The conclusion, then, is that interpretation is a choice. Is there any kind of control upon the choices to be made? Are there any guidelines, any parameters given by the text or available outside the text that would assure us we have chosen the right interpretation, or that our interpretation is at least "in the ball park" of truth? What keeps choices from being merely arbitrary? Believers hold that interpretation should be an informed choice made under the light of the Holy Spirit and faithful to the revelation already given. But what that means in detail remains to be seen.

8. What does Luke mean when he writes that Philip, "*beginning with this scripture passage,* proclaimed Jesus to him"? What did "beginning with this scripture passage" involve? In Luke's mind, did Philip mean to say that the prophet Isaiah was actually thinking about Jesus as Philip came to know Jesus? Was Isaiah thinking about Jesus at all? And if he was, in what sense? How specifically did he, in that distant time, prophesy? Or was Philip

5

just using the text as a "jumping-off point," his real interest being more in telling the official about Jesus than in interpreting the original author's intention? In other words, what were Philip's assumptions about the relationship of the text and its author? And about the relation of both to the Jesus that Philip proclaimed?

9. Then there is Luke himself, the author of this story. What are his assumptions? What "world" is he coming from? He is not a Jew, not even a Hellenistic Jew. He is a learned Greek. And what is his purpose is relating this story? How does it fit into his overall work, first of the Acts and then of the combined work of the Gospel and the Acts?

10. One of the judgments of our forebears was that not only Luke-Acts but twenty-six other books would take their place alongside it in a collection we call the New Testament, itself contextualized by reference to the Old Testament. Did this passage assume any further meaning by reason of the church's placing it along with the other books?

11. That brings it down to us. We come to the text, we the contemporary readers or listeners. What do we hear when we read or listen to this text? Luke was obviously writing for anyone who would care to read his work. What appeal is he making to the reader in this story? Is he asking the reader to do anything? The text itself, read in the light of Luke's double work, gives clues to answer those questions. But can the text answer the new and unique questions that come from our contemporary world? We live in the world of space travel and instant communication by satellite. Our world is a global village. We have more information than we know what to do with. Christianity is split into hundreds of denominations. We know more about psychology than the ancients did. What happens when the "horizon" of the ancient text meets our "horizon" today?

12. There is, of course, no *one* contemporary world. Anyone who has traveled to India or Africa or China knows that we don't have to return to misty bygone ages to find a different world. There are different worlds cohabiting our planet today. And each of those worlds has its own story, its own culture, its own values, its own hopes and struggles. Do those elements affect the process of interpretation? Would the text mean something different to a

Zulu than to the chief executive officer of an American corporation? And if so, can we speak about "objectivity" in the text at all?

13. Finally, Christians read this text as the inspired word of God. What does this dimension add to the discussion? How does it differ from the linguist's reading, the historian's reading, the sociologist's or the psychologist's reading? If Christians believe that God is the author of the text, is God's meaning coextensive with the author's meaning as embodied in the text? What assurance do we have that the interpretation we come up with is the meaning God had in mind? Is there one meaning or several meanings? And what does this have to say if and when this text is brought into a discussion not just of inspirational interpretation (such as one might get in prayer) but of doctrine? And is there any difference between our private reading of the text and our hearing it in the context of the liturgy?

Our purpose in this introduction is not to answer all these questions, only to pose them. For they are the questions of hermeneutics, the science of interpretation. One hopes the number of questions has not made the student/reader a cynical agnostic from the start but only provided a whetting of appetite. There *are* answers to these questions. The rest of this book wrestles with them.

Part 1

THE ROAD ALREADY TRAVELED

TWO

The Bible Interprets the Bible

Event and Interpretation

Because this book focuses on the interpretation of the Bible,[1] it is possible to think of interpretation solely in terms of interpreting a *text*. Most of our experiences in life, however, are not textual. We are constantly interpreting the ongoing events of our lives, for the drive to understand is endemic to being human. We want to arrive at truth that is not merely accumulation of knowledge but the reality of life and *our* life. Sometimes a distinction is made between the *report* of an event and its *interpretation*. But every report is already an interpretation. Even an eyewitness's *perception* of an event does not wholly capture the event, as we know from the fact that several eyewitnesses will give complementary versions of the same event. Even more so is this true of a report, though if it is the report of an eyewitness who is trustworthy, reasonable people will judge his testimony credible. Still, every report is selective and at least to that extent an interpretation. Thus it is difficult in practice to distinguish event and interpretation. For an uninterpreted event is an event without meaning, for meaning is constituted by relationship. We explore this dimension of life at greater length later. For the moment, suffice it to say that biblical interpretation is, for those who care to do it, a specialized function of the universal human search for meaning. What is proper to biblical interpretation is that it is the search for meaning in a *text* and a text that is itself someone else's the biblical author's) interpretation of one or more events or traditions or texts.

The Bible illustrates all these dimensions of interpretation. It is an interpretation of *events*, often events that have already been interpreted by a prior tradition, whether oral or written. The events at issue are the events of Israel's history. Unlike the gods of some other world religions, Israel's God revealed himself in actions on the stage of history. Israel's most ancient creed (or cultic anamnesis) was a recitation of historical events:

> My father was a wandering Aramean who went down to Egypt with a small household and lived there as an alien. But there he became a nation great, strong and numerous. When the Egyptians maltreated and oppressed us, imposing hard labor upon us, we cried to the LORD, the God of our fathers, and he heard our cry and saw our affliction, our toil and our oppression. He brought us out of Egypt with his strong hand and outstretched arm, with terrifying power, with signs and wonders, and bringing us into this country, he gave us this land flowing with milk and honey. Therefore, I have now brought you the first fruits of the products of the soil which you, O LORD, have given me. (Deut 26:5–10)

The event of the exodus has left no trace in the annals of secular history or even of Egypt's religious history, but Israel interpreted it as the major act of deliverance by its God, the Lord. It laid the foundation for the covenant of Sinai, giving the Lord the right to expect certain things of this people whom he had claimed as his own. The great festival of Passover celebrated—and interpreted—this event every year. And the Bible recorded that interpretation. The exodus was not merely a fortunate escape of an oppressed people. It was a call and an act of deliverance by a God who promised this people a brilliant future.

Joshua and subsequent priests and prophets told and retold the story of the exodus, and they also read the ongoing events of their people's history in the light of that event and the covenant that sealed it. Their history was either blessing for their fidelity to the covenant or chastisement for their infidelity. Prime examples would be Jeremiah's famous temple sermon (Jer 7), or Ezekiel's allegory of the faithless spouse (Ezek 16). The future was conditional: "*If you listen to my voice and keep my covenant...*" (Exod 19:5). This connecting of past, present, and future, conditioned by covenant observance, was a process of interpretation.

The Future: Past and Present Reinterpreted

Because of the covenant promise, conditional though it was in its Mosaic form, Israel was pointed to a future.[2] As the years passed, the hopes and expectations about that future grew. The institutions of Israel, such as the covenant, the king, the temple, and the cult, were projected toward a grandiose future. Thus Jeremiah would prophesy a new covenant (Jer 31:31–34); Isaiah would foretell the coming of the perfect king ruling over the perfect kingdom (Isa 7, 9, 11); Ezekiel would dream of the new temple and the new Jerusalem in majestic detail (Ezek 40–48) and Malachi of a new and purified priesthood (Mal 3:3–4). Not only the institutions but the events of the past would be repeated on an even greater scale. Second Isaiah announces the return from exile as an expanded replay of the Exodus (Is 43; 44:26–27; 51:9–11), even as a new creation (45:11–13). When read in tandem with Ezekiel 28:11–19, even the account of man's creation and fall in Genesis 2:4b:3–24 looks more like a program for the ultimate perfection to which all peoples are called. Or, as the Germans, proverbial inventors of catchphrases, have it: *Urzeit ist Endzeit*— primordial time is really a description of end-time. The ideal past, now lost, is a portrait of the ideal future.

Three successive chapters of Isaiah brilliantly illustrate the thrust and the complexity of this process of interpretation. A common opinion among biblical scholars today is that the prophecies in chapters 7, 9, and 11 of Isaiah are a progressive refinement of Messianic hope. In chapter 7, Isaiah confronts the faithless king Ahaz, whose kingdom is threatened by attack from the north. He is wavering in his faith in the Lord, having immolated his own son in fire-sacrifice (2 Kgs 16:3), a practice condemned by the Law and the prophets. Isaiah, wishing to win Ahaz back to faith in Yahweh, invites Ahaz to ask the Lord for any sign he wants to prove that the Lord will stand by his promise to protect and bless the Davidic king. When Ahaz hypocritically says he will not tempt the Lord by asking for a sign, Isaiah tells him the Lord will give him a sign of his own choosing: the *almah,* Ahaz's young bride Abi, will conceive and bear a son and name him Emmanuel, "God with us" (Isa 7:14). In other words, the promises made to David and his line, which Ahaz should have enjoyed, are now going to be transferred to the new king, whose conception and birth the prophet announces.

When the child is born and named Hezekiah, Isaiah sings lyrically of the future of this child and the kingdom he will rule. The Davidic promises will be realized in him:

> The people who walked in darkness have seen a great light....Every boot that tramped in battle, every cloak rolled in blood, will be burned as fuel for flames. For a child is born to us, a son is given us; upon his shoulder dominion rests. They call him Wonder-Counselor God-Hero, Father-Forever, Prince of Peace. (Isa 9:1–6)

However, Isaiah's dream of the perfect king was shattered when, toward the end of his reign, Hezekiah began to ally himself with Egypt, the ancient oppressor of Israel. But the promises were still there, and Isaiah was convinced they would be fulfilled, if not now, then at some future time. Thus he looked to a distant king on whom the spirit of the Lord would truly rest, one who would institute the kingdom of justice and faithfulness, where the wolf would be guest of the lamb and the leopard lie down with the kid (Isa 11:1–9). And it was probably in the light of this final Messianic picture that the prophet reread his earlier oracles. The oracles were true, the promises were available, but the kings did not live up to them. Result: they are transferred to the future.

We see here a process, even within the prophet himself, of reinterpretation as well as projection to the future. The future builds on the past, both in continuity and discontinuity. Continuity in the sense that it will be a Davidic king fulfilling the promises made to his ancestor David. Discontinuity in that for once the king will be the kind of leader through which the Lord can fulfill his promises.

Reinterpreting Texts for the Present

This process is what Northrop Frye has called the power of the Bible to recreate itself. This interpretation of the past was oral at first, but it was eventually committed to written form. Although sometimes the Bible simply quotes a text to establish the truth it wishes to convey (for example, 2 Kings 14:5–6 quotes Deuteronomy 24:16), in various places in the Bible we find previous texts rewritten to highlight their relevance for the contemporary scene. This can happen subtly by way of literary allusion, as when Isaiah 51:3–6 uses words from earlier texts of Isaiah 2:2–4 and Micah 4:1–4—the reader would do well to compare these texts and underline the similarities. At other times scholars have detected the hand of a scribe who inserted a correction or an interpretation into the text itself. For example, 1 Kings 15:5 begins by praising King David: "David had pleased the Lord and did not disobey any of his commands as long as he lived." The Septuagint (LXX) stops there, but the Hebrew text adds, "except in the case of Uriah, the Hittite." Scholars suspect that a scribe, aware of the scathing condemnation of David's sin in 1 Kings 11–12, inserted that qualification.

But sometimes the changes are more drastic. Thus Deuteronomy 1:19–36 rewrites Numbers 13:1–14:44, and the chronicler rewrites the major stories of the tradition to show their meaning for the community of his day (1–2 Chr). The Wisdom of Solomon (for example chapters 11–19) and Sirach (44–50) do the same.[3] The apocalyptic writers, like the author of Daniel, loved to find hidden meaning in older biblical texts. Thus the seventy years that Jeremiah prophesied for the length of the Babylonian captivity are reinterpreted as seventy weeks of years in order to show that the conditions of the earlier captivity are still being experienced by the Jews under their Greek oppressors (Dan 9:1–27).

What is going on here? The events of the past set the pattern and foretell greater events to come. And contemporary events are understood to be a replay of the past events, not in the Greek cyclical view of history but rather in the sense of fulfillment of a promise that was latent or explicit in events or words that went before. If event takes on meaning only in relationship, then the past *must* be related to the present. The New Testament sees this process coming to fulfillment in Christ. He is the new Adam (Rom 5:12–21; 1 Cor 15:45–49); the Passover lamb (Exod 12; 1 Pet 1:18–19; Rev 12:11; John 19:36; 1 Cor 5:7); the establisher of the new covenant (Luke 2:20); the true vine (Isa 5:1–7; John 15:1–10); the propitiatory (Lev 16:15–16; Rom 3:25); the new and eternal David (2 Sam 7:11–16; Luke 1:32–33); the rock from which the waters flow (Num 20:7–11; 1 Cor 10:4); the great high priest like Melchizedek (Heb throughout); the good shepherd (Ezek 34:23–24; John 10:14) the prophet like Moses (Deut 18:15; Acts 3:22); the new and final temple (John 2:13–21). In Matthew's Gospel Jesus makes two astounding statements: he has come not to abrogate the Law but to fulfill it (Matt 5:17) and not only did the prophets prophesy but the Law itself did—that is, it pointed beyond itself (Matt 11:13).

To the New Testament Christians, Jesus is the key to the puzzle of the Old Testament. It's as if suddenly everything that was dreamed of is realized and everything that was obscure becomes clear. In describing the rock in the desert, Paul says the rock *was* Christ (1 Cor 10:4). He does not even say that the rock was a type of Christ. Of course, we can interpret his statement metaphorically. Still Paul, like many of the other New Testament writers, sees Christ himself in the Old Testament institutions, images, and events. Two events, the one past and the other present or future, depend on each other for their ultimate significance.[4]

This same interconnectedness applies to other aspects of fulfillment associated with Christ. The flood becomes a type of baptism (1 Pet 3:20–21); the manna is fulfilled in the Eucharist (John 6:31–51); Jerusalem is the church (Gal 4:26); the sea of the exodus is the baptismal water, the cloud the Holy Spirit (1 Cor 10:1–5), and so on.

The texts that relate those Old Testament events are reread in the light of their fulfillment. Looking back to the Old Testament from the perspective of the New Testament fulfillment justifies combining Old Testament texts at times. For example, Matthew 11:10 combines Exodus 23:20 with Malachi 3:1 and applies the fused text to John the Baptist. This reflects the practice of the writers of the Aramaic Targums in the first century. In copying the Hebrew text, the scribes faithfully transmitted what lay before them, even to the point of copying misspellings; but in the Targums, which were commentaries written into the Aramaic translation, the scribes were very free so as to make a contemporary application.

Paul describes the gospel as the manifestation of the justice of God (Rom 1:17). God's justice here means his fidelity to his covenant promise of salvation. Thus the gospel is not just some new word of salvation. It is the fulfillment of a promise made long ago, a fulfillment for which the entire Old Testament was a preparation. We cannot therefore understand the New Testament at all without entering into the world of the Old Testament. That is why the early church instructed even its gentile converts in the Old Testament.

The psalms, in their composition and reuse, are another illustration of this interpretative process. In most cases we have lost the original historical context in which each psalm was written. Later generations didn't care much about that, because the saving event that was celebrated, or the lament that was expressed in the old psalm did just as well when it came to celebrating a later saving event. Once in a while, of course, a psalmist wrote a "new song" (see Ps 33:3; 40:3; 96:1; 98:1; 144:9; 149:1), but even such songs soon became "old songs," because they were used and reused in new contexts. Instead of writing a new psalm every time there was something to be celebrated, Israel would pull out an old song and sing it—just as we do with our hymnals and even with our national anthem in a multitude of different situations. The idea behind this reuse in the psalms was that the same God was doing the same thing over again. The story was moving forward, but it was just another chapter in the book the Lord was writing.

Theological Presuppositions

When we speak of one *event* typifying another, we must remember that we are discussing an event *as narrated*. Thus Jonah, for example, can be a type of Christ (as in Matt 12:40), even though contemporary scholarship understands the story to be a realistically told dramatic parable rather than one with actual historical reference. Erich Auerbach calls this procedure "figural interpretation," and he notes that temporal progression or interconnectedness (such as intervening historical development) is not necessary, since the two are related in God's plan:

> Figural interpretation establishes a connection between two events or persons in such a way that the first signifies not only itself but also the second, while the second involves or fulfills the first. The two poles of a figure are separated in time, but both, being real events or persons, are within temporality. They are both contained in the flowing stream which is historical life, and only the comprehension, the *intellectus spiritualis,* of their interdependence is a spiritual act.
>
> In this conception, an occurrence on earth signifies not only itself but at the same time another, which it predicts or confirms, without prejudice to the power of its concrete reality here and now. The connection between occurrences is not regarded as primarily a chronological or causal development but as a oneness within the divine plan, of which all occurrences are parts and reflections. Their direct earthly connection is of secondary importance, and often their interpretation can altogether dispense with any knowledge of it.[5]

This process of event-projection and event-interpretation implies a continuity of purpose in Israel's history. It is certainly different from the modern view that sees history as a series of random events due to the percolating of natural causes or human arbitrary choices rather than the purposefulness of some divine plan. At the heart of the biblical view is an understanding of God that supposes several things:

1) God is the creator. The universe in its entirety issues from his will, and he is totally transcendent. He is not subject to the processes of nature but on the contrary is the source of them. As the supreme intelligent being he is the source also of a rational and intelligible order that may be *understood*. The Genesis creation account is a theological interpretation of that intelligible order.

2. God has a plan for the universe and intervenes to achieve it. Despite the currency of chaos theory,[6] even evidence-bound scientists admit to the marvelous design of the universe (the product if not the process); but that there is design to human history is much harder to admit, given the obvious role of human freedom. The presupposition of a God who has a plan and intervenes is rejected even by many who accept that there is a creator. But it is the clear presupposition and repeated affirmation of the Bible.

3. God's plan can be known, at least in its essentials, because he has revealed it within human history. God has revealed himself through the persons and events recounted in the Bible. He is the God of Abraham, the God of Isaac, and the God of Jacob, and ultimately the God of Jesus Christ.

4. Because God pursues a plan that ultimately aims to draw all people to himself, there is a consistency in his guidance and interventions and indeed a pedagogy about them. That is why the Bible can see one event as related to another, one event pointing to and preparing another, and that other event fulfilling a previous event. Biblical history is like an expanding telescope; an earlier event contains and mysteriously produces another like it. Thus we can speak of biblical events as being *open.* They are open to future fulfillment and open to being further understood. Later writers will speak of the earlier events or things being *types* of events and things to come.[7]

Those acquainted with the philosophy of Plato may wonder if this relating of type and fulfillment is just another way of talking about the shadow and the real. There are similarities here with Platonic thought in the sense that two things, one often imperfect, the other perfect, are related. But there are significant differences. Plato considered the material universe to be a shadow of the real world, the world of ideas, which lies above and beyond our sensory perceptions. To oversimplify, Plato thought of the relation as one between a world *here* and a world *there,* spatially, as it were. The Bible sees this relation rather in temporal terms— as between a *now* and a *then,* whether the *then* be past or future. The earlier event or thing is not a shadow but a reality with meaning in itself; but it sets the pattern for a later event or thing that will repeat or improve upon the former both in itself but also as an instrument of revelation, that is, for being *understood*. History therefore is the critical stage on which this process is played out.[8]

All of this supposes that history, sacred history at least, is proceeding according to a plan fashioned by a loving and faithful God. There is a vertical dimension to all human existence that involves a personal relationship to a personal God. Interpretation is reading events in the light of this personal relationship. To put it another way, more in keeping perhaps with our experience, since God has our good at heart and communicates his goodness by successive acts in time, his every gift is also a promise of a greater gift to come. And because of God's consistency, one can glimpse something of the coming gift in the present one. The Bible is a unique instance of this interpretative reading. This is the Bible's implicit and often explicit claim.

This claim, though, raises a lot of questions. Is the Old Testament *nothing but* prophecy or type? Is there any part of the Old Testament that does not point forward to Christ? Does the Old Testament have a value in itself, prior to and independent of Christ? Doesn't the figural interpretation run the risk of depreciating the meaning-in-itself of the earlier event? And by what authority do Christians read the Old Testament differently from the Jewish community, which does not see the scriptures fulfilled in Jesus?

In answer to the last question, the entire Bible is, in the view of Christians, a Christian book. Marcion's view that the Old Testament was opposed to the revelation of Jesus and Paul was never accepted. According to the Gospel of Matthew, Jesus himself accepted the Law and the prophets but brought them to fulfillment by his teaching and by his life. Jesus revised some of the old laws, abrogated others, and in some cases raised the demands he made on his own disciples (see Matt 5–7). The old law was valid, but only according to the interpretation that Jesus gave it. The church followed suit in setting aside certain of the Old Testament prescriptions, notably circumcision and the dietary laws, understanding these to have been only of temporary relevance. There was, then, a selective reading of the Old Testament from the very beginning—or better, a reinterpretive reading, since the church did not excise the passages it no longer considered normative but saw them as tokens of a divine pedagogy that it had now outgrown.

Such is the view of Paul in Galatians when he says the law was the *pedagogue* leading to Christ (Gal 3:24). The Greek pedagogue was not the teacher. He was a slave who escorted the child to school, carrying his books or supplies. Once the child was in the presence of the teacher, the pedagogue's role was finished. The law fulfilled this important but passing role, for now we are in the presence of Christ and justified by faith in him.

Yet all of this is true only in Christian retrospect. Jews today live from the enduring validity of much, if not all, of the Torah. They certainly accept the Ten Commandments and the interpretation given in the Old Testament books of their sacred history. The Orthodox Jews observe even all the dietary laws and many of the other detailed prescriptions of the Law that Reformed Jews no longer find necessary. This shows that the Old Testament can have meaning and give direction to people who are not Christian. Obviously the Christian interpretation of the Bible is not the only possible interpretation, though Christians believe theirs correctly fulfills the Old. This confirms, in an indirect way, what we said earlier about the Old Testament events and things having a meaning in and of themselves and not *merely* as pointing forward to Christ. Theoretically, Christians would maintain that the Ten Commandments would be eternally valid even if Christ had not come.

The fact, though, that the New Testament sees so much of the Christ event foreshadowed in the Old will open the door for an extension of this "typical" kind of interpretation to many other details of the Old Testament in the post–New Testament period, which we see in the next chapter.

Revisionist Interpretation

Not only is Old Testament revelation progressive and forward pointing. It is also at times radically revisionist. Job challenges the blessing-curse theology of Deuteronomy hammered at him by his "friends." Qoheleth challenges the prophetic longing for a better future, saying that it is better to enjoy the present moment and find God there. Exodus 34:7 had said that the punishment for sin extends to the third and fourth generation, but Ezekiel 18 says that only the wicked person will be made to pay for his crime. The earlier prophets proclaimed judgment upon the nations surrounding them, but Jonah, coming toward the end of the prophetic period, hails God's patience and mercy extending salvation to the gentiles.

The New Testament revises much of the Old even in the process of proclaiming its fulfillment. This is most evident in the Sermon on the Mount, particularly in Jesus' command to love one's enemies.[9] But revisionism, or at least reinterpretation, appears in many other places as well. For example, Psalm 8, echoing the creation account in Genesis, had hailed God's making humankind a little less than the angels and putting all things under man's feet, but Hebrews 2:5–9, like Paul elsewhere, realizing that not everything is actually under man's control in this life, inserts into the quotation the words, "for a little while," indicating that Psalm 8 was a divine promise that reaches fulfillment only in Christ. To the devil who invites Jesus to jump from the temple pinnacle by quoting a Psalm verse, Jesus replies, "Scripture also says...."

The biblical texts themselves, therefore, raise the question as to which text has the final word, or is the truth somewhere between the tension of the differing texts? And then who decides which text is the better one or where, between the two positions, the truth lies for a contemporary application? The seeds of future controversies are here, as also the groundwork for what will later be called "canonical criticism."

Translation as Interpretation

The Jewish tradition and scriptures came into contact with other cultures long before the writing of the New Testament. In Alexandria around 250 BC a group of scribes began translating the Hebrew scriptures into Greek, and this work, called the *Septuagint* (after the "seventy" scribes who were presumed to have done the work, abbreviated as LXX), became the Bible for public reading in the synagogues of the Greek-speaking Jews.

While the quality of the translation varies and may at times be more accurate than the extant Hebrew text, the translators experienced what every translator experiences: the constraints of the new language are different from the old. It's as if a metal that was poured into previous molds of a certain size must now be remelted and poured into molds of a different size—some larger, some smaller. For example, in Isaiah 7:14, the text says, "Behold the *almah* will conceive and bear a son...." In Hebrew *almah* means a young woman of marriageable age; it does not necessarily mean virgin. But when the Septuagint translators put the phrase into Greek they chose the Greek word *parthenos*, meaning "virgin" in the more restricted sense.[10] This is the text Matthew would use to speak of the virginal conception of Jesus.[11]

Was this translation accidental, or was there a real theological development at work? Other passages reveal the theological development that was taking place in Judaism, especially in the doctrines of the resurrection and angelology. For example, the Hebrew of Job 42:17 reads, "Then Job died, old and full of years." The LXX adds, "And it is written that he will rise again with those whom the Lord raises up." Or the replacing of the enigmatic *elohim* (God, gods) in Psalm 8:6 with "angels."[12] But it is possible in some cases that the LXX translation is based on a Hebrew text that is earlier than the Massoretic text commonly assumed to be prior.

If we turn to the New Testament a similar phenomenon of Jewish tradition in Greek garb takes place. Jesus spoke Aramaic, yet the Gospels, in fact all of the New Testament books, are in Greek. What happened to the original meaning? It is the meaning of the Greek that the church takes as inspired, not the Aramaic "original," the reconstruction of which would be a good deal of guesswork anyway. Something was lost and something was gained by the recasting of the early tradition into Greek. Lost: For example, in the text, "God can raise up sons (children) to Abraham from these very stones" (Matt 3:9), some scholars have suggested that the reconstructed Aramaic would read for "sons" *banim* and for "stones" *abanim*, an obvious play on words. Gained: In John 3:5, "Unless one be born again of water and the Spirit, he cannot enter the kingdom of God," the Greek word translated here as "again" can also mean "from above." Which meaning was in the evangelist's mind? In a gospel so given to multiple levels of meaning, perhaps the evangelist meant both. In the story of Susanna there is a double pun in Greek, which doesn't work in Hebrew, making it doubtful that the story was translated from the Hebrew.[13]

Casting the gospel tradition into Greek happened long before the Gospels were written, for the Greek-speaking Jewish Christians (Hellenists) must have put the gospel stories and the teachings of Jesus into Greek as soon as they became Christians. Hence the cross-cultural and cross-linguistic process of interpretation was there from earliest hours. It would continue in the next centuries as the gospel, which bore a new message even in Greek, met the Greek world of religion and thought, as we shall see in the next chapter. But the task of interpretation accompanies any attempt to translate from the original into other languages, such as we find in the many English versions today.[14]

The Heritage of Jewish Methods of Interpretation

That the Bible itself requires interpretation was appreciated by the various Jewish interpretive communities in the early pre-Christian and Christian period. Aside from the Septuagint already discussed, there were apocalyptic writings such as Jubilees, 1 Enoch, the Assumption of Moses, 4 Ezra, 2 Baruch, all of which show Essene influence. Study of these documents has been very helpful in illuminating certain passages of the New Testament. 1 Enoch, for example, identifies the "Son of Man" of Daniel with the Messiah. 4 Ezra overlays extensively the image of a mother with the city of Jerusalem, an image already found in the latter part of Isaiah but also figures prominently in the Apocalypse and even in the Gospel of John.

Then there are the Targums, Aramaic commentaries or expansions of the original biblical text to accommodate a contemporary audience. Most of these are post-Christian, but the Targumic method was surely at work in New Testament times. One text from the Targum Neofiti, plausibly dated to the first century, can illustrate the Targumic method. Genesis 1:2 in the Hebrew reads, "A mighty wind (or: the spirit of God) swept over (or hovered over) the waters." Neofiti (1, I, ad loc.) reads, "And a *spirit of love before the Lord* was blowing over the face of the waters." Today the *Living Bible* uses a similar method by writing a commentary or expansive explanation into the text of the Bible itself.

Of great interest to us are the methods revealed in the Dead Sea Scrolls, especially the Pesher commentaries, which we discuss following. And finally, there was the allegorizing method used by Philo of Alexandria.

Following Richard Longenecker,[15] we can distinguish four principal methods of Jewish exegesis.

1. *Literalist.* Beyond simply taking the law at its face value, the interpretation at times is extended in ways even other rabbis considered excessive. For example, the school of Shammai taught that "in the evening all should recline when they recite [the Shema], but in the morning they should stand up, for it is written, 'And when thou liest down and when thou risest up.'"[16]

2. *Midrashic.* A method that goes beyond the literal, to examine the spiritual sense of the scriptures, and to derive meanings that may not be immediately obvious. Eventually seven rules were developed that enabled the interpreter to get at the deeper meanings. Use of these methods can be detected at times in the gospel and Acts,[17] and in Paul. In 2 Corinthians 3:1–4:6, Paul uses one of the seven methods, that of *gezera shava.* He connects passages in which the same word or expression appears to explain one another, even when their individual contexts might suggest something different.[18]

3. *Pesher.* This method, used particularly at Qumran, meant identifying an Old Testament word or reality as a mystery, the meaning of which remained unknown even to the writer but is now revealed, charismatically, as it were, only to the community. Thus,

God told Habakkuk to write down what would happen to the final generation, but He did not reveal to him when that time would come to fulfillment. And as for what He said, *That he who reads may read it speedily*: the interpretation *(pesher)* concerns the Teacher of Righteousness, to whom God made known all the mysteries of the words of His servants the Prophets.[19]

In the Gospels Jesus often speaks Pesher language when he says that certain texts were referring to him: the stone that the builders rejected (Ps 118:22–23); the striking down of the shepherd that scatters the sheep (Zech 13:7); John the Baptist as the messenger of Malachi 3:1 and Isaiah 40:3, where, in Matthew 11:10, Jesus says explicitly, "This is he of whom it is written..."(Matt 11:10). Paul too uses Pesher when, for example, he says that "the rock was Christ" (1 Cor 10:4).

4. *Allegory.* In Alexandria Philo the Jew encountered gentile writers who sought to salvage the unethical parts of the Greek myths by resorting to allegory, and he used this method extensively to make the Jewish scriptures attractive to the gentiles. What is the deeper meaning of the seventh day of creation, the day of rest, Philo asks. Because it is a perfect number, it represents the mind that dominates the unruly passions represented by the other six days.[20] Such an interpretation was calculated to appeal to the Stoic mind, though it is obviously reductionistic, that is, artificially making a biblical passage illustrate a philosophical idea.[21]

Paul uses allegory in Galatians 4:21–31, but we will see it used extensively in the Alexandrians and even in Augustine.

Globalization has brought an increased interest in the Islamic interpretation of the Qur'an, even among Christians, who would be particularly curious about its similarities and differences from the Bible (for example, Mary, the Mother of Jesus, is mentioned more times in the Qur'an than in the New Testament) and the hermeneutics discussed in this book. That is beyond our present focus, but interested readers might start with a book titled *The Bible and the Qur'an*.[22]

What interests us here is the development of the Christian tradition of interpretation, and for that we turn to the patristic period.

THREE

The Wealth of the Word:
The Fathers Interpret the Bible

To speak of the patristic period as "post–New Testament" could be misleading if we envision it as all the writings that occurred after the books in the New Testament were written and compiled.[1] Some of the New Testament books, considered by the church as having apostolic authority, may well have been written *after* the earliest writings of the "fathers." For example, the first letter of Clement of Rome is dated by most authorities around AD 95, while the Second Letter of Peter may well come from the early part of the second century. At that time there was no "New Testament" as we understand it today—a collection of the twenty-seven books beginning with Matthew and ending with the Apocalypse. There were rather individual gospels and letters that circulated and were read as having apostolic, and therefore inspired, authority. But not every church possessed a copy of every book, nor was there universal agreement on which books enjoyed that authority. For example, there was a long hesitation before the Epistle to the Hebrews and the Apocalypse of John were accepted.

So as we enter the second and subsequent centuries we need to be aware of the fluidity that marked this period. Though probably no part of the New Testament was written after AD 125, what exactly constituted the New Testament was not clear. The "Muratorian Fragment" (so called after Ludovico Muratori, who discovered it in 1740) has been commonly dated to the end of the second century (ca. AD 198) as a Roman listing of accepted books, though a recent opinion has suggested that it is a fourth-century Eastern list.[2] A fragment, it begins in mid-sentence and breaks off abruptly at the end. It lists the four Gospels and Acts, the thirteen letters of Paul (excluding Hebrews), Jude, 1 and 2 John, and the

Wisdom of Solomon. It accepts not only the Apocalypse of John but the (now noncanonical) Apocalypse of Peter, though admitting that not everyone in the church accepts the last two. James, 1 and 2 Peter, and 3 John are passed over in silence. Its major concern was to reject books of gnostic, Marcionite, and Montanist origins. This same concern for a canonical listing is found in Eusebius,[3] writing around AD 300. He categorized the books under three headings: (1) books accepted without qualification; (2) disputed books; and (3) heretical books. The disputed books are James, Jude, 2 Peter, 2–3 John, and five other books that no longer belong to our canon: the Acts of Paul, the Shepherd of Hermas, the Apocalypse of Peter, the Epistle of Barnabas, and the Didache. He said that the Apocalypse of John could fall either under the accepted or disputed category.

I have gone into some detail on this issue, which really belongs to the question of canonical interpretation treated later, because it illustrates the fluidity that reigned at this period. If the church was concerned about correct interpretation of the apostolic tradition, it was important to know first of all which witnesses to that tradition were to be trusted. As the churches gradually moved toward a consensus, their very selection of books was an act of interpretation! The role of the church, and the Holy Spirit in the church, was crucial in determining which books she read as the word of God.

Questions They Asked

The questions asked by the writers from the second century onward were little different from our own: How do we find a *now* meaning in a *then* text? How do we as Christians make use of the Old Testament? This was a burning question, especially in the light of Marcion's claim that the Old Testament was of no value to Christians, that only Paul and the New Testament witness should be read and listened to. A gnostic, Marcion made a list of all the "shocking" statements in the Old Testament to justify his rejection of the whole. On another front, Christians in dispute with Jews had to use the Old Testament and thus were obliged to see how the two testaments were related. The question of the relevance of the Old Testament has surfaced in our day in a new way. Some Zionist Jews and some evangelical Christians maintain that God's promises to give his people the land of Canaan still hold and that the modern state of Israel and its claims are the fulfillment of those promises. In response, some Christians, especially among the Palestinians, have maintained that the Old Testament is nothing more than a religious and secular history of a particular people and it has no abiding authority. Latin-rite Patriarch Michel Sabbah addressed this question in a lengthy pastoral letter in November 1993, which merits reading on this particular issue.[4]

The fathers had other questions: How can the Jewish scriptures be understood in Greek culture and thought? How do we apply the gospel to situations not experienced by the writer? How do we deal with problematic passages of the Old Testament, like the incest of Lot's daughters or Abraham's lie to Abimelech? And even when the literal sense is obvious, is there also a deeper meaning available in the text? (Recall that the symbolic process was already at work in the Gospels themselves; for example, John sees in the cure of the man born blind a symbol of baptism.)

Most of the early writers practiced interpretation without theorizing about it. But in the East, the schools of Alexandria and Antioch were major centers of interpretation theory as well as practice. And in the West, Augustine wrote the first comprehensive treatise on Christian hermeneutics.

Clement of Alexandria (185–254): Bridge to the Greeks

Alexandria, whose population has been estimated at three-quarters of a million, was the largest city in the East, rivaled only by Rome in the West. Cosmopolitan, it attracted every philosophical school and religious cult of the ancient world—Greek, Roman, Egyptian, Mesopotamian. It was a major center of gnosticism. Above all, it was a hotbed of intellectual activity, boasting a library of seven hundred thousand volumes, incredible for its day. Here Euclid wrote his famous book on geometry. Home to a substantial Jewish community, it was the base for the Greek translation of the Hebrew Bible beginning around 250 BC. And it was there that Philo the Jew wrote his numerous works.

And there, in the late second century AD, appeared a cultured Greek philosopher and scholar who had converted to Christianity: Clement of Alexandria. With his thorough knowledge of the pagan religions and Greek literature (he cites 348 authors), he was the first to attempt to construct a systematic bridge between the Christian faith and the Greek world. To claim the whole Bible for the church, he attempts to parallel the different levels of biblical interpretation with those of Platonic philosophy. In so doing he speaks of scripture texts as containing a type, a sign, a precept, or a prophecy.[5] Some have seen this statement of Clement as the forerunner of the four senses that became so popular in the Middle Ages, but the text is too obscure for certainty in the matter.[6] What is certain is that Clement makes ample use of allegory in his exegesis. In his commentary on Deuteronomy 22:10, which forbids the yoking of ox and donkey for tilling the soil: "In my view this is an allegory, meaning that we should not share the cultivation of the Logos [Christian community] on equal terms between the pure and the impure, faithful and faithless, as the ox is accounted a clean animal and the donkey unclean [referring to Philo, *On Virtue*, 145]."[7]

Though he repeatedly uses the term *gnosis* and *gnostic* for the perfect Christian, Clement dissociates himself from classical gnosticism and holds to the common tradition of the church: "This gnosis will be advantageous to us, in accord with 'the glorious, majestic norm of tradition' [quoting Clement of Rome, *First Letter to the Corinthians*, 7.2]."[8] He does, however, approach gnosticism when he introduces into the Christian gnosis the knowledge of revelation secretly transmitted from the time of the apostles[9] or hidden in scripture under symbols that only allegorizing exegesis can interpret. This runs close to putting the "gnostic" Christian in opposition to the mere believer.[10] Nevertheless, this pursuit of authentic gnosis leads to *apatheia*, the Stoic ideal[11] and charity.[12]

Clement, like the rest of the fathers, sees biblical interpretation in the service of building up the body. His method is pastoral exegesis and interpretation. He is not interested in the intention of the author as modern historical critics are, but in what immediate relevance the text has for Christian doctrine and practice—and for this, allegory is a quick and ready tool.

Allegory was highly prized in his age. Pagan authors had used it to reinterpret the myths in Homer and Hesiod, in terms that would protect the gods from the accusation of immorality. Apollo's arrows are pestilence; Athena pulling Achilles' hair to check him is an allegory of the hero's state of mind; the gods' plot to bind Zeus is an allegory of the interaction of air and water.[13] In our day Joseph Campbell and others have interpreted the myths in terms of Jungian psychology.

Philo the Jew, as we noted in the previous chapter, while accepting literal historicity of the biblical stories, is always looking for allegorical meanings. This is particularly true when he finds the literal meaning base or unworthy, but he finds even other passages a rich field for hidden meanings. Abraham's migrations, for example, are an allegory of a soul that loves virtue in search of the true God. Circumcision is an outward symbol of the duty of excising passion from our lives (note the appeal to Stoicism here).[14]

Clement may be called the founder of the Alexandrian school of exegesis, but it would be made famous by his successor, Origen.

Origen (185–254): The Old Testament Is Gospel

Whether Origen was a pupil of Clement is not clear. He certainly knows Clement's writings, and he uses the allegorical method extensively, but he differs from Clement in important aspects, especially by giving scant attention to *apatheia,* the Christian version of the Stoic ideal of indifference to pleasure or pain. He is undoubtedly the outstanding and most creative theologian of the East. No single writer would have the impact Origen had on future generations of interpreters in the East or West.

Appointed by his bishop, Demetrius, to be a catechist, Origen operated a school—an activity that reinforced his concern for the spiritual and pastoral sense of the scriptures. But he was also a scholar concerned for textual accuracy. He created the Hexapla, parallels of six texts and translations—the Hebrew text, its Greek transliteration, the Septuagint, and the versions of Aquila, Symmachus, and Theodotion. He did not despise the literal sense. To establish it he draws on history, geography, philosophy, medicine, grammar—what exegetes today call the "auxiliary sciences." Particularly was this important for scripture's moral injunctions, which must be taken to the letter.[15]

> Let no one suspect that we hold that Scripture does not contain real history, or that the precepts of the Law are not to be observed to the letter, or that what is written of the Savior did not happen in reality....Much more numerous are the truly historical passages than those which are to be taken in the purely spiritual sense.[16]

In this he differed from the author of the Epistle of Barnabas, who held that only the spiritual sense, that is, the transferred allegorical sense, was meant by the Old Testament author.[17] Eusebius tells us that Origen took Jesus' instruction about not wearing sandals so literally that he himself went barefoot for several years.[18] In his youthful but misguided zeal, Origen even took literally Jesus' saying about those who make themselves eunuchs for the kingdom (Matt 19:12) and mutilated himself—a practice that in his elder years he violently condemned.[19] Thus he did not deny the inspired character of the literal sense.

But he was keenly aware that to truly understand the text, to hear God speaking a *now* word to the hearer or reader, one needed more than human science. Only if the same Holy Spirit who inspired the writer inspires the reader as well, giving one the mind of Christ, will one rightly interpret the gospel.[20]

> The Scriptures were written under the action of the Spirit of God, and apart from their obvious sense they have another sense, which escapes most people. For what is described there is both the figure of certain mysteries and the image of the divine realities.[21]

33

That which comes from the Spirit is fully understood only through the action of the Spirit.[22]

Another way of putting this is to say that the reader/interpreter must have some experience of the reality revealed in the text if he or she is to understand it at all. Regarding the Gospel of John, Origen dares to say, "No one can understand this gospel, unless he has rested against the breast of Jesus [John 13:23] and taken Mary for his mother [John 19:27]."[23]

Origen, however, does not believe that the interpreting Spirit comes extrinsically, as it were, and certainly he does not believe the interpreter is authorized to impose an arbitrary meaning on the text. Rather the spiritual meaning is hidden in the text itself: "It is...in the very text of the Scriptures that the reader who has 'the spirit of Christ' will discover 'what is beyond what is written.'"[24] Origen humbly confesses that at times he is not sure whether he has come to that understanding. Only prayer will let one perceive the meaning of difficult passages. "When we are seeking something of the divine meanings and cannot find it, then let us make this fervent prayer for the visitation of his Word and say: 'Let him kiss me with the kiss of his mouth.'"[25] This deeper meaning he calls variously *spiritual, mystical, true, intelligible, reasonable,* as opposed to *material, corporeal, visible, perceptible,* or in the nouns *symbol, type, image, enigma.* He included in the spiritual sense any metaphorical expressions used by the sacred writers themselves (which Thomas Aquinas and today's scholars would include in the literal sense).[26] In his commentary on the Canticle of Solomon he faithfully seeks the literal sense first (which he considers love songs composed for the marriage of King Solomon) but then moves on to the spiritual, which for him is the allegorical sense. It is his mystical thirst and his pastoral concern that moves him to do so—a concern with which any homilist can easily sympathize.

This procedure can be illustrated by the way he handles the troublesome text concerning Lot's daughters in Genesis 19:30–38. The reader who expects both Lot and his daughters to be exemplary is offended when they conspire to get their father drunk so they can have intercourse with him and assure their own progeny. Origen discusses first the literal meaning of the text and the moral responsibility of the three characters. Lot was not aware of his intercourse but was responsible for getting drunk. The daughters were responsible for their incestuous project, but their guilt could be lessened because they did it only to have off-spring and not out of lasciviousness, for they did not repeat their actions. A modern interpretation of this story is given in the *New American Bible* note on this text: "This Israelite tale about the origin of Israel's neighbors east of the Jordan and the Dead Sea was told partly to ridicule these racially related but rival nations and partly to give folk etymologies for their names." Obviously modern interpreters, who follow a progressive model of revela-tion, see no need to exculpate the characters or to retrieve a moral lesson from the story. Crouzel comments, "It does not seem Origen was aware that there was in the Old Testament evolution and progress in respect of moral and religious standards."[27]

So what does Origen do with the story? He continues:

We referred Lot himself indeed to the rational under-standing and the manly soul, but his wife, who looked back, we said to be the flesh given over to concupiscence and pleasures. Do not, O hearer, receive these things carelessly. For you ought to watch lest perhaps even when you have fled the pleasures of the world and have escaped the fires of the flesh…and you have ascended to the height of knowledge, as to some mountain peak, beware lest those two daughters be in wait for you, who do not depart from you, but follow you even when you ascend the mountain. They are vainglory and her older sister, pride. Beware lest with their embraces those daughters constrict you, deprived of sense and sleeping, while you seem neither to perceive nor know. They are called daughters because they do not come upon us from outside, but proceed from us and from a kind of innocence, as it were, of our acts. Be vigilant, therefore, as much as you can, and watch lest you beget sons from these daughters, because those who have been born from them "shall not enter the church of the Lord"

[Deut 23:3]. But if you wish to beget, beget in the spirit, since "he who sows in the spirit shall reap life everlasting" [Gal 6:8]. If you wish to embrace, embrace wisdom and "say wisdom is your sister" [Prov 7:4] that also Wisdom may say of you: He "who shall do the will of my Father who is in heaven, he is my brother and sister and mother" [Matt 12:50]. Jesus Christ our Lord is this Wisdom, "to whom be glory and sovereignty forever and ever. Amen" [1 Pet 4:11].[28]

Notice how Origen not only uses allegory to teach a lesson elsewhere contained in the scriptures in a literal sense but works his way to a christological climax. This is typical of his method.[29]

There are other cases where Origen finds nothing salvageable in the literal sense and moves immediately to the allegorical. Thus in the story of Abraham lying to Abimelech that Sara is his sister:

If anyone wishes to hear and understand these words literally he ought to gather with the Jews rather than with the Christians. But if he wishes to be a Christian and a disciple of Paul, let him hear Paul saying that "the Law is spiritual" [Rom 7:14] and declaring that these words are "allegorical" when the Law speaks of Abraham and his wife and sons [cf. Gal 4:22–24]. And although no one of us can by any means easily discover what kind of allegories these words should contain, nevertheless one ought to pray that "the veil might be removed" from his heart, "if there is anyone who tries to turn to the Lord" [2 Cor 3:16]—"for the Lord is Spirit" [2 Cor 3:17]—that the Lord might remove the veil of the letter and uncover the light of the Spirit and we might be able to say that "beholding the glory of the Lord with open face we are transformed into the same image from glory to glory, as by the Spirit of the Lord" [2 Cor 3:18].[30]

He goes on to say that Sara stands for the virtue of the soul and Abraham calls her his sister because he wishes not to keep her to himself but to share her, as every virtuous person wishes to share his virtue.

Two things should be noticed about this text:

1. The meaning of a text is to be sought in the *community* that interprets it. Origen does not approve of individual interpretation isolated from tradition and the community of believers. Even when he sets out his own interpretation, he frequently deprecates it with expressions like, "We pass no judgment on those who have been able to perceive something more sacred from this text."[31] In this case, failing to find any literal meaning for the Christian community, Origen leaves it to the Jewish community to explain.

2. Origen gives here, as he often does elsewhere, his justification for a spiritual, that is, allegorical, understanding of the text. His defender and forerunner is Saint Paul, who at times uses allegory when this is helpful to elucidate the meaning of a pericope, for all meaning now comes from Christ, who is the "spirit" contained in the Law.[32] Therefore, if one approaches the text prayerfully, one will encounter in it Christ the risen Lord and will be transformed into his image.

Origen thus salvages the Old Testament in all its parts because he is not bound to a literal interpretation. Even when he can find a literal interpretation he will often prefer a "spiritual" (that is, allegorical) one which enables him to make the Old Testament text *an instance of the gospel*. Not, obviously, that the Old passage is as clear as the New Testament. Basing himself on Hebrews 10:l, "The law has only the *shadow* of the good things to come, and not the very image," Origen, followed by Ambrose and the medieval tradition, sees three levels of the gospel: (1) the ultimate level, the "realities" *(pragmata)* that belong to the next life, and that Origen, following Revelation 14:6, calls the *eternal* gospel; (2) the *temporal* gospel, which is the gospel as experienced in this life after the coming of Christ. It is the participatory *image (eikon)* of the eternal gospel, differing not in substance but only in the way it is known, "through a glass darkly," from the eternal realities seen "face to face"; and (3) the Law, which offers the *shadow*, the hope, the intimation of the realities to come.[33] Origen considers his hermeneutical task to bring what was shadow into the light. And where the typical sense does not suffice he uses allegory. This procedure he found useful for preaching, catechesis, and prayer. Sometimes, as in this case, his allegorizing seems arbitrary and far-fetched. By the same token, however, the historical-critical model that has recently ruled the field, often shows only how far in time the scene is from our contemporary world and thus reduces its potential for contemporary application.

If we today find many of Origen's allegories untenable, as did the school of Antioch a century later, it is because we have a better appreciation today of the role of the human authors in the composition of the Bible. For Origen, the Holy Spirit is the author of the Bible. It is that simple. There is only one God, who is author of both the Old and the New (a point the fathers make repeatedly against Marcion). The role of the human author was more like that of a secretary taking dictation. We know now that such was not the case, that the authors were true authors, that the composition of the Bible was the work of centuries, that however Spirit-guided the tradition may have been, it evolved and was reworked and deepened as new crises faced the people. Our problem today is how to retrieve meaning from texts we now know are snapshots or paintings or "freeze-frames" of a drama constantly moving. Study of Old Testament history, of literary forms, of culture and the sociopolitical scene helps us to situate a given text. But any homilist realizes as much as Origen did that such auxiliary sciences do not assure that the reader or listener will experience the spiritual impact of God's word. When the liturgical readings parallel an Old Testament passage with one from the Gospels, is not the homilist being invited to do precisely what Origen did—to find in the Old Testament text an instance of the gospel?

However much we may find Origen's application of allegory to the minutest details of the Old Testament unhelpful, we cannot escape the problem. Nor can we dismiss what all the fathers took seriously—that the fullness of revelation is not in a book, not even in the New Testament as text. It is the person of Jesus Christ. And the early church's experience of Jesus Christ as Lord authorized measuring the Old Testament by that experience and interpreting it in the light of that experience. Jesus was now the hermeneutical principle of the Old Law, the key to it all. Vatican II would say the same. But how, in detail, this principle is to be applied—*voilà le problème!* Does every passage of the Old Testament have a christological meaning—or only certain ones? And if only certain ones (the messianic prophecies, for example), what of the other parts?

Chrysostom (347–407): The Literal Exhorter

Alexandria was not the only center for intense biblical study. Since the days of Lucian, martyred in 312, there had been at Antioch in Syria a tradition of Bible study that paid close attention to the literal sense. Perhaps it was the closeness of the Syriac environment, itself closer to Palestinian Aramaic, that accounted for this difference from Alexandria. In any case, the chief theologians of what came to be called the Antiochene school were Diodore of Tarsus (ca. 330–ca. 390), Theodore of Mopsuestia (ca. 350–428), and Theodoret (ca. 393–460). If the Alexandrian school could be accused of rampant allegorizing, the Antiochene school could be accused of opening the road to a rationalism that minimized mystery, as Newman pointed out.[34] That is probably an unfair assessment through the spectacles of the Enlightenment.[35] But one can see the school's method best applied moderately by Saint John Chrysostom (ca. 347–407), who was trained in Antioch before assuming the see of Constantinople.

The Antiochene theologians and preachers felt that allegory as practiced in Alexandria was a misguided effort in interpreting the Bible. As Frances M. Young says, they broke up the narrative context by allegorizing individual words: "The objection to Alexandrian allegory is that it treats texts as a collection of arbitrary tokens, not as 'mirroring' in its narrative coherence the truths which may be discerned within it."[36]

But the Antiochenes also knew that the historical sense alone was not always sufficient. In place of allegory they spoke of *theoria,* which J. N. D. Kelly translates "insight."[37] They accepted typology, that is, the fact that certain *things* as well as words could be prophetic. Chrysostom, in fact, coined the classic definition of a type as "a prophecy expressed in terms of things."[38] But for *theoria* to be preserved from abuse, three conditions must be observed: (1) the literal sense should be preserved; (2) there should be a well-founded correspondence between the historical fact or type and its fulfillment; (3) these two objects should be understood together, though in different ways. These principles, they maintained, would head off rampant allegorizing.

This allowed liberties in discerning types beyond those given in scripture. For example, Diodore could see Cain as prefiguring the synagogue and Abel the church.[39] Theodore could discern in the blood sprinkled on the Israelites' doorposts a type of our deliverance by Christ's blood. In doing this they were following an earlier common tradition—Irenaeus, for example, extends the Adam-Christ typology to Mary as the New Eve. But otherwise the Antiochenes were quite rigorous in limiting Messianic interpretation of both prophecies and things in the Old Testament. Chrysostom and Theodoret were less rigid in applying the principles of the school, but they too avoided what they considered the excessive allegorizing of the Alexandrians and their followers.

Chrysostom's love for the literal derives in part from his understanding of scripture as an extension of the incarnation—the "condescension" *(synkatabasis)* or "weakness" *(asthenia)* of God—meaning the divine acceptance of human limitations in the mystery of becoming man and, analogously, speaking to man in human words. A better rendering of the idea might be God's "considerateness,"[40] that is, his clothing of the divine message in the flesh of human words—a motif for which Chrysostom was especially appreciated by Pope Pius XII and Vatican II.[41] Acceptance of the limitations of the human-divine word is in one sense liberating, for one is not obliged to find scientific or historical accuracy in every text but only that truth which "the love of God provides for the sake of our salvation," an expression of Chrysostom that Vatican II would use in the Constitution on Divine Revelation.[42]

But reducing one's expectations of the word, now enfleshed in human words, raises again the problem: If we cannot use allegory, what method do we use to discover the *now* meaning? Chrysostom's answer: Exhortation. And exhortation involves exploring first all that is implied in the text by way of questions, comparison, contrast, examples, and all the rhetorical tools at his command. His habitual homiletical method is to comment on the text line by line, mining it for all it is worth, and then concluding with a flourish.

In treating the daughters of Lot, Origen had examined the literal sense, finding both father and daughters partially guilty, and then he plunged into allegory, letting Lot stand for the rational soul and his daughters for vainglory and pride. What does Chrysostom do with the same text? He refrains from any allegorizing but exculpates entirely both Lot and his daughters, Lot's excessive drinking because of depression, the daughters because they thought they were the only ones left to repopulate the world (the latter being already Philo's explanation).[43] Although this minimizing of moral responsibility is a departure from Chrysostom's usual practice, ironically Origen is closer in this case to modern historical critics who see in the story a severe judgment on the incest of Lot's house and the intended put-down of Israel's neighbors. Chrysostom, though, finds a moral by way of contrast as he goes on to say that today we should be concerned to leave a memorial not of children but of good works. Chrysostom, who doesn't like to find fault in his biblical heroes, passes over the issue of Abraham's lie to Abimelech.[44] Instead, he moves from Abraham's fear of death to the Christian's liberation from it by the death and resurrection of Christ. Thus, like Origen, he proceeds from the Old Testament to the New and a christological emphasis, but in a different way, namely by parallels between the biblical experience and those of his audience.[45] From these examples we can see that *theoria* meant the significance of the literal sense for the contemporary audience, a significance that the Holy Spirit enables the interpreter to perceive.

It would be unfair to judge Chrysostom, or any of the other writers of this period, on the basis of a problem-text of the Pentateuch. More characteristic of Chrysostom would be the rhetorical heights to which he soars in commenting on the letters of his hero, Paul.[46] After reading Paul's own rhetoric about the foolishness of the cross being wiser than human wisdom, and its weakness stronger, Chrysostom soars:

> How greatly did Plato labor, endeavoring to show that the soul is immortal! Yet even as he came he went away,

41

having spoken nothing with certainty, nor convinced any hearer. But the cross achieved persuasion by means of unlearned men. Yes, it convinced the whole world— and not about common things but it wrought its conviction discoursing about God and the godliness which is according to truth, and the gospel way of life, and the judgment of the things to come. And of all men it made philosophers: the very rustics, the utterly unlearned. Behold how "the foolishness of God is wiser than men," and "the weakness stronger"! How stronger? Because it overran the whole world, and took all by force, and while men were endeavoring by tens of thousands to extinguish the name of the Crucified, the contrary came to pass: the name of the Crucified flourished and increased more and more; while the persecutors perished and wasted away. The living at war with the dead were powerless.[47]

Though Chrysostom and Origen differed on the allegorical method, they were united in basic typology rooted in the conviction that the Old Testament was a rehearsal for the New.

The allegorical method became entrenched decades before the Antiochene school reacted against it. As might be expected, it influenced the Alexandrian fathers from Dionysius to Cyril. But it also left its mark on the Palestinian and Cappadocian fathers, who, like Origen, followed the literal sense but also used allegory extensively. Through them the allegorizing tradition passed to the West, as can be seen in Hilary, Ambrose, and especially Augustine.

Jerome (ca. 340–420): The Spirit in the Text

The greatest biblical scholar of the fourth and early fifth centuries was undoubtedly Jerome. Master of Latin, Greek, Hebrew, and Chaldaic, he was a meticulous student of the original languages, translating the Old Testament from the original Hebrew (and later, under pressure, the books of the Septuagint that were not available to him in Hebrew) and the New Testament from the

Greek in a Latin version called the Vulgate. Although classified as a Western father because he got his early education in Germany and Rome and wrote in Latin, he spent a great portion of his life in the Holy Land, where we would expect him to have a greater sense of the historical roots of the scriptures and therefore for the literal sense. But he is also a Christian, and therefore he shows a solid commitment to the Christian interpretation of the Old Testament.

In fact, he is very much in the furrow of Origen. To properly interpret the scriptures one needs the same Holy Spirit that inspired the writer:

> Even if he does not stray from the Church, anyone who…understands Scripture otherwise than in the sense demanded by the Holy Spirit in whom it was written can be called a heretic; his choice belongs to the works of the flesh, for he has chosen the worst.[48]

The truth of the text—that is, its *spirit*—is to be found deeper within the text, not outside it. But to arrive at it often requires prayer. Thus, in his explanation of the account of the transfiguration, he says, "*After six days.* Pray to the Lord that I may interpret these words in the same spirit in which they were spoken."[49] What that means concretely is that the spiritual meaning of all scripture lies in its relationship to Christ:

> For us, the spiritual man, who judges all things and is judged by no man, is the one who knows all the mysteries of the Scriptures and understands them in a sublime manner: he sees Christ in the divine books and takes no account of Jewish tradition.[50]

It should be obvious from these texts that for Jerome the "spiritual sense" is not a matter of private interpretation; there is an "objective" spiritual sense in the interior of the text, and it corresponds to the consciousness not of the individual interpreter as such but of the church. At the same time, his position seems to give little or no place to the horizon of the Old Testament author or to the progressive nature of revelation.

Augustine (354–430): Personal Transformation and the Reign of Charity

The most comprehensive treatment of hermeneutical theory in the West was Augustine's *De Doctrina Christiana*. It set the tone for the practice of interpretation during the entire Middle Ages. The Bishop of Hippo begins by stating that revelation or doctrine involves either realities or signs of realities. The ultimate reality is of course the Holy Trinity, but other examples would be the church, persons, and the love of God. Signs are of two types: words and things. Words point to the realities, and so can things. Biblical types fall under the latter category. The end of all is the enjoyment of God, and everything else is useful to the extent that it leads to God. This principle affects not only man's journey to his eternal home, requiring constant purification of heart. It also affects his reading of scripture, for scripture has one end, to lead to the love of God and neighbor. "Whoever, therefore, thinks he understands the divine Scriptures or any part of them so that it does not build the double love of God and of our neighbor does not understand them at all."[51]

On the other hand, even a mistaken interpretation can build up charity and thus reach scripture's goal. "If [a person] is deceived in an interpretation that builds up charity, which is the end of the commandments, he is deceived in the same way as a man who leaves the road by mistake but passes through a field toward the same place to which the road itself leads."[52]

Is then the meaning of scripture a matter of indifference? Is there no need to find out what the text is actually saying? Augustine adds, "But he is to be corrected and shown that it is more useful not to leave the road, lest the habit of deviating force him to take a crossroad or a perverse way."[53] Augustine is thus aware that there are right and wrong interpretations, and he later sets about the exposition of rules to determine them. Getting in the habit of making wrong interpretations can dispose one to error and missing the goal.

But Augustine is adamant about the end of scripture. He even goes so far as to say that if one has a firm hold on faith, hope, and charity, one does not need scripture, except for the instruction of others, because there are "three things for which all knowledge and prophecy struggle: faith, hope, and charity."[54] Hence acceptance of this end is necessary for anyone who would approach the reading of scripture securely.[55]

Once the goal is clearly established—that is, the reality toward which all points, namely the enjoyment of God through faith, hope, and charity, Augustine then turns to the signs that are means to attain the goal. Scripture is one of those signs. The purpose of scripture is not to inform or entertain but to transform the reader, readying him or her for the vision of God. To approach scripture fruitfully, a conversion is needed, especially from pride.[56] Scripture leads the reader through a seven-step process. It first instills a fear of God in recognition of his will, then through piety, knowledge, fortitude, mercy (teaching us to love our enemies), the cleansing of the eye so that it may see God, it finally brings one to wisdom, where the reader enjoys peace and tranquility. Augustine elsewhere calls the effect of scripture "medicinal."[57]

For one serious about the interpretation of scripture, this transformative process includes a study of auxiliary sciences— natural and secular history, philosophy, ancient arts and sports, original languages, including the symbolism of numbers, previous translations, and the context of given passages, so that the writer's intention can be discerned.[58] Becoming a student of scripture, then, involves personal dispositions and objective knowledge:

> A man fearing God diligently seeks His will in the Holy Scriptures. And lest he should love controversy, he is made gentle in piety. He is prepared with a knowledge of languages lest he be impeded by unknown words and locutions. He is also prepared with an acquaintance with certain necessary things lest he be unaware of their force and nature when they are used for purposes of similitudes. He is assisted by the accuracy of texts which expert diligence in emendation has procured. Thus instructed, he may turn his attention to the investigation and solution of the ambiguities of the Scriptures.[59]

The difficulties and obscurities one finds in scripture are all part of this function of transformation, for they lead to humility in the search and prizing the truth when it is found.[60] If there is ambiguity in the literal sense, Augustine advises consulting the "rule of faith," which means to look at the clearer passages of scripture and the authority of the church.[61] Consultation of other passages is important, for "hardly anything may be found in those obscure places which is not found plainly said elsewhere."[62] As for the authority of the church, the faith of the Christian community is then like the banks of a river that contain interpretations within a clear channel. This includes the determination of which books are inspired. Augustine lists as canonical the books of the Septuagint.[63] His recommendation that the student read *all* of scripture and check his interpretation against the wider canon[64] is a forerunner of what today is known as "canonical criticism." If the whole Bible is held by the church to be inspired, then the interpretation of one book must be contextualized by its place among all the others.

In terms of objective meanings, Augustine finds four levels possible: "In all the holy books we must perceive the eternal realities that are intimated there; what facts are narrated; what future realities are predicted; and what things we are commanded or warned to do."[65] This fourfold formula, refined by Cassian, will become the classical reigning model during the Middle Ages.

When it is not clear whether a passage is to be taken literally or figuratively, then

> whatever appears in the divine Word that does not literally pertain to virtuous behavior or to the truth of the faith, you must take to be figurative. Virtuous behavior pertains to the love of God and of one's neighbor; the truth of faith pertains to a knowledge of God and of one's neighbor.[66]

For "Scripture teaches nothing but charity."[67]

Where does Augustine get this principle? Probably from the words of Jesus that the double commandment of love sums up the whole teaching of the law and the prophets (Matt 22:40).

Augustine thus enjoys a wide liberty in dealing with the Old Testament texts. All or almost all of the Old Testament is to be taken figuratively as well as literally.[68] This enables him to find typology everywhere and to use the allegorical method where we would never think of using it today. In the Canticle of Solomon we read, "Your teeth are like a flock of ewes to be shorn, which come up from the washing, all of them big with twins, none of them thin and barren among them" (4:2). A modern scholar would simply classify this as an extended metaphor in a love song. But Augustine sees in it "the teeth of the church cutting off men from their errors and transferring them to her body after their hardness has been softened as if by being bitten and chewed." And the shorn sheep have "put aside the burdens of the world like so much fleece, and as ascending from the washing, which is baptism, all to create twins, which are the two precepts of love, and I see no one of them sterile of this holy fruit."[69]

Like the earlier fathers, Augustine seems to be little aware of any other real author of the Bible than the Holy Spirit. The Bible is a two-dimensional picture without topography. Was Augustine aware at all of the progressive nature of revelation? Only minimally it seems when he justifies Abraham's polygamy as permitted in a previous dispensation,[70] or when he says that we may take as literal what scripture praises, even though it is not to be adopted after the coming of Christ.[71] In other words, the whole of the Old Testament is seen as a temporary or preparatory dispensation, not as containing within itself discernible degrees of revelation, which would take into account the intention of the human author at a given period in the development of biblical revelation.

Augustine's simple rule that every interpretation should promote charity and lead to the enjoyment of God reflects, it seems to me, what happens when most Christians prayerfully read the Bible. Sometimes the sense that strikes them is the literal one. At other times a particular phrase may carry a meaning for the reader that the author had not intended but because of a particular circumstance in the reader's life this phrase strikes home as a "word from the Lord" for his or her particular need. Usually such a meaning corresponds to a truth found elsewhere in scripture, and as long as it falls under the rule of faith (Augustine's other guideline), it is not only harmless but helpful. When one attempts, however, to discern the *teaching* of scripture on a particular matter, a more serious attention to the literal sense is required. Even for such a study, Augustine would say, faith, humility, and a whole personal transformation is required or effected by the word of God.

Conclusion

The problem for the fathers was how the Old Testament was to be related to the New. They knew that the Christ-event threw a new light on the Old Testament, and their solution was to use the Old to illustrate the New. The historical critical method has taught us to think diachronically, that is, limiting the meaning of a text to what the authors said at the moment of their writing, based on pre-texts used in their original sense or moved to a new register—but rigorously excluding what may have come later, either in terms of reuse, relecture, reinterpretation of the text or the event narrated. However, the fathers thought of the Bible synchronically, or better, achronically, and this enabled them to see the interconnectedness of texts unmediated by the unfolding of time. This they understood to be the true meaning of any text, because its full meaning was now more clearly available, and this is the meaning God intended all along, because in God there is no past or future but all is present. Passages that appeared Messianic they took as foretelling the New directly; other passages would be used as catechetical tools to illustrate what they had come to know through the New Testament. With little or no understanding of the progressive nature of revelation, where the literal sense would not suffice, they resorted to allegory or to *theoria* (Chrysostom and the Antiochenes). Their legacy would be carried on and systematized in the Middle Ages.

FOUR

Climbing the Tower:
The Middle Ages

The Middle Ages would be noted for significant developments in theology.[1] But for a long time theology was held to be nothing else than commentary on scripture, for all revelation was understood to be contained in the scripture. Bonaventure even said, "Sacred Scripture which is called theology"[2] and Thomas Aquinas the reverse, "Theology which is called Sacred Scripture."[3] The influence of Origen and especially of Augustine dominated the hermeneutics of medieval Europe. Since scripture is a well of many meanings (an "infinite forest," Jerome had said[4]), any interpretation was acceptable provided it conformed to truth and charity.[5] "In what you understand in the Scriptures charity is obvious. In what you don't understand, charity is hidden."[6] And the goal of all scripture is to lead one into the mystery of God.

The Four Meanings of Scripture

The four senses distinguished by John Cassian (d. 435) became classic in the Middle Ages: the historical (literal), the allegorical (which included the typological), the moral or tropological, and the anagogic or eschatological (the heavenly realities of Augustine). Although these divisions were not rigid and were applied in different ways, a Latin verse, originated by Augustine of Denmark became the student's catchword:

> Littera gesta docet, quid credas allegoria,
> Moralis quid agas, quo tendas anagogia.

49

("The literal sense shows what happened, the allegorical what you are to believe, the moral what you are to do, the anagogical where you are destined.")

The *literal sense* concerned not the author's intended meaning as we understand the literal sense today but rather the events narrated, what happens in the text, hence they also called it the "historical sense." This is a very crucial insight for our understanding of the fathers. Since they understood the literal sense of narrative to be the *facts* narrated, they were compelled to find another way to get at the spiritual meaning of the text. Thus, for example, Augustine in commenting on the wedding feast of Cana, after explaining the literal meaning undertakes to show the *mystery* underlying this event, which is that it is a symbol of the messianic marriage feast, the sign of the New Covenant.[7] Similarly, Jerome distinguishes between *historia* (or *littera*) and *mysterium*.[8] But today, exegetes would understand this meaning of the wedding feast of Cana to belong to the literal sense—that is, what the author was intending to convey by the way he told the story.

This understanding of the literal sense—what happens in the story—at least was the case in the earlier Middle Ages. When they spoke of *historia* they did not mean what we mean by "historical criticism" today. Unlike modern scientific research into history, the purpose of studying history, even secular history, in precritical times was not the determination of facts in their particularity, nor even the interrelation of events. History was studied for the lessons it contained. If this was true of the study of secular history, it was all the more true of the study of biblical history.[9] The events of history were more for *formation* than for information. For this reason there was little interest in verifying historical details by the study of contemporary documents, and archeology and historiography in the modern sense were unknown. In this precritical stage the biblical narratives were assumed to tell straightforward happenings, and since virtually all history was narrated from a pedagogical viewpoint, in which the listener/reader was assumed to be involved, history is the story in which the meaning of human existence is played out, and the stakes are decisive. This explains why history was recorded in epic and saga rather than in positivist details, and even prose history followed the same pattern. In this view there was little reason to question either the facts or the interpretation given them.

As far as the Bible itself was concerned, the medieval authors considered the historical sense like the foundation of a tower, necessary but only a condition for arriving at the summit, which was the spiritual or allegorical sense, or what they often called the "mystery." Only when this literal sense was repugnant (in Augustine's sense) could it be bypassed. The spiritual sense was, however, founded not in the text itself but in the *events* related by the text. Thus, because God is the author of history and not just of the inspired books, "the works speak...the facts, if you would understand, are words."[10] What the Bible says of Abraham, for example, is both "event and prophecy."[11] Or, in the words of Cassian, "Those things which in reality were done, are said to have prefigured the form of another mystery."[12] Today we would say that because God is the author of sacred history, earlier events were prophetic of later events.

The Allegorical Sense

The word *allegory* was used, not because it was the best word in the secular vocabulary of the day, but because Paul had used it in Galatians 4:24 concerning Sarah and Hagar. In the common secular usage, the word meant simply a continuous metaphor or "the designation of one thing by another." In patristic usage it was interchangeable with *mystery*. Applied to the Old Testament, it meant that everything that was related there pointed forward in some way to Christ: "Everything contained in the sacred books announces in words, expresses in deeds and confirms by examples the coming of our Lord Jesus Christ."[13] Allegory was then no longer merely a matter of words but also of deeds that instructed and gave understanding of the primordial self-revelation of God, Jesus Christ. The mystery of Christ also included, of course, the mystery of the church, as the Letter to Ephesians had already noted. The fathers and the medievalists never said they were "reading back" into the Old Testament the mystery of Christ. On the contrary, both word and event in the Old Testament contained within them the coming mystery, like the ark of the covenant that was contained within the temple.[14] Or, using the example of Albert the Great, in commenting on Mark's story of the man let down through the roof, the house is scripture and the roof is the historical sense, which must be passed through to reach the mystery, Christ.[15] In the Joseph story in Genesis, the silver cup is the spiritual sense hidden in the sack of the literal.[16]

In this it is obvious that Christian "allegory" was different from the pagan or secular practice of interpreting the myths as allegories of nature, or abstract thought, or philosophical or psychological truths. Christian allegorical method focused wholly on Christ in a way vastly different:

> One is led by a series of individual events to another singular Event; a series of divine interventions, each of which has a meaning in itself, leads to another kind of divine intervention, equally real, more profound and decisive. Everything culminates in the great Event which, in its uniqueness, has multiple repercussions, an Event that dominates history and brings the fullness of light and spiritual fruitfulness: the Event of Christ.[17]

Although often accused of Platonism, the medievalists insisted more than Plato and the neo-Platonists on the reality of the "type." It was not just a shadow. Although it pointed forward, it had a meaning in itself.

Allegoria quid credas. "Allegory indicates what you are to believe." The sense is that the spiritual interpretation of the Old Testament reveals the mystery of Christ and the church, hence the very content of the Christian faith. The purpose is not so much to bring one to faith as to build up and further instruct the faith already received. As one uncovers the inner meaning of the things or events, one grows in one's appreciation of the revelation God has made in Christ.

However, this understanding of Christ was not the kind of dispassionate exercise of the intellect that a positivist scientist might have. For Origen and those who followed in his wake in the Middle Ages, to read the scriptures, Old or New, was to meet Christ, the beloved. The lover tends to see his beloved everywhere, in the wind, the flowers, the sky, the stars, the sun. Or, if not yet seeing, he asks himself how those things image his beloved. This is a projection, seeing a metaphor of the beloved in something else. Origen uses this image of the lover/beloved in his approach to scripture, but he would hardly think of it as a projection. The beloved is really there, waiting to be found. Commenting on the Canticle of Solomon, he says that the soul seized by love for the word of God is at first distressed by the enigmas of the text, but she comes to sense that he approaches and she hears from on high the sound of his voice. Taking courage as the light from on high illumines her, she cries, "Behold He comes, bounding over the mountains, leaping over the hills!"[18] It is the beloved in person that one seeks in the text: "Christ himself is the secret and hidden meaning."[19] Reading and studying scripture was for Origen and the great medievalists, a mystical experience.

The last two senses, the moral or tropological and the anagogical, are really aspects of the spiritual or allegorical sense. For revelation is not only a word about God and his actions in history; it is a call to a new life for the believer, and therefore conversion. And the anagogical is simply the "not yet" of the mystery presently leading the pilgrim through time to its full fruition in eternity.

The Tropological or Moral Sense

Tropological comes from the Greek verb *trepein,* meaning "to turn" and its noun form, *trope,* "turn." There is, in every passage of scripture, a call to conversion—whether this be initial or ongoing. The focus here is on *response* to the mystery elaborated in the allegorical sense. And this response-meaning is not a list of moralizing directives. Rather it is the soul, or the church, or Mary as an image of either, united mystically with Christ, so that what happens in him also happens in his members. Obviously behavior is implied, but it flows from mystical union with Christ. It is the mystery lived out in the church and the individual soul.

That means a daily re-enactment of what happened once, historically, in the past. Each day, in the depths of our being, Israel leaves Egypt, each day it is nourished with the manna, each day it fulfills the Law, each day it must engage in combat, each day the promises that were made to this people in a carnal way are realized spiritually in us....Each day the Lord comes, each day he approaches Jerusalem....[20]

It is here that the fathers understood the word to touch the reader/listener with a personal here-and-now message. The purpose of God's actions in history, and the revelation of their meaning in Christ, was all for one end: to reach the human soul. It is here that meaning and understanding and life-changing power are experienced. It is here that one meets God. "God walks with me in paradise when I read the divine Scriptures."[21] The fruit of this encounter is growth in charity.

Hans W. Frei has expressed this in more modern terms:

In figural interpretation the figure itself is real in its own place, time, and right, and without any detraction from that reality it prefigures, the reality that will fulfill it. This figural relation not only brings into coherent relation events in biblical narration, but allows also the fitting of each present occurrence and experience into a real narrative framework or world. Each person, each occurrence is a figure of that providential narrative in which it is also an ingredient.[22]

When moderns speak of scripture not as a window but as a mirror, they are only echoing a tradition going back to Augustine, one that became widespread in the Middle Ages. In scripture we see ourselves in relation to our creator and redeemer; our own experience is touched.[23] The most brilliant of scholars may read and seem to understand the scriptures, "but they do not yet understand them through experience."[24] In other words, to understand the text one must have some experience of the reality being

54

expressed. Edmund Husserl later will say, "No one knows himself unless he reads the Bible."[25]

The Anagogical Sense

The *anagogical* sense referred to the consummation of the mystery. (*Anagoge* means "leading up," that is, to heaven, the final goal.) Christ's coming in the flesh was the "allegorical" meaning of sacred history; his coming to the soul of the believer was the tropological meaning; his coming at the end of time is the anagogical. If the allegorical meaning built up faith, and the tropological built up charity, the anagogical fired supernatural hope. At times the anagogical meant the final realities themselves, at other times the contemplation of them in heaven, a contemplation begun already here below.[26]

As an example of how the four senses could be teased out of a single passage, note the following text of Thomas Aquinas:

> When I say, "let there be light," literally referring to material light [of the first creation], this belongs to the literal sense. If "let there be light" is understood as Christ being born in the church [baptism was known as "illumination"], this is the allegorical sense. If "let there be light" means that through Christ we are led to glory, this is the anagogical sense. If "let there be light" means that by Christ we are illuminated in mind and inflamed in heart, this is the moral (tropological) sense.[27]

On the text of Sirach, "He who created me rested in my tabernacle (tent)" (Sir 24:8, Vulgate), Saint Bonaventure writes:

> According to the literal understanding this fits the virgin Mary, in whose tabernacle the Lord rested bodily. According to the allegorical sense it fits the church militant, in whose tabernacle the Lord rests sacramentally. In the moral sense it fits the faithful soul, in whose tabernacle the Lord rests spiritually. In the anagogical

sense it fits the heavenly court, in whose tabernacle the Lord rests forever.[28]

John Cassian had already illustrated the four senses in the city of Jerusalem. In the literal sense Jerusalem is the historical city; in the allegorical sense the church, in the moral or tropological sense the Christian soul, in the anagogical sense the heavenly Jerusalem.[29]

The four senses were arrived at largely through wrestling with the meaning of the Old Testament for the Christian. Once it was clear that the New Testament was not only new but also "ever ancient," that is, the flower and fruit of the Old, the Hebrew Bible became a revered source of interpretation and inspiration. Bonaventure expresses the general view: there is also a spiritual sense to scripture because the Holy Spirit is its author and the Spirit has put multiple meanings in every word.[30] Paul's use of the allegorical or typical method justifies and commends its use in further elaborating scripture's meaning.[31] The medievalists' admiration at times becomes lyrical: scripture is the great eagle of the Apocalypse, "and its two wings are the two Testaments, which are given to this Woman, that is, made intelligible to her, that her heart might be lifted to heaven."[32] In the promised land we find "milk and honey, that is, the two testaments in the church."[33] The two breasts of the church or of her spouse are the two testaments.[34]

To sum up the senses graphically:

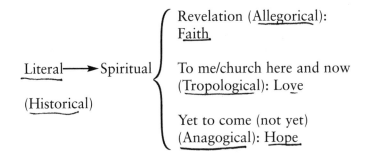

Literal ⟶ Spiritual
(Historical)

Revelation (Allegorical): Faith

To me/church here and now (Tropological): Love

Yet to come (not yet) (Anagogical): Hope

Meaning and Personal Transformation

It should be clear now from our examination both of the patristic and medieval evidence that the tradition sees a correlation

56

between interpretation and personal transformation. On the one hand, the word of God provokes conversion. When, on hearing the words *tolle, lege* ("take and read"), Augustine picked up the Bible and read Romans 13:13–14, his life was changed forever. But the converse is also true, that as one grows in the spiritual life, the scriptures themselves seem to grow. John Cassian affirms what many others held: "As our spirit is renewed by the meditation of the scriptures, the face of the scriptures themselves also begins to be renewed, and the beauty of a more sacred meaning begins to grow as we progress."[35] Gregory the Great would say, "The words of Sacred writ grow with the spirit of the readers."[36] The notion of correlation and personal transformation will become very important in the Reformation, especially with Calvin. Walter Wink is noted for his work on this dimension of interpretation in the twentieth century. Bernard Lonergan, as we will see, speaks not only of conversion but emphasizes that the richer the resources of the reader are (and in this he would include eminently the reader's personal holiness) the better will he or she understand scripture.

Later Developments: Thomas Aquinas

One of the most significant moves of Aquinas is his proposal that the author's intention extends to metaphor as well. We remember that earlier authors considered metaphor to belong to the spiritual sense. But for Thomas the literal sense is not the figure of speech but its content—a point that had already been made by Alexander of Hales[37] and Saint Albert the Great.[38] This means a greater respect for the literal sense and its potential meaning. Thomas's innovation was due not only to the influence of Aristotle but also to that of the Jewish expositor Maimonides who brought a more contextual understanding to many of the obscure passages of the Old Testament. For example, earlier Christian commentators had great difficulty making literal sense of Exodus 23:19, "You shall not boil a kid in its mother's milk." Augustine gave up any hope of meaning in the literal sense and, faithful to his principles, brought his allegorical genius to bear on the passage and interpreted it as a prophecy that Christ should not perish in the slaughter of the innocents.[39] Thomas simply says, "It would savor of heartlessness if the mother's milk, which was intended for the nourishment of her offspring, were served up on the same dish."[40] Another example: Gregory the Great and other expositors had given ample allegorical interpretation to the book of Job. Thomas simply sees its literal aim as showing "by probable reasons that human affairs are governed by divine providence." Since this is the purpose of the book, it does not matter whether Job was an actual historical figure or not, although Thomas says that Ezekiel (14:14) seems to treat Job as a historical person.[41]

Thomas's moving of metaphor into the literal sense was a distant harbinger of the inclusion of various literary forms and narrative structures within the literal sense, which allows for a more spiritual sense to be found not beyond but within the literal sense itself. For example, John's story of the cure of the man born blind is surely, at the symbolic level that is *part of the intention of the text,* a catechesis on baptism. And the fourth evangelist surely is capable of encoding more than one meaning in the literal sense of the text.

Another consequence of taking the literal sense seriously was the possibility of *progressive revelation.* In the prologue to his commentary on Job, Thomas writes, "As in things produced in the course of nature, gradually through the imperfect the perfect is reached, so it happens to man in his understanding of truth."[42]

Finally, Thomas concludes that there is nothing necessary for the faith in the spiritual sense that is not somewhere contained in the literal sense.[43] Hence, in argumentation, only the literal sense has the validity of proof.[44] The key words here are *necessary for the faith.* Only the literal sense may be used when the truth of the faith is at issue. He is not saying that tradition cannot contribute to the formulation of the faith (in the *Summa* he quotes the fathers as much as he quotes scripture), but rather if one uses scripture for that purpose one must stick to the literal sense. However, once that basis is assured, multiple meanings can be discerned, for "the Holy Spirit has impregnated scripture with truth greater than any man can discover."[45] The reason for this is that by "author" Thomas means God, as he says explicitly when discussing the intention of the author: "The literal sense is that which the author intends...

and the author of Sacred Scripture is God."[46] Therefore nothing prevents God from using the things to which the words refer in the literal sense, to symbolize other things.[47] Note the shift from the text to the reality to which the text refers to explain the spiritual senses. Thomas uses this principle to defend the four traditional senses. This means that while the sense the human author intended is also the sense of the divine author, the divine author can have in mind more than the human author can see (and this revelation, giving the spiritual sense of the earlier text, will be found later in scripture in the literal sense).[48]

It would appear then, that the literal sense is available to anyone who might study the text with the tools of "objective" science. That is why it alone can be used for argumentation, either with those outside the Christian community (for example, the Jews) or within the community concerning doctrines of the faith.[49] Where the scripture itself uses the allegorical or typical sense, this is explicitly contained in the literal sense somewhere else in scripture. What then of the spiritual senses (allegorical, tropological, anagogical) that postbiblical authors find but are *not* found elsewhere in scripture in the literal sense? These function *ad aedificationem fidei* ("for the upbuilding of the faith"), as several authors say. That means that within the Christian community they can profitably be used as illustrations of the faith, or enrichments of the faith. These are valid meanings, if only within the structure of faith already established on other grounds.[50]

Thomas's precision about the senses can be seen in one of three texts in which he expressly treats the matter:

> The spiritual sense is threefold. For as the Apostle says to the Hebrews (10:1), the old law is a figure of the new law; and the new law itself is a figure of future glory; also in the new law those things that take place in the head [Christ] are signs of those things which we are to do. Hence inasmuch as the things of the old law signify those of the new, this is the allegorical sense; inasmuch as those things that took place in Christ, or were signified by what Christ did, are signs of what we are to do, this is the moral [tropological] sense; inasmuch as they

59

signify those things that belong to eternal glory, this is
the anagogical sense.[51]

Did the fathers and the medievalists think that every passage of
scripture held the four senses? No, the tradition was aware that
some passages were more fittingly interpreted in one sense than in
another.

In this period, while commentaries of scripture were still being
written, scholars began to systematize theological questions either
in *Sentences*, like those of Peter Lombard, or in "Summaries" called
Summae, of which Thomas's *Summa Theologica* is the best-known
example. Thomas himself never lost his rootedness in the word of
God, for he consecrated the first hour of each day to commenting
the scriptures. But as the practice of systematization into *Doctrina
Sacra* developed, gradually the freshness of immediate contact with
the word of God faded, a trend that Roger Bacon deplored.[52] The
development of the natural sciences gave impetus to the new movement, so that considerations outside the scriptures began to have a
greater impact on theology. The way was being prepared for the
Enlightenment. In terms of theological method, using the scriptures
for proof-texts was on the horizon.

The Apocalypse: A New Approach

Joachim of Fiore (ca. 1130–1202) set in motion a new
approach to interpretation that has survived vigorously into our
day. He divides all history into three ages according to the three
persons of the Trinity. The Old Testament was the age of the Father,
the age of fear and servile obedience, which he also characterized as
the age of the married and the aged. The New Testament was the
age of faith and filial obedience (the age of the Son, also identifiable
as the age of the clergy and the young), and the age of the Holy
Spirit, to begin around 1260, which would be the age of love and
liberty, the age of monks and infants. While this periodization of
history has not survived, his method of approaching the
Apocalypse has. In his commentary on this prophetic book he read
predictions that would be fulfilled in specific persons or events in

the near future of the church. Augustine had said that the Apocalypse covers all the time from the first to the second coming of Christ.[53] But Augustine never applied the principle in the way Joachim did, nor especially as did the followers of Joachim. For Augustine and the tradition until Joachim, the figures of the Apocalypse are to be taken in a general sense of the church and its enemies of all times. But now the heads of the beast become the leaders of each of the seven ages of the world and the seven persecutors of the church: Herod, Nero, Constance the Arian, and so on. The "silence in heaven" signals Julian the Apostate, who closed churches. Mohammed is the beast rising from the earth. The horses in chapter 19 are the military orders; the "first resurrection" is the foundation of the mendicant orders. And so on. Tying the apocalyptic figures to specific past or contemporary historical figures becomes not merely a novel pastime, it becomes a new form of revelation. Scripture is not a place to find God; it is a place to find the answers to one's curiosity. Hal Lindsey with his *Late Great Planet Earth* and David Koresh would have felt perfectly at home in the atmosphere of this development. Raising his voice in protest, Dennis Ryckel returned to the generalizing, spiritual interpretation of the earlier age.[54] By the end of the century the method had fallen into contempt. Thomas Aquinas answers it briefly.[55] But it has had a persistence in popular circles to our day.

Perhaps even more significantly, the temptation to interpret history in periods, usually culminating in the exaltation of the interpreter's present *Zeitgeist,* is one that many secular theorists have not resisted. Shorn of theological categories, this motif has enjoyed enormous prestige and use in the West. It became the basis for the Enlightenment's breakdown of history into ancient, medieval, and modern, for Comte's notion of history moving from theological through metaphysical to the positivist scientific eras, and for the National Socialists' symbolism of the Third Reich. Closer examination reveals that these interpreters were doing exactly what Joachim was doing to scripture: imposing meaning improperly on texts and historical persons and things.[56]

Decadence

In the fourteenth century, Peter Lombard's *Sentences,* which had been the basic textbook for the University of Paris, now assumed an authority nearly equivalent to that of scripture. It was hailed as clearing up scripture's obscurities. The four books of which it was comprised were the four rivers of Paradise! Creativity lapsed, replaced by repetition of formulas that became laws in themselves. The dialectical method became an end in itself. Theology was becoming wholly argumentative, divorced from its contemplative roots, with proof-texts imported often without regard for their literal meaning. Even Pope Boniface VIII fell into the method by invoking the passage about the two swords in Luke 22:38 to prove the papal right to temporal as well as spiritual power—an obvious abuse of the literal sense. The severity of the Inquisition was often justified by the Psalm text that the Messiah would rule the nations with a rod of iron (Ps 2:9).

What was happening here? Allegorical interpretations, often of the most bizarre type, were being used argumentatively as proof for positions taken. Augustine and Aquinas had said that only the literal sense should be used in disputes about the faith. Now the allegorical prevailed, untethered to any concern for the literal sense. Wholly arbitrary interpretations were being used, not "for the building up of the faith" but for the winning of theological arguments. A tinder box was being prepared for the reaction of the reformers. A special irritant to them was use of the two-swords text to claim absolute authority for the papacy.

Barthelemy Arnoldi of Usingen, teacher of Luther who condemned many of his errors, admitted that in his day "most theologians have put so much water into the wine of sacred doctrine that it has lost almost all its taste."[57]

Meantime, in another development, Marcil Ficin (1433–1499), and his disciples John Pic and John Reuchlin (1455–1522), though skilled in languages and given to devotion, used the methods of the Jewish cabala to explore the Christian scriptures for their mystical meanings. The tendency bordered on the occult; it was part of the current of an age that included astrology, divination, alchemy, magic, and even demonology. Numbers and letters of the scriptures have secret meanings. (Today's "Bible Code" project is not far from this method.) The interpreter is not concerned with the literal sense of the statements but with occult meanings that can be derived by combinations of letters. At the extreme, the Bible has become a tool of superstition.

It is clear then that theology was becoming increasingly divorced from what earlier authorities understood it to be: an articulation of what was accepted and experienced in faith—in other words, its contemplative function. Francis Martin has shown that the roots of this shift lay in several factors. The exclusion of women from the universities (Bologna being the only exception) meant that women's contributions, especially those of the great medieval mystics, were marginalized and further development discouraged. The model for the masters of theology was the brotherhood of the military orders! And along with that came a growing distance of the monks and clergy from the laity, with the latter's participation in the liturgy moving from actors to listeners to spectators.[58]

Erasmus

Erasmus (1466–1536) was revolted by the paganization of a Christendom that preferred to be inspired by Catullus and Ovid than by Moses and Paul.[59] He was also revolted by the theological decadence of his age and wished to bring new life to the study of scripture and theology. That meant going back to the fathers and to the example of Saint Thomas Aquinas. As for scriptural interpretation, he respected the literal sense, emphasizing that it was necessary to work from the original languages (which meant Hebrew or Greek and not the Latin Vulgate),[60] that the original text should be accurately established,[61] that obscure passages should be interpreted in the light of those more clear,[62] that scripture should be understood (that is, interpreted) in light of its "natural, or historical and grammatical sense."[63] But he wanted to arrive at the spiritual meaning that alone suffices to nourish the soul.[64] The influence of the *devotio moderna* on Erasmus is noticeable here, for he is less interested in the collective mystery of salvation than in scripture's meaning for individual piety.[65] His use of the allegorical method at times approaches the allegorizing of the pagan myths, though this appears chiefly when he deals with the origins of the race in Genesis, where he suspects he is dealing with something that is not pure history.

Erasmus defends the allegorical method of the fathers, but attacks the abuse of it when authors violate the natural meaning of the words. He thus defends both the literal and the allegorical sense and only attacks the excesses of those who would hold only to the literal sense (which he considers a Judaizing tendency) or those who carried the allegorical to excess. To sum up, Erasmus returns to the spirit of the fathers, always seeking spiritual nourishment in the scriptures, all of which ultimately speak of Christ.[66] Erasmus's theology is pastoral, for he writes not for the scholars in their cells but for preachers in the churches.

This positive portrait departs considerably from the bad press Erasmus has suffered, being caricatured as a humanist, free thinker, romantic, precursor of Luther. More recent sober scholarship has rehabilitated him.[67]

Conclusion: Are the Four Senses Retrievable?

The modern historical-critical method has so influenced biblical scholars of the twentieth century that most have summarily dismissed the theory of the four senses, though it reigned for more than a thousand years. But widespread contemporary dissatisfaction with the historical method has also given rise to a number of other methodologies, all of which in some way are trying to recoup the life that earlier Christians found in the Bible. Is there any way to retrieve what was lost?

First of all, we should note that what many of the early writers meant by the literal sense was really the "historical" sense, that is, the actual events recorded—what the text says, not what today's scholars would call "historical criticism." When Alexander of Hales, Albert the Great, and Thomas Aquinas extended the meaning to encompass the metaphorical, they were moving the understanding of the literal sense closer to what we understand it to be today: the meaning intended by the author as evidenced in the text. This is still literal, but the focus has moved from event related to authorial intention and the literary form used.

That being granted, can we admit that there are senses imbedded in the literal sense that may not have been foreseen by the human author but that are retrievable from some other source? If scripture itself often finds a typical (allegorical) sense in its earlier texts, can this method be practiced legitimately by postbiblical authors? And if so, by what authority? To say that God intended other senses besides what are contained in the literal is not very helpful, for how do we find out what other senses God intended?

Here the ancients' distinction between the *functions* of the literal and spiritual senses may point the way to an answer. The literal sense, they said, is important for argumentation and for determining the content of the faith; the spiritual sense is "for the building up of the faith." The fact that the literal sense can be used for argumentation, even with nonbelievers, suggests that the literal sense is not only the guide to the Christian community within but also the interface with the world outside, and thus falls in the category of the universal language of humankind. It belongs to the universal human community. And this is so even prior to and independent of assent of the listener to the speaker's proposition, though it allows for the speaker to use reasoning or signs to convince the listener of the truth of the proposition.

On the other hand, communication is also limited by the codes proper to each community. An American visiting Australia will sometimes be amazed when the locals laugh at one of his expressions that has a very different meaning in their usage. An immigrant family newly arrived in a foreign country will have its own "language" (expressions, customs, meaning-making events) not available to the outside world unless one enters and is socialized into the family.

This distinction may help retrieve the respective values of the literal and the spiritual senses maintained for the first thousand years of the church. Medievalists insisted that the literal sense was the foundational one, the sense usable in argumentation, hence in the community of the world at large as well as for its own foundational creed. But the literal sense was also the gate to the spiritual senses, which belong as it were to the enclosed garden, access to which is available only to those who pass through the gate, which is faith. To pass through that gate is to enter into another community, where the spiritual senses are real senses, though meaningful only in the context of the believing community. These, as the authors said, are for "the upbuilding of the faith." If we further admit that the community and it members are guided by the Holy Spirit, then senses that build up the faith in fidelity to the foundational sense but elaborating it, are indeed legitimate senses, though they belong to the "domestic" community and are accessible only within it. The literal sense therefore faces both outward and inward. The spiritual senses only inward.

That does not mean that every spiritual meaning derived by any preacher or Christian is of equal value. The value of a spiritual interpretation would depend not only on its ability to build up the faith but also on the degree of its coherence with the faith and with the literal sense. Several authors in the tradition protested against the indiscriminate or frivolous use of the allegorical sense. The allegory Augustine paints on the Canticle text about the ewes coming up from the washing with twin lambs (which we saw in the previous chapter) could hardly be classed with the image of Mary as the New Eve, an early type derived from the scriptural witness of Christ as the new Adam.

Understood in this way, the four senses are retrievable. If this understanding were acceptable, it would liberate the historical critics from demeaning the spiritual meanings that Christians find so nourishing for their devotional life, and the devout from condemning the "sterility" of the historical-critical method.[68]

The Unity of the Bible

Basic to what Auerbach and Frei have called "figural" reading of the Bible—that is, seeing the earlier events prefiguring the later ones (whether explicitly mentioned in the Bible or not) is the belief in the divine inspiration of the scriptures, or, in other words, that God is the ultimate author of the Bible, and that beyond the horizons of the individual books God has a broader horizon that he only progressively reveals—and the fullness of which we do not know even now but must await at the end of time. This is a great leap, of course. Is there any justification for it in the Bible itself? Yes, in part. For the biblical authors were quite aware that they were in the <u>flow of a history</u> being written <u>by the Lord.</u> As many of them looked back on their history, reading it in light of the promises and threats of the covenant, they discerned something of a pattern (for example, the allegory in Ezekiel 16). But they were also aware that *every gift of God is* <u>*also a promise of a greater gift to come.*</u> And while they only vaguely glimpsed the shape of that future gift, they were certain of its existence. So there is *some* basis for figural interpretation in the very world expressed by the texts.

However, it takes more than the authors' or the texts' forward thrust to enable the reading of the whole Bible as a narrative. In fact, the ordinary reader, even in the light of the New Testament, would be at a loss to see how the extremely diverse parts fit together narratively unless there were some other light by which to read them. To say that they were written by God, and recognized as such by the church, attests extrinsically to their unity, but has he given any hints to the intrinsic unity, that is, to the story line of this overarching narrative? This question will occupy us in the chapters on <u>canonical</u> criticism and the spiritual senses of the scriptures.

FIVE

The Path of Independence: The Reformation and the Enlightenment

Nominalism and Anti-intellectual Piety

New trends often carry within themselves the seeds of later developments of unimagined proportions. Such was the case of the ideas proposed by William of Ockham, an English Franciscan who lived from about 1285 to about 1349. To put his case most radically, for him words are just words. They do not name a reality. Or, if they have a reference, it is without significance. Impressed with the transcendence and the incomprehensibility of God, he posited a distinction between the truths of faith, which are credible but unknowable, and the results of scientific knowledge or dialectics, which are knowable. We cannot know God's mind but only the decrees of his will as contained in scripture; hence what is now sinful might later be commanded. He can even predestine to hell. We just don't know. Though they may argue with each other, faith and reason are two totally different realms. An effect of this is that all universal or abstract terms (whether used of God or of the world) are mere necessities of thought or conventions of language and therefore exist as names only and have no general realities corresponding to them. They are, as it were, labels that can be applied and removed at will. By the end of the fourteenth century the regnant philosophy in the universities of Europe was nominalism. Theology was dealing with words rather than things. And reason and faith, once happily married, were now living in their own worlds, meeting largely as embattled debaters. A form of nominalism has revived today, as we

68

shall see, in those theories of hermeneutics that exclude extratextual reference from their horizon.

At the same time, piety in men like Meister Eckhart, Suso, and Gerson was taking a strong anti-intellectual trend—understandable given the aridity of the dialectics of a decadent scholasticism. The disgust of Thomas à Kempis for theological disputes in *The Imitation of Christ* makes sense in the light of the ideological environment of the day.

The Impact of Martin Luther (1483–1546)

In the first part of this chapter we pay particular attention to the development of critical and hermeneutical theory in the Protestant tradition for four reasons: (1) given the Protestant claim that the Bible alone was sufficient as the medium of revelation, more energy was necessarily expended upon it; (2) in the Catholic camp, though there were notable exceptions, the reaction to the Protestant focus on scripture alone led to an emphasis more on the sacramental and devotional life and a de-emphasis on the role of the Bible, not to say an avoidance of it; (3) the Protestant tradition, at least in Europe, seemed to be closer to the philosophical spirit of the times, which was emancipation from authority; (4) in the professional biblical circles and the ecumenical climate since the second half of the twentieth century, a meeting and mutual fecundation of Catholic and Protestant streams has been taking place, so it is important even from a Catholic point of view to know some of the basic stages of the development of hermeneutics in Protestant thought.

Luther was both traditional and revolutionary in his thinking about biblical interpretation.[1] On the one hand, he clearly lined up with the tradition going back to Origen that Christ is the Bible's central theme and that Christ is present in the text in such a way that the reader/listener can hear the living voice of God in the text before him. In light of the deterioration of biblical interpretation in the fourteenth and fifteenth centuries, this reaction was quite understandable. Luther also reactivated the patristic practice, if not the theory, that the Bible is primarily a book for preaching, and philological and historical research should serve this end. The written text stands between the apostolic preaching, which was done orally, and the contemporary preacher who also conveys his message orally. Holding that the literal or historical—or "grammatical" sense, as he preferred to call it—is the only sense, and rejecting the other three senses of the patristic and medieval periods, he held that the function of the written word is primarily to control the contemporary preacher by the apostolic tradition. This was, in fact, the only control.

Luther insisted on the priority of scripture itself over any other authority. Hence, neither tradition nor the inner witness of the Spirit (as the enthusiasts claimed) nor church authority nor philosophy are to be consulted in interpreting the Bible, and certainly they are not to determine its meaning.[2] Rather the Bible itself is to judge both tradition and the church. That means that scripture authenticates itself and is its own interpreter (a principle, incidentally, for which no text of scripture gives warrant). Scripture is "through itself most certain, most easily accessible, comprehensible, interpreting itself, proving, judging all the words of all men."[3] The Swiss reformer Zwingli (1481–1531) would argue the same. Scripture is thus clear in itself, the meaning of all of scripture being clarified by Christ as contained in the scriptures. By "Christ" Luther understands the gospel of God's free mercy justifying the believer by faith. Justification by faith then becomes the absolute principle in the light of which all else in the scripture is to be judged. Because Paul, especially in the Epistle to the Romans, is the one who spoke of this most clearly, those texts that speak of Christ in Pauline terms have authority over any other text. This is what led Luther to reject the Letter of James: "His [James's] authority is not great enough to cause me to abandon the doctrine of faith and to deviate from the authority of the other apostles and the entire Scripture."[4] For this reason, James cannot be an apostle.[5]

While Luther accepted the typical sense of Old Testament passages identified elsewhere in the literal sense (thus enabling them to maintain the unity of the Bible presumed by the canon), Luther's prioritizing of Romans established a canon within the canon. Till the end of his life he continued to put a different value on the books he had put together at the end of his Bible than on the "main books."[6] This principle was applied in another way in Luther's distinction between law and gospel, both of which are found in each of the Testaments. "Law" expressed God's expectations, both in the Old and in the New Testament (for example, the Ten Commandments and the Sermon on the Mount). It convinces people of their own unworthiness and need of grace and thus drives them to Christ. "Gospel" is the good news of justification by faith in Jesus Christ, and it was present in the Old Testament under the form of *promise,* in the New Testament as *fulfillment.* Luther can thus hold to the literal sense but at the same time maintain what he calls "the spiritual sense," which is the reference to Christ. He is critical of the traditional allegorical sense, however, maintaining that the early fathers by ignoring the literal meaning of the words discovered meanings totally alien to the text.[7] From what we have seen of the fathers, this was an indiscriminate accusation. He prefers the words *sign* or *type,* finding his justification in John 3:14: "As Moses lifted up the serpent in the desert, so the Son of Man must be lifted up."[8]

John Calvin (1509–1564)

Calvin introduced to the hermeneutical question the principle of the "internal testimony of the Holy Spirit."[9] For Calvin, it is not the text that is inspired. The text only communicates and informs. It is the reader who is inspired to discern the written word to be God's word. The written word is clear enough, but it takes the Holy Spirit to connect the reader with the message. Calvin's method is a correlation of text (then) and context (now) grounding the interior witness of the Holy Spirit, that is, the interiorization of faith as affective certitude.[10] He also sees the figural sense not as dependent on retrospect from the New Testament but as already imbedded in the Israelites' forward-looking hope as they clung to the promises that at the time they saw as material blessing.[11] In this he clarifies what was presupposed in the fathers' hermeneutics, namely that every gift of God, besides being a gift in itself, is also a promise and often a figure of a greater gift to come. And thus their clinging to the Lord in the covenant that promised blessings was in itself a forward-pointing instance in a lived narrative, of which they had at least some intuition. This would help explain how God's authorship of the Bible, far from being an extrinsically imposed narrative pattern, was in reality experienced immanently by his people, albeit gradually, and progressively interpreted by the biblical writers.

Luther's and Zwingli's insistence that scripture was its own interpreter, and Calvin's reliance on the inner witness of the Holy Spirit, would lead to the Catholic accusation that such a principle would amount eventually to private interpretation. But one should note that Calvin's stress on the interior witness of the Holy Spirit approaches what Vatican II in *Dei Verbum,* article 12, says: "Holy Scripture must be read and interpreted in the same spirit in which it was written." The difference is that the discernment of that Spirit in *Dei Verbum* takes into account a series of controls, especially the tradition of the church. Calvin, however, bypasses church tradition. And yet unconsciously he assumes it when he defends the totality of the canon as authoritative over against Luther's demeaning certain books. For Luther also thought he was guided by the Holy Spirit in making his choices. "Whether he realized it or not, Calvin allowed himself to be guided in this matter by ecclesiastical tradition much more than by his own principles."[12]

But even among the Protestants there were those in the wake of the great reformers who would claim a more-than-literal sense. The Pietists believed that the devout person could perceive, beyond the literal and figural sense and supplementary to it, a deeper meaning quite beyond the grammatical or ordinary sense of the words. This position differed from that of Calvin, who held that the inner testimony of the Holy Spirit enabled one to connect with the single meaning of a given passage (whether literal or figural). The Pietists came to believe that their "spiritual" interpretation, equally inspired by the Spirit, could have an authority equal to the grammatical sense.[13] Even a Lutheran critic like J. A. Ernesti would react against the lurking subjectivism of this approach.[14]

To the Catholic Church, the Pietist strain appeared as a rejection of the community of the past (tradition) and of the community of the present (the authority of the church). The emphasis on scripture alone would also have the effect of putting the principal responsibility for scriptural interpretation on exegesis, and this would have enormous impact on the development of exegesis and hermeneutics in the succeeding centuries.

Focus on the Text

Since the text now had to stand alone, independent and even critical of tradition and the church, more and more emphasis was placed on verbal inspiration and inerrancy.[15] Every word is inspired, and if the sciences disagreed with the Bible, the sciences must be wrong. This stream would carry on to our day in fundamentalism. However, there were those who took the opposite position, for the focus on the self-standing text also led to the discovery of the historically limited nature of the Bible. The Bible's emergence in a specific time and place and culture raised the question of its validity for all times and places and cultures. Independence of authority in religious and biblical matters went hand in hand with the spirit of free enquiry and rationalism that characterized the Enlightenment. Rather than being read to nourish the faith or for personal or corporate transformation, the Bible is to be read as a historical document. That is, it should be read as any other document of history should be read, by scholars who profess value-neutral objectivity. This led to historical criticism in its various forms—text criticism, form criticism, historical background studies, redaction criticism—which we examine in detail in later chapters. All these methods supposed the genetic principle, that is, that the key to meaning in the text was an understanding of the origin and development of the text and the tradition from which it came. They also supposed that the practitioners of these methods were free of their own subjective viewpoints, which later generations would show were as historically limited as were the texts they were examining. Gradually scriptural interpretation was moving from the pulpit to the professor's chair.

When the intellectuals of the Enlightenment took their stand on positivist grounds, they naturally discarded the three "spiritual" senses of the patristic and medieval periods. But they also began to find fault with what had been called the literal sense.

This sense, we remember, was identified in the patristic and early medieval period, with the _historical_, that is, the _gesta_, the events that took place in the story. Of course there was an awareness of metaphor and parable, but generally the historical facticity of the accounts (for example, the book of Jonah) was not questioned. This, however, was now beginning to look different under the microscope of independent historical research. The positivists, of course, came with their own presuppositions, namely, that meaning is historical meaning, as they reconstructed it.

Spinoza and Cocceius

There were those who sought to "save" the Bible by confining it to the safe shores of inspirational reading. Benedict de Spinoza (1634–1677) was one of these. Admitting the historical unreliability of many biblical passages, he wrote:

> Scripture does not explain things by their secondary causes, but only narrates them in the order and the style which has most power to move men, and especially uneducated men, to devotion; and therefore, it speaks inaccurately of God and of events, seeing that its object is not to convince the reason but to attract and lay hold of the imagination.[16]

And even when the literal meaning and the historical reference of a passage are the same, the historical meaning is unimportant, since knowledge and love of God should come from "general ideas, in themselves certain and known, so that the truth of a historical narrative is very far from being requisite for our attaining our highest good."[17] Thus there is a difference between literal and historical interpretation.

Spinoza's position was really a reflection of the earlier humanist position that rhetoric and persuasion are the overriding principle in biblical interpretation. Read the Gospels as literature meant to persuade; other questions are secondary or irrelevant. Modern rhetorical criticism finds an early root here.

The Dutch professor at the University of Leiden, Johannes Cocceius (1603–1669), an ardent disciple of John Calvin, worked out a careful periodization of biblical history, from creation to the end of the world, with Christ at the center, and even, Fiore-like, extending the fulfillment of biblical prophecy into his own day in the death of Sweden's king Gustavus Adolphus. Since there were many other themes besides the Christ-centered one in the Old Testament, Cocceius resorted to extensive figural reading to bring everything into his thesis. Instead of understanding himself as in the flow of the biblical narrative in a real but undifferentiated way, Cocceius reveals the anxiety to prop up the biblical witness with something outside it, a different world. "And so…the Bible's own story becomes increasingly dependent on its relation to other temporal frames of reference to render it illuminating and even real."[18]

The Scientific Revolution and the Enlightenment

Once the Bible was no longer exclusively in the hands of ecclesiastical authority or tradition or the pastorally oriented preacher or catechist and placed in the academy, it had to take its place on a par with the religious literature of the world and its historical claims to be judged by the scientific tools that were rapidly being honed. Already in 1605 Faustus Sozinni, reacting both to the external norm of papal authority, on the one hand, and the appeal to inner experience on the other, published a catechism in which he held that "nothing may be asserted which contradicts sound reason or contains a contradiction in itself."[19] Although this sounds innocent enough to someone who believes God is the one author both of revelation and of reason, in practice it amounted to reducing what can be known with certitude to reason. On the level of the physical sciences, the impact of Sir Isaac Newton (1642–1727) was bringing a wholly new way of understanding the universe itself. Aristotelian physics, which had ruled for two thousands years, now was faced with an alternative, one that would understand all reality in terms of a single complex of laws. Even the existence of the creator could be established by consideration of the laws of the universe. Christian apologists were quick to seize this principle to show that natural philosophy alone was sufficient to establish the existence of God. It was a Pyrrhic victory, however, for while the tradition held that the existence of God could be proved by human reason, the notion of God the *creator* needed the light of revelation and faith. They tacitly accepted that the Christian faith neither established nor defended its own first principle, that of God the creator, but relied on natural philosophy to do that.[20]

But then along came French encyclopedist and philosopher Denis Diderot and Baron Paul d'Holbach and others who argued persuasively that the principles of Newtonian physics showed that the universe could be explained coherently without recourse to a supreme being. Thus while religion needed physics to establish its first principle, physics did not need religion. This insight signaled the rise of modern atheism.

This development had a significance for biblical interpretation that was wider than the Bible itself, for it attacked the very foundation of religion itself. The biblical authors assumed the existence of God the creator, and the whole development of interpretation, whether within the Bible itself, or by others, assumed that because God is creator he can and does intervene in history, and since his interventions reveal a saving purpose, he can and does make one event open to another for which it prepares, and the later fulfills the promise of the former. But a mechanistic view of the universe had no place for such "fantasy." And as more and more scientific discoveries demystified the secrets of nature, intellectuals gradually came to believe that ultimately there would be no more mystery, that science could explain everything and ultimately solve every human problem. Since in their view religion grew out of humanity's need to cope with mystery, in this new understanding there was no place for a Supreme Being and no need for his saving intervention.

In England and Germany

In England Deism questioned the very notion of revelation itself.[21] In its place natural religion, common to the whole human race, was the only authentic religion. The Deists likewise questioned the historicity of the biblical accounts of miracles, since the presumption of the "scientific age" was against them, particularly in the view of natural law that admitted no exceptions. In response to this, efforts were made to find archaeological or historical evidence confirming the biblical witness, for example of the great flood.[22]

John Locke (1632–1704), the empirical philosopher-friend of Newton, affirmed that reason alone must be the judge of all truth, including anything that claimed to be divine revelation. Under Locke's disciple Anthony Collins, the argument about the meaning and interpretation of biblical narratives turned into one about the *reference* of these narratives. The meaning of a history-like narrative is to be judged according to the historical criterion alone.[23] Meaning is identified with reference to independently establishable (that is, empirical) fact claims.[24] Hence, "the art of conveying through narrative the divine dimension of events and their relation to one another could make no sense in terms of Lockean (and later a Kantian) epistemology."[25] Hence, Old Testament prophecies had only one reference, either to a contemporary or a future event, but not to both. This marked the breakdown of the figural or typical sense, since in this view one cannot escape the limits of one single meaning to a biblical proposition. Thus it severed the unity of the two testaments, discarding as it did the possibility of a divine author having more in mind than the human author's literal and univocal meaning. At the same time it abetted the process of measuring the meaning of biblical narrative by historical accuracy.[26]

What was at issue here was not so much the critical study of the Bible. For already in this period Richard Simon (1638–1712) and later Jean Astruc (1684–1766) were doing that in a remarkable way—albeit not without nervousness on the part of ecclesiastical authorities. What was at issue was the very nature of the *meaning* of biblical narrative. Since the understanding of the Bible was totally dependent on whether an event actually happened in precisely the way it was narrated, the study of the Bible, like history in general, was to be modeled on the physical sciences, where autonomous intelligibility, in chronological and causal context, was the norm.

Immanuel Kant (1724–1804) sought to overcome the subject/ object dichotomy posited by René Descartes (1596–1650) by maintaining that the mind does not discover but imposes structure or order on the world, thus blocking access to anything-in-itself. If what one knows is only one's ideas and not the external world, then words are simply the expression of one's ideas or, more precisely, language expresses the subject's *experience* but not *what* is experienced. The knower is isolated on an island, confronted by a chaotic, unlimited, and untrustworthy sea. And the knower imposes order on this flux rather than receiving and perceiving an order already there.[27] In keeping with this theory, Kant proposed that the biblical narratives were ideas in story form, hence allegories, meant to convey moral teaching. This placed them basically in the category of myth, and even his contemporaries, aware of the historical setting and commitment of the Bible witness, were not willing to follow him that far. But Kant's retreat from the historical anticipated later attempts to find meaning in the Bible by bypassing history in favor of eternal or existential truth.

Religious thinkers, for their part, were often inadequate to the task of responding to this challenge of the positivists. Apologists frequently accepted the tenets of Newtonian mechanics and scrambled to find concordances between the physical sciences and what was known of secular history on the one hand and the Bible on the other. At issue was an unwillingness to admit that there could be a distinction between an *autonomous* world and an *independent* one. Autonomy means that nature operates by its own laws. It is not a lifeless marionette moving only when an invisible "god" pulls the strings. Independence, however, means that the universe is self-explanatory; it neither posits nor depends on a creator. The Second Vatican Council made very clear its position on nature's autonomy and the corresponding autonomy of the sciences that explore it:

> If by the autonomy of earthly affairs is meant the gradual discovery, exploitation, and ordering of the laws and values of matter and society, then the demand for autonomy is perfectly in order: it is at once the claim of modern man and the desire of the creator. By the very

nature of creation, material being is endowed with its own stability, truth and excellence, its own order and laws. These man must respect as he recognizes the methods proper to every science and technique. Consequently, methodical research in all branches of knowledge, provided it is carried out in a truly scientific manner and does not override moral laws, can never conflict with the faith, because the things of the world and the things of faith derive from the same God. The humble and persevering investigator of the secrets of nature is being led, as it were, by the hand of God in spite of himself, for it is God, the conserver of all things, who made them what they are. We cannot but deplore certain attitudes (not unknown among Christians) deriving from a shortsighted view of the rightful autonomy of science; they have occasioned conflict and controversy and have misled many into opposing faith and science.

However, if by the term "the autonomy of earthly affairs" is meant that material being does not depend on God and that man can use it as if it had no relation to its creator, then the falsity of such a claim will be obvious to anyone who believes in God. Without a creator there can be no creature. In any case, believers, no matter what their religion, have always recognized the voice and the revelation of God in the language of creatures. Besides, once God is forgotten, the creature is lost sight of as well.[28]

Because the apologists, like their adversaries, were unable to grasp the human dimension of biblical narrative, they were unable to stem the tide of the worldview that accompanied the historical-critical method, nor offer an alterative to it. Pressed by the scientific skepticism about the miracles of Jesus, apologists offered as an alternative the "moral" miracle of his exalted teaching and exemplary character. Or they appealed to the evangelists' trustworthiness, the lifelikeness of their reports, their apostolic origin, and the congruence of the miracles with natural religion.

While in eighteenth-century England the search was on for external confirmation of the biblical message, in Germany the emphasis was on the internal, that is, the literary-historical approach to the text. Interpretation means understanding what the statement says, and there is only one meaning, which is retrievable by the methods used in examining all other nonbiblical texts. Obviously by this time the spiritual senses, whether of the patristic variety or later, were discredited. What is significant, though, is that at this very period a flood of books on hermeneutics began to appear.[29] While eighteenth-century hermeneutics was more a theory of exegesis and its application,[30] it became increasingly evident that historical exegesis of itself, pursued in a positivist sense, was creating a hermeneutical vacuum that somehow needed to be filled.

By the end of the eighteenth century critics were either defending the positivity of the biblical miracle stories (that is, the stories relate actual occurrences), or at the other extreme, explaining that, while the authors intended to describe miracles, it was according to their limited worldview, and the modern scientific worldview cannot accommodate them.[31] It must be said in all fairness that the vast majority of the eighteenth-century critics still had a religious reverence for the Bible and were convinced of its religious significance. Hermann Samuel Reimarus (1694–1728), who held that the gospel story was a tissue of errors on Jesus' part and of lies by his disciples, stood with a handful of like-thinkers in solitary splendor among those who on the contrary defended the lasting value of the Bible as a religious document.[32]

Even so, what was happening on all sides of the debate is that the meaning of a gospel narrative was being sought outside the narrative itself, whether by the critic's reconstruction of the probable historical sequence or by the congruence he perceived in the story with the general religious truth of humankind. That the narrative itself might be seen as conveying meaning apart from its ostensive reference was overlooked, and no cognizance was taken of the literary and narrative shape of the Gospels. And this, despite the fact that the eighteenth century, in England at least, showed a marked interest in the realistic novel so popular at the time. Though there are profound differences, the realistic novel would have provided an alternative base of comparison for the biblical narrative, which likewise from the beginning presented itself as an overarching unit of episodes (real and figural) moving toward a conclusion at the hand of a (divine) author. This is Hans Frei's critique,[33] but it would seem to assume either a divine author of the entire Bible or some kind of consciousness on the part of an individual or a community (the church) that identifies the books of so varied types as integral parts of a consistent and unified narrative. And, of course, to think of the Bible *only* as narrative could lead to equating it with myth and denigrating its serious historical claims.

But there was another consequence of this movement to seek the meaning of the Bible outside itself. J. S. Semler in a series of essays published between 1771 and 1775[34] aimed his critical guns at the canon itself. Since each book of the Bible is to be considered in its historical context, many of the books are of merely archival and not of religious interest, and Semler sets up a criterion for judging them accordingly. And therefore the determination of what books belong to the canon is of mere human, not divine, authority. (We remember that the gradual acceptance of books into the canon in the early centuries was dictated primarily on doctrinal and apostolic grounds.) Obviously here Semler sets up himself, rather than the ecclesial community, as the arbiter of the religious value of the books.

Furthermore, since the Bible had now been cut free from its doctrinal overseer, whether Catholic or Protestant, it was now exegesis that determined dogma and not dogma exegesis. Johann Philipp Gabler was the first to express this hitherto latent conclusion.[35] But this would obviously involve some judgment as to the relative authority of texts, especially when these are in tension with one another. Whose judgment, then, prevailed?

Thematic Progression: An Alternative Key to the Unity of the Bible?

Figural interpretation, we have noted, affirmed the unity of the testaments in the fact that one event had meaning not only in itself but also as forward-pointing to a later fulfillment, and this

81

because of the plan of God, who is the ultimate author of the Bible. Although a given event was part of an overarching story, it did not matter if there were a great lapse of time between the earlier event and its later fulfillment. But this figural approach had by now long been dismissed. Scholars then searched for an alternative key to the unity of the Bible. Several believed they found it in a specific theme that could be found, to a greater or less degree, in every book of the Bible. Although this approach flourished in the mid-twentieth century, its roots can be traced to the late eighteenth century. It consisted in following a central theme of the Bible, from the earliest text to the latest, showing its gradual development. Walter Eichrodt found the central theme to be covenant, Oscar Cullman time, Gerhard von Rad salvation. Frei has accurately described the difference of this approach to that of figural narration:

> Biblical unity is not the enactment of a single pattern of meaning through a specific set of interactions constituting a single story consummated over a temporal span [figural narration]. It is the history of the tradition of the writings about the events depicted.[36]

As fruitful as the works of these scholars proved to be (and I myself wrote a book tracing the theme of the Spirit from Genesis to Revelation), the fact that different scholars found different centers and that not every book of the Bible could easily be squeezed under the umbrella of the theme proposed indicated that the single-theme approach was inadequate to account for the Bible's unity. The Pontifical Biblical Commission in its 2002 document, *The Jewish People and Their Scriptures in the Christian Bible,* used a multiple-theme approach to show the continuity of the Old Testament to the New, without proposing a single theme as the central one. The one-theme approach also demanded a certain amount of historical reconstruction, which, of course was not always acceptable to other members of the academy, much less comprehensible to the nonspecialist. In a later chapter we discuss how proponents of a canonical approach sought to remedy the problem of the Bible's unity by finding it in the community's reception of the various books.

Fact or Myth

By the end of the eighteenth century, then, biblical interpretation evinced two directions: either the biblical texts were explained by reference to historical facts (whether they did or did not happen) or they were considered nonrealistic accounts whose value lay in their moral or religious teaching. The critical work of the German biblicists in particular raised the question of how the Christian faith could be related to historical events whose actuality had become more and more elusive under their critical examination. The issue reached a climax when David F. Strauss published his *Life of Jesus* in 1835.[37] He asked two questions: (1) Is the foundation of the Christian faith, namely the truth of the Gospels, necessarily connected with reliable historical knowledge of Jesus or the church's claim to his unique relation to God? (2) If so, can it be shown that the supernatural events that confirm this claim really or probably happened? Strauss did not accuse the gospel writers of deception. He simply said that they were captive of the time-conditioned consciousness out of which they wrote, which was a mythical worldview. His understanding of "myth," however, was not the commonly accepted definition as the history of the gods (which could find no place in the Bible), but the intervention of the divine into the human without mediation—in short, what others would call the miraculous.[38] The miracle stories of Jesus were the product of a mind and a culture that had not yet risen to abstract thought. The narratives are the expression of philosophical or historical or poetic myth. Unlike the Romantics who had a positive interest in myth, Strauss was interested in myth largely as a means of discrediting the historical reliability of the Gospels. His attack was based less on available comparisons outside the Gospels, material that was too sparse to be significant, than on internal criteria, among which were his comparison with the general experience of natural, historical, and psychic occurrences in the modern age. We don't experience miracles today of the sort reported in the Gospels; hence the likelihood that they did not "really" happen. Not wishing to cast Christianity and the Bible out as a whole, he maintained that dogmatic claims need have no basis in the factuality of the gospel

83

accounts, and in the conclusion of his book he said that the doctrine of the God-man "really means the eternal incarnation of the divine Idea in the human species as a whole and its historically developing general consciousness."[39]

The "mythophiles" like Strauss so stressed the difference of the ancient worldview from the modern that there appeared to be little possibility of retrieving contemporary meaning from them. Prior to this sea-change, it was generally assumed that the literal sense of the Bible, particularly of the Gospels, was adequate for contemporary applicability. But now, as the *distance* of the text's world was being more and more stressed, the rise of hermeneutics proper, that is, a second stage of understanding, began to come to the fore. Hermeneutics as making sense and application of an ancient text was now becoming something clearly separate and distinct from textual analysis.

Hans Frei summarizes the critical positions at the beginning of the nineteenth century:[40]

> 1. Those who held that the meaning of the narratives lay in *the real spatio-temporal world* to which they refer (ostensive reference), and these critics fell into three subcategories:
> a. The "Supernaturalists" took the narratives *literally*, that is, if miracles are related they actually happened that way
> b. The "Naturalists" who maintained that *behind* the related supernatural event was some natural occurrence on which the supernatural account was based [Paulus in his 1828 *Leben Jesu* maintained that the angels at the nativity were phosphorescence, the narratives of healings omit their natural causes, and the transfiguration story is the product of sleepy disciples who saw Jesus talking with two unknown persons during a beautiful sunset.[41] Some more recent commentators have suggested that Jesus' multiplication of loaves was merely an invitation to the crowds to share the food they had brought.]
> c. Those who (like Reimarus) claimed that the accounts did intend to relate actual events but were *deceptions*

2. Those who held that the narratives were *religious or moral truths in story form*. These in turn fell into two groups:
    a. Those who held that it was actually the author's *intention* to write these fables or allegories
    b. Kant, who dismissed any concern about the author's intention as well as any concern about the genesis of the accounts, and held that the meaning of the narratives lay solely in the *ideas* they represent
3. The *mythophiles* who rejected any ostensive reference in the narratives and the significance of the author's intention, for the latter was captive of the mythological worldview no longer tenable today. That is, the biblical authors saw whatever they were describing or experiencing inescapably in the clothing of myth.

Behind all these positions was a common assumption shared by all the debaters: that the *meaning* of a text is found somewhere other than in the text itself.[42] At the end of his analysis of this entire period, the narrative critic Hans Frei attempts to elucidate that which was overlooked in the entire quest:

> The literary parallel between history writing and history-like writing is perfectly clear: in each case narrative form and meaning are inseparable, precisely because in both cases meaning is in large part a function of the interaction of character and circumstances. It is not going too far to say that the story is the meaning or, alternatively, that the meaning emerges from the story form, rather than being merely illustrated by it, as would be the case in allegory and in a different way, in myth. A great theme in literature of the novelistic type, like a pattern in a historical sequence, cannot be paraphrased by a general statement. To do so would approach reducing it to meaninglessness. In each case the theme has meaning only to the extent that it is instantiated and hence narrated; and this meaning through instantiation is not *illustrated* (as though it were an intellectually presubsisting or preconceived archetype or ideal essence) but *constituted*

through the mutual, specific determination of agents, speech, social context, and circumstances that form the indispensable narrative web.

If one used the metaphorical expression "location of meaning," one would want to say that the location of meaning in narrative of the realistic sort is the text, the narrative structure or sequence itself. If one asks if it is the subject matter or the verbal sense that ought to have priority in the quest for understanding, the answer would be that the question is illegitimate or redundant. For whatever the situation that may obtain in other types of texts, in narrative of the sort in which character, verbal communications, and circumstances are each determinative of the other and of the theme itself, the text, the verbal sense, and not a profound, buried stratum underneath constitutes or determines the subject matter itself.[43]

Historical Criticism in the Later Nineteenth Century

Before moving to the next chapter we must say a word about the state of historical criticism in the remainder of the nineteenth century. F. C. Baur, professor of historical theology at Tübingen from 1826 to 1860, was strongly influenced by Hegel's thesis-antithesis-synthesis thinking.[44] He applied this to the genesis of the New Testament: the earliest Christian Jews wanted a thoroughly Jewish Christianity (thesis); this was challenged by Paul who conflicted with their narrow ideas (antithesis); finally the two were reconciled in a synthesis represented by the Gospels. In France, Joseph Ernest Renan's (1823–1892) *Vie de Jésus* also followed the positivist trend. But there too in response to the liberals, J. B. Pérès used the methods of the positivist scholars to "prove" that Napoleon never existed. In Germany Julius Wellhausen proposed his famous theory known as the "four sources" of the Pentateuch, which would affect Old Testament research to our day. Adolf Harnack continued the either/or tradition: "Either the Gospel is in all respects identical with its earliest form, in which case it came with its time and has departed with it; or else it contains something that, under differing historical forms, is of permanent validity."[45] He strongly harkened back to the spirit of the Reformation, rejecting all formal, external authority—of councils, priests, and the whole tradition of the church.[46] Hence, the supremacy of individual interpretation, or of the academy.

One thing that all the critics we have studied in this period agreed upon was that no external authority like the church or tradition should impinge upon the free interpretation of the scriptures. To that authority and tradition, which stood outside the text, they substituted other extratextual "authorities" according to their particular methodological presuppositions. In the meantime, what was going on with the Catholic Church and among Catholic scholars? To that question we now turn.

SIX

The Bible and the Church: The Catholic Response

Given the climate of the time, development of hermeneutical theory in the Catholic camp in the sixteenth and seventeenth centuries was influenced largely by the need to respond to the cataclysmic threat that the Reformation presented to the church. The tendency was twofold. First, Catholic apologists insisted that it was not from scripture alone that the church draws its certitude concerning revelation. Tradition too must be taken into account even in the interpretation of scripture, and that tradition also involves the authoritative decrees of councils over the centuries. Second, the use of scripture in the polemical climate of the day tended to be proof-texting, that is, finding support in individual scripture passages for church doctrines being threatened by the Reformation.

There were, of course, Catholics who found much worthwhile in the new critical approach to the scriptures. The Jesuit Maldonatus (d. 1583) produced a sober and excellent commentary for the time. Richard Simon (1638–1712), ordained a priest of the Oratory in 1670, wrote his *Histoire critique du Vieux Testament* ("A Critical History of the Old Testament") in 1678, in which he tackled the problems involved in the composition of the Pentateuch. It provoked a strong reaction from both Protestant and Catholic theologians (Bossuet violently opposed him), and as a result he was expelled from the Oratory. In retirement he published several works under pseudonyms. He seemed to have no problem reconciling his critical studies with his Catholic faith, which he never abandoned. John Astruc, a Catholic doctor, continued the critical discussion of the Pentateuch in 1753. The work of Julius Wellhausen (1844–1918) on the sources of the Pentateuch shook the conservative community, both Catholic and Protestant. Underlying his valuable critical work was the presentation of the evolution of <u>Yahwistic religion</u> from a naturalist point of view, from the monolatry of Moses' time to the monotheism of the prophets, <u>leaving no place it seemed to divine revelation.</u> This <u>appeared to Catholics and orthodox</u> Protestants as a complete <u>rejection of their religious view of the</u> Old Testament.

Ernest Renan (1823–1892), Brittany-born Catholic and one-time seminarian of the Oratory, made outstanding contributions to the study of Semitic languages. In 1863 he published his *Vie de Jésus* ("Life of Jesus"). Written in an engaging style, it was widely read in France. Renan presented Christ as an "incomparable man" (the expression that cost him his professorship at the Collège de France in 1862), and in the end he denied the supernatural, the divinity of Christ, and the existence of a transcendent God. The Dominican M.-J. Lagrange, founder of the École Biblique in Jerusalem, answered him in a full-length book.[1] Renan concluded that because of the contradictions in the Bible it cannot be a divinely inspired book:

> In a divine book, everything is true, and since two contradictory statements cannot be true at the same time, there must be no contradictions in it. Now the attentive study that I made of the Bible, while revealing historical and aesthetic treasures to me, also proved to me that this book was no more exempt than any other ancient book from contradictions, mistakes, errors. In it there are fables, legends, traces of purely human composition.[2]

Later interpreters of a more conservative bent would have to deal with the problem of inerrancy in historical and scientific matters and the expression of differing, even contradictory viewpoints in the Bible. And they would. But for Renan, these kinds of errors or contradictions nullified the possibility of divine revelation.

It was largely the naturalistic ideology that accompanied the historical-critical method that provoked such a strong reaction on the part of the Catholic Church authorities. Writings of rationalist critics were put on the Index of Forbidden Books, Pope Pius IX issued his Syllabus of Errors in 1864, and Pope Leo XIII warned of the errors of liberalism in his 1893 encyclical *Providentissimus*

Deus. When Father Lagrange expressed interest in the documentary hypothesis of the Pentateuch, he was silenced for a time, and he turned to specializing in the New Testament.

Modernism

But just after the turn of the century a new form of rationalism developed in the Catholic community, ironically as an attempt to cope with rationalism's attack on religion. "Modernists," as they were called, felt that the future of the church depended upon its accommodation to the assured results of modern science, in particular the results of the preceding century of historical criticism. They claimed as their ally not only science but John Henry Cardinal Newman in his essay on the development of doctrine. Newman, now dead, was unable to correct the errors of his modernist interpreters. In *L'Évangile et l'église* ("The Gospel and the Church"), Alfred Loisy sought to answer Harnack's *Das Wesen des Christentums* ("The Essence of Christianity"). On the one hand he defended tradition: "We know Christ only by the tradition, across the tradition, and in the tradition of the primitive Christians....The mere idea of the gospel without tradition is in flagrant contradiction with the facts submitted to criticism."[3] But at the same time he explained away many New Testament passages as without basis in history, he denied the actuality of miracles (they occurred only to the eye of faith), and he attacked the role of the church in authoritative interpretation of the Bible. He calls the latter "traditional" exegesis and says it stands "in permanent contradiction with the principles of a purely rational and historical interpretation."[4] Yet he tried to save both kinds of exegesis by implying that each was right in its own sphere, coming close to positing a separation between faith and knowledge. Loisy was excommunicated for his views, and Pope Pius X condemned modernism in his encyclical *Pascendi Dominici Gregis* (1907). Among the errors condemned was the view that the inspiration of scripture did not prevent error in it. To this point we shall return later.

One of the most fruitful effects of the modernist crisis was the establishment of the Pontifical Institute for Biblical Studies in Rome and the establishment in 1901 of the Pontifical Biblical Commission. The latter was a commission that involved a large number of biblical experts as consultors. The commission was to monitor developments in biblical studies and publish its decisions as a guide to Catholic biblical study. In the climate of the modernist crisis, the decisions of the commission, up to the publication of Pius XII's *Divino Afflante Spiritu* in 1943, were exceedingly cautious and by today's standards unnecessarily so. Moses was directly or indirectly the author of the Pentateuch, the arguments for Isaiah 40–55 being from a different hand were not decisive, the formation of the first woman from the first man was to be taken as historical truth, and so on. By the middle of the century the climate had so changed that these earlier decisions were no longer considered normative for exegetical research, even by officials of the Pontifical Biblical Commission.[5]

But such was the atmosphere of the modernist crisis. Neither naturalistic nor historical positivism nor the modernist attempt to answer it was satisfactory, in large measure because there were philosophical underpinnings that were unacceptable to the Catholic faith.

The Form Critics: Bultmann, Dibelius, and Friends

Meantime, Protestant exegesis was taking another turn. After the First World War, Rudolf Bultmann, heavily influenced by existentialism, concluded that to win the postwar culture to the gospel it was fruitless to insist on the historicity of the gospel accounts, which could not be proved anyway, and that what was needed was a proclamation of the gospel message according to what it really is: proclamation or *kerygma*. The mythological matrix of the Gospels needed to be purged. He called this "demythologizing," and he used the Bible's assumption of a triple-decker universe—heaven above, earth here, hell below—as an example of a mythological worldview that is irreconcilable with modern science. The

Gospels' historical content *(historisch)* was neither provable nor relevant. Instead the *historic (geschichtlich)* meaning of the proclamation is the only retrievable element, and it is this that, confronting modern man, will offer him the option of authentic existence. And for Bultmann, that meant *remythologizing* the gospel into the categories of existentialism. This reductionism accounts for the negative reception in many quarters of the contributions Bultmann made in form criticism.

Though Bultmann is the best remembered, there were other German contemporaries in the form-critical movement: M. Dibelius, K. L. Schmidt, P. Albertz, and G. Bertram, all of whom published about the same time (1919–1922). Their great contribution in the critical study of the Gospels was their calling attention to the role of the early Christian communities in the formulation of the Gospels. What we have in the Gospels is not an unmediated contact with Jesus but rather the faith expression of early Christian communities. And the Gospels are collections of various units, which can be classified according to their literary *forms* (for example miracle stories, pronouncement stories, legends, and so on). These can then be studied in terms of their development in the earlier, largely oral, life of the church up to their present shape in the Gospels. The English term for this method is *form criticism,* but the German *Formgeschichte* is more accurate: "the history of forms." Bultmann held that the creative work of the communities was primary, that fidelity to a normative tradition going back to Jesus was minimal. For this he would come under fire later by some of his own disciples. But his positive contribution was to highlight the role of the early church in the shaping of the gospel tradition.

Though this chapter is concerned primarily with the reaction of the Catholic Church, note should be made of the influence of Heidegger (whom we treat in the next chapter) and the Protestant revolt against liberal rationalism led by Karl Barth's 1921 publication of *Romans.*

While distrust of Bultmann's proposals was widespread, a number of conservative scholars found his insights valuable. Vincent Taylor's commentary on Mark utilized the insights of the form critics without swallowing either the hypothesis of total creativity or the philosophy of existentialism. So too Joachim Jeremias's and C. H. Dodd's work on the parables of Jesus. Significant studies by Catholics began to appear, for example K. H. Schelkle's study on the passion of Jesus and A. Descamps on the concept of justice in the New Testament.

Divino Afflante Spiritu

Though there was a stormy period in the 1920s between the Roman curia and the exegetes, with some works put on the Index of Forbidden Books, biblical study was now advancing upon a less threatening terrain. Protestant exegesis was becoming less tendentious and radical; in fact it was becoming more interested in the religious message of the gospel, Catholic scholars were showing by the very nature of their publications that the new approaches could enrich the faith rather than oppose it, and on the popular level the biblical movement was growing in intensity and depth. As often happens, the floodgates of a more moderate approach were opened by an attempt to shut them firmly. An Italian priest circulated an anonymous forty-eight page pamphlet severely attacking the use of scientific, historical, and critical methods to study and interpret the scriptures. He targeted especially the Pontifical Biblical Institute. The Biblical Commission felt compelled to answer this attack in a letter dated August 20, 1941. Substantially it prepared for the pope's encyclical two years later. Against the pamphlet's extolling subjective and allegorical meanings, the commission upheld the literal sense as foundational for the Bible's meaning, that is, for any other senses that might be drawn from the text. The letter further upheld the authority of the original texts, thus removing the Latin Vulgate from the unique dominance that the pamphlet proposed (on the basis of an exaggerated interpretation of the Council of Trent), and consequently the importance of textual criticism and the study of Eastern languages and the auxiliary sciences.

These principles were taken up and expanded in Pope Pius XII's liberating encyclical, *Divino Afflante Spiritu* in 1943, issued exactly fifty years after Leo XIII's biblical encyclical

Providentissimus Deus. He listed a number of conditions for biblical exegesis and interpretation that would be both scientific and Christian: (1) a return to the original texts; (2) a proper interpretation of the sacred books based on the literal sense. While affirming that there is a legitimate theological and spiritual sense, for this the exegete should take into account the fathers and doctors and great exegetes of the Catholic tradition; (3) commentators should take into account the personality of the author, the literary forms he uses (including the ancients' understanding of history), and the contributions of archeology, history, and the literature of other peoples of biblical times; (4) finally, the pope gives guidelines for the teaching of scripture to the faithful and to seminarians.

The encyclical opened the way to a revival of Catholic biblical studies unparalleled in the history of the church since patristic times.[6] It also marked the beginning of a more positive attitude on the part of the Roman authorities concerning the acquired results of biblical research. For example, in 1948, responding to a question about the historicity of the first eleven chapters of Genesis, the Pontifical Biblical Commission wrote:

> To declare *a priori* that these narratives do not contain history in the modern sense of the word might easily be understood as meaning that they do not contain it in any sense, although they relate in simple and figurative language, adapted to the understanding of mankind at a lower stage of development, the fundamental truths presupposed by the economy of salvation, as well as the popular description of the beginnings of the human race and the chosen people.[7]

Though today the expression "lower stage of development" sounds condescending and culturally chauvinistic, the Commission's response marked a real breakthrough in affirming an understanding of Genesis 1–11 in terms of its literary form—a *popular* description, which therefore need not mean scientific or historical exactitude. Furthermore, in stating that the stories in those chapters related in simple and figurative language the *truths* of salvation, the statement clearly affirmed their *literary* character as key to interpreting their meaning. Though by no means denying their historical foundation, the commission accepted what was becoming increasingly obvious to the scholarly community, that these introductory chapters were concerned to show humanity's need for salvation by portraying the origins of the world and the race in narrative forms familiar to the ancient world. This could mean that the writers were acquainted with the mythologies of the surrounding peoples from which they could borrow motifs to illustrate the monotheistic and salvific faith of Israel.

In the wake of this liberating atmosphere, Catholic scholarship developed with an explosive rapidity. While many felt free to pursue their historical-critical research without concern about synthesis, others found that their research into the literal, historical sense could render a service to the church that, far from undermining the faith, could nourish and strengthen it. On the popular level, the Catholic biblical movement kept pace with scholarly research. The new insights would bear fruit at the Second Vatican Council in its Constitution on Divine Revelation *(Dei Verbum),* which we examine later, in the document on *The Historical Truth of the Gospels,* and in the 1993 documents of the Pontifical Biblical Commission, *The Interpretation of the Bible in the Church* (1993), and *The Jewish People and Their Sacred Scriptures in the Christian Bible* (2002), which we also discuss further on.

SEVEN

Hermeneutical Theory: From Text to Subject to the Hermeneutics of Understanding

Friedrich Schleiermacher: Meeting the Spirit of the Author

Biblical hermeneutics in the late nineteenth and twentieth centuries would be heavily influenced by *general* hermeneutics, that is, the theory or philosophy of how human beings derive understanding and meanings from any text or communication. Immanuel Kant's ideational theory of interpretation was universally rejected, but his focusing on the relationship between subject and object in the process of knowing marked a philosophical divide that would influence hermeneutical theory from the nineteenth century onward. Although the positivistic trends of the previous century continued right into the twentieth century, Friedrich Schleiermacher (1768–1834) initiated an approach that would gain him the title of the father of the general hermeneutics of understanding. He moved the hermeneutical question from a preoccupation with finding meaning in an objective world outside the text (as we saw in chapter 5) to the exploration of the very nature of the understanding process, namely what happens intersubjectively in the process between the author's creative moment and the subject's interpretative moment.[1] It is to Schleiermacher's credit that he views the text not as an object to be dissected as in a laboratory but as the creation of a human person. And thus interpretation has an inescapably interpersonal dimension. For Schleiermacher, the interpreter recreates the discourse in such a way that it is no mere mechanical copy but is penetrated by the interpreter's own understanding. So true is this that Schleiermacher said the interpreter's task is to "understand the discourse first as well as and then better than its originator."[2] In the act of understanding there is an immediate communion of interpreter and author in the latter's self-expression without the intervention of time or transmission. Interpretation is more of an art than a science because it is an intersubjective act. As such it can only be an approximation, and thus the process is never complete. Although the interpreter moves from the author's discourse to his thought, thus reversing the process by which the discourse was created, still the process is also a divinatory one by which one turns oneself as it were into the other by the kind of intuition appropriate to esthetic or artistic understanding. And as the interpreter probes beyond the author's mere act of creation and even his intention to its source in the author's life, its organic development, its cultural connections and its wholeness, the interpreter can indeed understand the work better than the author unless the author himself decides to become his own interpreter, which is a function subsequent to his authoring. Schleiermacher does not discount the role of the grammatical or linguistic analysis but suggests that there needs to be an oscillation between that activity and the psychological/intuitive/esthetic for understanding to happen. How these two relate in themselves is never clear in Schleiermacher's thought—they come together only in the interpreter's stance of understanding. Because understanding ultimately involves the fusion of author and interpreter, the distinction between explication of a text (what it meant) and its application (what it means to me here and now) is no longer significant because both take place in the act of understanding.

In this view, it is neither the ostensive reference nor general ideas that is important in interpretation but rather the grasping of the spirit of the author. This is of course easier in the nonnarrative portions of the Bible because the spirit of the author is more immediately available than in the narratives, which are presented as reports of external happenings. As far as narratives are concerned, Schleiermacher prefers the Gospel of John because the author's spirit is more patent than in the Synoptics, which seem to be more collections than organic works. The author's spirit is itself a reflection of the consciousness of Jesus, which is diffused in different ways in all the authors of the New Testament. He draws a strange conclusion from this fact: "The holy books have become the Bible in virtue of their own power, but they do not forbid any other book from being or becoming a Bible in its turn," since the person of Jesus Christ is all that is normative.[3] This consciousness of Jesus accounts for the unity of the canon. Narrative continuity thus lies not in the interaction of character and setting and external events but in consciousness, of which the narrative is the self-manifestation. This amounts to discounting the significance of the action or interaction of author and his social context. If "consciousness" totally defines what it means to be human, then the social bond, the solidarity with the author's world, even when he differentiates himself from it, fades from view. And that means that the author's narrative is more like a series of windows through which one can view the author's spirit.

This theory is what led Schleiermacher to imply that the death of Jesus upon the cross was only apparent. In part, this posture, which made the resurrection less than miraculous, may have come from the spirit of the age, which was totally skeptic regarding miracles. But more important, as Frei remarks, this position makes the narrative story of Jesus ludicrously anticlimactic, thus destroying its narrative unity. But it is not incompatible with Schleiermacher's hermeneutical theory, if indeed the only thing holding the narrative together is the consciousness of Jesus in its various manifestations. For the death of Jesus would have been a foreign intrusion, something beyond his power to control, no matter what his "consciousness." Others, who claimed that Jesus did indeed die, had the problem of relating the resurrection to the consciousness of Jesus, for it obviously involved the intrusion of God into the story, so that it was no longer Jesus' consciousness but God's, so to speak, that takes over.

It becomes clear, then, that Schleiermacher's reaction to his predecessors did not guarantee his freedom from their basic supposition: that the meaning of the biblical narratives lay outside the narratives themselves—not in their facticity or ideas but in the spirit of the author. This led him ultimately to acknowledge such a difference between thought and language that the latter suffers at the expense of the former. Language must be taken seriously, but it must be passed through to reach the spirit of the author.

One of the concepts basic to Schleiermacher's theory was that of the *hermeneutical circle*. When we read a sentence, for example, the meaning of the individual words depends on the sentence as a whole. And yet the sentence as a whole depends on the meaning of the individual words. Logic would seem to say that you must understand one before you can understand the other. But such is not the case. *Intuition* enables you to comprehend both whole and parts in a single act of understanding, the way a child understands a new word. This interrelation between the whole and the parts is what is called "the hermeneutical circle." Applied to the process of interpretation, this means that we must come to a text already with some pre-understanding of what it is talking about or we will not understand it at all. We bring our personal history, our previous experience, to our understanding of the text, and the text as "other" challenges our world. Perhaps this is the greatest contribution made by the German scholar—not his "psychologizing," that is, trying to get into the mental processes of the author, but his awareness of the process of understanding in the reader/hearer, especially the world that the latter brings to her encounter with the text.

The pertinent point for hermeneutics is this: For Schleiermacher, language expresses the subject's *experience* but not *what* is experienced. Since God is beyond categories and words, these can only express our experience of God and not God in himself. In other words, when we talk about God we are talking about our *experience* of God, not about God as he really is in himself. Ockham and Kant are the ancestors of this view, but through Schleiermacher they will have an immense progeny. Since words are only labels for the individual's experience of God, the question immediately arises: Whose experience is authoritative? Evidently none. One person's experience of God is just as authoritative as another's. The consequences for building a universal community based on an authoritative revelation are dire. And as for scriptural interpretation, the text becomes only a triggering device to put the reader's experience in contact with the experience (the "consciousness") of Christ. But there is no apparent norm by which anyone's understanding of that experience is better than another's. As Donald Senior has pointed out in a more contemporary context, if the world in front of the text can be recontextualized in a series of diverse and equally competent readings, it is impossible to deny an apartheid or antifeminist reading an equal hearing with a feminist reading.[4]

Wilhelm Dilthey:
Human Sciences and Historicality

Though interest in hermeneutics continued in legal and philosophical studies, it waned in biblical studies after the death of Schleiermacher in 1834. But toward the end of the century it resurfaced in the work of Wilhelm Dilthey (1833–1911).[5] As Palmer observes, Dilthey reacted strongly to the positivist tendency to apply the norms of the natural sciences to humane studies. And at the same time he was unhappy with the idealist tendency to take speculation as a starting point of the human sciences (what he called *Geisteswissenschaften*—literally, the "sciences of the spirit," what we might call the social sciences today). But in his concern to discover "objectively valid" interpretations of "expressions of inner life" (that is, mental life), he was trying to bring together opposite, perhaps even contradictory expectations. In any case, he maintained that the starting point for his method must be concrete experience.

Though he was very concerned with the knowing subject, he disagreed with Locke, Hume, and Kant in their tendency to restrict knowing to the cognitive faculty without reference to feeling and will. He was critical of their tendency to abstraction and generalizations that their universal laws and principles involved. Moreover, the Kantian categories in *The Critique of Pure Reason* are not suitable for the human sciences, for the study of man must take into consideration his historicality *(Geschichtlichkeit),* that is, his insertion into the flow of past, present, and future, where we experience life not in the static categories but in individual moments of "meaning." *Experience (Erlebnis)* for Dilthey is full of meaning prior to our reflection upon it, and it already contains within itself horizons of past and future, though this becomes sharpened by reflection—the past as recollection, the future as anticipation. The temporal unity—that is, the connectedness of the experience to past and future, is not something the mind imposes on the experience (as the Kantians would have it). Reflection merely brings to light what is already there.

Dilthey argues that human living is not a mass of disconnected facts. It is encountered everywhere as already organized, structured, interpreted, and therefore meaningful. Thus the human sciences are necessarily hermeneutical, for they are a grasp of the principles of this structure of the life-world. There is in human beings a persistent tendency to achieve a comprehensive interpretation, in which one's picture of reality is combined with a sense of its meaning and value. This "world-picture" *(Weltanschauung)* is a subjective event, and it sets up the conditions for understanding any human event, including a text. These conditions are twofold: first, we must be familiar with the mental processes through which meaning is experienced and conveyed, beginning with concrete context (for example, if we do not love or abhor something, we cannot understand love and abhorrence). Second, we need to know the social and cultural context that controls the expression of the experience. Hence, when this experience is *expressed* in language, it goes beyond being simply a disclosure of the person; it reveals a sociohistorical reality of life itself and thus enables the understander to commune with the speaker/author's world because of his analogous human experience. Finally, understanding is the process by which we comprehend living human experience or meet another person (the author, speaker, artist) in his or her lived human experience.

Is this Schleiermacher *redivivus*? Yes and no. Like Schleiermacher, Dilthey believed that the proper human achievement is the understanding of another person, but unlike Schleiermacher, that understanding was of the other's "world," that is, the complex of feelings and reactions and values that one comes to share. The natural sciences may at times study the same facts or objects, but the social sciences are interested in what these mean for the inner life of the human person. The former may "explain" things. The latter alone enable understanding: "We explain nature; man we must understand."[6]

In the end, Dilthey's theory is that understanding is a subjective experience of intersubjectivity. Though he rejected Kant's categories because they were empirical generalizations, he substituted his own "categories of life" as the principles by which we organize our experience. Thus we interpret events in terms of some prior relationship (for example, part and whole, means and end, value, purpose). These categories exist "below consciousness," and inasmuch as we use them to organize our experience, they serve the same purpose as Kant's categories, the imposition of the mind on the world. Dilthey is still caught in Kantian subjectivism that goes back to Descartes.

A critical aspect of Dilthey's theory of understanding is man's historicality. He posits not only that history is the only vehicle of understanding who he is ("What man is only history can tell him"[7]), but that man has no fixed nature and is yet undetermined. He will decide not only how he will develop but what he will be. This leads Dilthey to historical relativism. As Palmer reads him, "History is ultimately a series of world views, and we have no firm and fixed standards of judgment for seeing the superiority of one world view over another."[8] This leads to his own view of the hermeneutical circle. Human understanding of our history, and therefore of ourselves, is historically conditioned and therefore changes with time. Each moment of human life is but a freeze-frame in a constantly moving scene. When we today look back on a given period or culture, we become aware of how historically conditioned were the people living in that time, and yet even they were moving. But the same holds for ourselves. We are conditioned by our "world," which is a kind of lens through which we view the past, and we too are constantly moving. Think of two fighter planes in a dogfight. They are both moving targets, and a freeze-frame of either of them is only a momentary blip in a constantly moving scenario. Or think of two celestial bodies moving around one another. The position of each in relation to the other is constantly changing.

A consequence of this hermeneutical circle, as Dilthey applies it to life, is that there is no presuppositionless understanding. We are always contextualized by our horizon. Gadamer will later point out that this limitation or "prejudice" does not negate the possibility of truth, for some presuppositions are obviously "truer" than others. Authority is not necessarily wrong just because it is authority. But we are getting ahead of our story.

Another positive consequence is the reality check that this "historicality" provides upon our contemporary judgment of past societies and cultures. We realize how easily we can become chauvinistic, despising other cultures, past or present, as "primitive," while being myopic about the limitations of our own. On the other hand, we can be so persuaded of the constantly changing scene that we conclude that there is no permanent truth that transcends historical limitations, others' or ours. And there is much in our contemporary experience that fosters this assumption. In the medical field for example, women were once advised to take hormones to replace those lost in menopause. Now it is said that such therapy is dangerous. Once eggs were part of a wholesome diet, then the cholesterol scare said they weren't, and now they've been rehabilitated as part of a healthful diet. This heuristic approach in the fields of science easily gets universalized as a dictum that all truth is at best only momentary, what is true today may be false tomorrow, and vice versa. This is clearly historical relativism. There is nothing outside the successive worldviews, as Dilthey sees it, by which to judge the superiority of one over the other. Events and the persons who interpret them are both moving targets. And particularly this unmoored system makes difficult if not impossible historical continuity and authoritative interpretation in a community like the church.

As far as the Bible is concerned, or any definitive determination of doctrine for that matter, one can play the "historical limitation" card and dismiss any continuity or permanence of truth that one chooses. Somewhere one needs to deal with the possibility of organic development of tradition, or, to be more specific, the possibility of a discontinuity occurring within a broader continuity. Another word for growth. But, just as the acorn's fruit in the tree may be infected by disease, or by the intrusion of a choking vine, and thus deteriorate, so also tradition, for not all change in an organism is necessarily organic.

Is it possible, then, to avoid drowning in a historical relativism? Bernard Lonergan offers an alternative in his development of the critical role of judgment, which we discuss further on. In sum, Dilthey's major contributions were to set hermeneutics within the human sciences and to highlight the historical conditions that affect both the event and the interpreter. He will have a major influence on Heidegger, Gadamer, and Ricoeur.

Martin Heidegger: Hermeneutics as Ontology

With Martin Heidegger (1889–1976) there is a new development. He extends the concept of hermeneutics beyond a particular discipline, even beyond a method for the human sciences (Dilthey), to encompass being itself. To use "understanding" in this sense will be new to the person who has always understood it to mean an intellectual endeavor to comprehend what is heard or read. For Heidegger, being itself is self-disclosing. Technically, Being *(Sein)* discloses itself in being-there *(Dasein),* which is human being.[9] Understanding is not projecting meaning onto phenomena. Rather, what appears is an ontological manifestation of Being itself. Hermeneutics as the methodology of the human sciences is only a particular manifestation of the hermeneutics of existence. Heidegger's concept of understanding differs from that of Schleiermacher, for whom understanding meant identifying with the speaker/author's inner reality. It also differs from Dilthey, for whom understanding was a grasp of lived experience or of life itself. Even more does Heidegger differ from Kant, for whom the subject imposes order on the object that is otherwise not attainable in itself. For Heidegger understanding constitutes one's possibilities for being within the life-world in which one exists. It is not something one possesses but a way of being-in-the-world.[10] It is not the subject that controls the object (Kant) but Being that discloses itself in being-there *(Dasein)* and in so doing activates the subject's potential for understanding and language.

For Heidegger, as for Dilthey, one's understanding is always contextual. We are immersed in our "world," which for Heidegger is not the external environment but rather the world that is part of our self, like an invisible lens through which we see everything. We cannot grasp it as object because it is present in our every act of knowing. It is prior even to subjectivity, because subjectivity supposes a subject-object relationship. We notice the elements of our world, as we notice a part of our body, only when they break down. This world is the "place" where Being translates itself into meaning, understanding, and interpretation as language. Not that words or the logical system of language are sufficient of themselves; they point beyond themselves and express meaningfulness already there in the network of relationships of world. In applying Heideggerian ontology to texts, it is not man who confers meaning on reality (the object); rather reality (the object) conveys meaning to man by giving him the ontological possibility for words and language. Heidegger here seeks to overcome the subject/object dichotomy by pulling the object into the realm of the subject's very constitution. That means, for example, that I do not create a meaning for some object that I encounter, for it already comes to me clothed with a network of relationships and I understand it prior to any mental statement I make about it. Ontic interpretation is simply the explicitation of understanding in the form of language. And language itself already has a "shaped way of seeing." One then expresses one's understanding and interpretation in conventional codes that are extrasubjective.

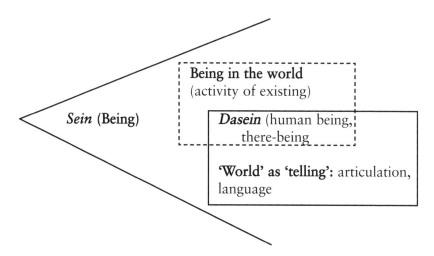

Being discloses itself as there-being *(Dasein)*, which is human being, and this prior to language or articulation.

The presupposition of the positivists was that they were in a hermetically sealed environment separated from the world they were examining. This is misleading, Heidegger says, because the observer is part of the very world he is observing; he is mostly unconscious of the fact but acts upon that basis like fish in water. It is not that he conceptualizes being and thus understands it. Rather, like a grinder transforming pork into sausage, Being speaks itself through him and thus passes into language.[11] The value of this insight is that indeed the observer is already more identified with the "object," the world he comes to know, prior even to his understanding it, than he may suspect. The caveat is this: Does Being flow through him so overwhelmingly that he has little or no judgment of what is passing through him, and is he aware of his own possible distortions as he constructs Being into language?

The point soundly made by Heidegger, following Dilthey, is that there is no presuppositionless interpretation. This idea has been called the fallacy of the empty head. When I interpret a text, for example, there are all kinds of presuppositions at work. Why did I choose to interpret this text rather than some other? What preconceptions do I have as to what the text should say? What categories are in my mind by which I might classify this text? And so on. The presuppositions of the positivists of the eighteenth and nineteenth centuries were that they were approaching the Bible without presuppositions!

For Heidegger, there is more to an object than the mind's classification of its essence or the assertion of its properties (for example, "The hammer is heavy"). For once one has objectified what one perceives, one no longer receives the thing in its totality but only in one aspect, and the thing's "Being" recedes. (An Indian proverb says, "Once you have taught a child the name of a bird, he will never see that bird again.") There is more to Being than can be expressed in language. Similarly, in reading a text, what is important is not to "understand the author better than the author understood himself" (Schleiermacher) but to understand what he said and what he didn't say, to get in touch with the "nothingness" out of which the creative expression came, to get beyond objectified or ideational thought as a way of controlling Being and rather responding to what is there in a contemplative kind of way. The later Heidegger speaks of Being as a gift from the side of Being rather than a product of man's inquiry and grasping.[12] Real understanding is not the result of analysis but rather the result of waiting for Being to disclose itself. Heidegger even posits that it is not man that speaks but language itself speaks, that language is not the expression of man but an appearance of Being. Thinking does not express man, it lets Being happen as language event.[13]

One begins to wonder whether this isn't German romantic idealism applied to language. Thomists and other philosophers criticize Heidegger at this point for identifying Being itself *(ipsum esse)* with intentional being *(esse intentionale),* for collapsing the real and the intentional order, and also for neglecting the role of the subject's judgment in the understanding process.[14] Nevertheless, Heidegger provides a corrective for Kant's domination by the subject over the object (as if meaning is *imposed* on the object by the mind) and provides for a more receptive, contemplative approach to interpretation.

In terms of exegesis, since Heidegger is interested in language as a disclosure of Being, it is not sufficient for him to analyze what a text says but what it leaves unsaid. In his own commentary on the "Ode on Man" from Sophocles' *Antigone,* he writes:

> If we content ourselves with what the poem directly says, the interpretation is at an end. Actually it has just begun. The actual interpretation must show what does not stand in the words and is nevertheless *said.* To accomplish this the exegete *must use violence* [that is, go beyond what is explicitly said]. He must seek the essential where nothing more is to be found by the scientific interpretation that brands as unscientific everything that transcends its limits.[15]

We often discover that our words fall far short of the reality that gave rise to them. At wakes we may even apologize for the inadequacy of our words to express our grief or our compassion for the grieving. In similar situations we may speak of ourselves "being left speechless." This comes close to what Heidegger calls the "breakdown of Being." Loss of language often reveals the "real presence of Being."[16] We also know what this is like in various kinds of art. Intentional gaps in narrative; empty space in advertisements; the power of a moment of silence in liturgy. Some of the most powerful messages in the parable of the prodigal son come from what is not explicitly expressed. For example, why does the story end leaving the reader wondering whether the elder son will enter the feast or not? Even the traditional title of the parable, "The Prodigal Son," as one of my students pointed out, has limited our understanding of the whole story by focusing on the one son to the neglect of the other (who is really more lost than the returning son) and even of the father. Heidegger's thesis that Being is not captured by words but lies beyond them echoes the *via negativa* or apophatic tradition of theology (that our language is better at telling us what God is not than what he is), and the sense of mystery that the human words of scripture open up.

Because poetry exemplifies better than prose the power of the what is indirectly said, it was for Heidegger the highest form of human communication or of the linguistic disclosure of Being. Beyond what the poet *decides* to leave unexpressed there is Being that he *cannot* express, for it eludes his grasp. Yet it is somehow said. Put in another way, Heidegger means what is *there* but *unsaid*—not what is chosen to be left aside or negated in the proposition. For example, "Thou shalt not kill" excludes murder, but it also affirms a whole unspoken world of values, history, and more.

In summary, Heidegger accounts for several new trends in hermeneutical theory. Chief among these is his ontological view of hermeneutics, that is, his use of hermeneutics in understanding Being itself. It is not the interpreter who gives meaning to Being. It is Being that interprets the interpreter. Heidegger is reacting to the vaunted hegemony of the positivists who presumed to stand above their "objects," analyzing and thus attempting to control them. This is not true understanding or interpretation. There are no presuppositionless interpretations. The interpreter's world is a prereflective complex that responds to the world opened up by the object, or the text—or simply, being. And the interpreter must be open not only to what is directly said by the text but also to what was not expressed, or only indirectly expressed. What Heidegger said about the self-disclosure of Being would be all the more applicable to biblical texts that purport to be a disclosure of subsistent Being, which we call God.

Heidegger had a great influence on Gadamer, whose hermeneutics we examine next.

Hans-Georg Gadamer: Dialectical Hermeneutics and Language as the "House of Being"

In 1960 the appearance of the original German edition of *Truth and Method* by Hans-Georg Gadamer (1900–2003) marked a further significant development in general hermeneutics, one that would have dramatic influence on the theory of biblical hermeneutics as well. Gadamer was not interested in discussing the rules of hermeneutics but rather in hermeneutics as the structure of human existence itself, hence the philosophy of understanding that is prior to and explicative of every other human endeavor, including the special hermeneutics of the sciences and the arts. The application of this philosophy to the hermeneutics of texts (which is of interest to us in biblical interpretation) was profound. It is not the mind of the author that gives meaning to the work, nor the work itself "divorced from its constantly renewed reality of being experienced"[17] that leaves it abstract, but its "effective history," that is, its influence on all succeeding generations:

> The purpose of my investigation is not to offer a general theory of interpretation and a differential account of its methods...but to discover what is common to all modes of understanding and to show that understanding is never subjective behavior toward a given "object", but towards its effective history—the history of its influence; in other words, understanding belongs to the being of that which is understood.[18]

In other words, the effect on others is part of the very object's being, as the sun's rays touching the Earth are part of the sun's "being." To give an example that I have not drawn from Gadamer: We will not know what "really happened" at the resurrection of Jesus until the end of time, because the effects of that event are still being felt. We are in the flow of its influence. Or, to use a secular example, those who were closer to President Nixon in his White House years do not have a better understanding than those who understand his presidency from its effects a hundred years later. As far as scripture is concerned, some fundamentalist groups in their concern to build their faith on "the Bible alone" discount the two millennia of "effective history," beginning with the rich commentaries of the church fathers. The latter stood much closer to the time and the culture of the texts and modeled the task that every generation of biblical interpreters has had to face, namely, to determine what the word of God means in the light of evolving cultures and questions totally unforeseen by the biblical authors.[19] The Bible more than any other book has influenced history, especially that of the West.[20] Yet one must also ask the question: What of misinterpretations or misuses of the biblical text that have wreaked historical havoc? Are these too part of the "meaning" of the text? We return to this later on when discussing the role of judgment in chapter 8, on critical realist hermeneutics. Stay tuned.

Another aspect of Gadamer's thought is his rejection of the subject/object dichotomy so characteristic of modern technological thinking. The Greeks—and we might say most ancient peoples, including the Hebrews—"did not take subjectivity as their starting point and then ground the objectivity of their knowledge on it. Theirs was a more dialectical approach that tried to allow itself to be guided by the nature of what was being understood."[21] Gadamer thus opposes this "dialectical" approach to the modern "method" approach, which prestructures answers by the very way it asks questions of the object.[22] In Gadamer's dialectic, it is the object that asks the questions and the subject responds. Heidegger's influence is evident here.

Gadamer begins his monumental work with the question of truth as it emerges in the experience of art. In contemplating a work of art, there is more than feeling or aesthetic pleasure in some kind of timeless truth that happens to be embodied in this work. We ordinarily do not separate out the "truth" of the art work (whether a picture, a play, a poem, or any other work of art) from the particular form in which it is embodied. Rather, the work of art itself opens up a world for us, the artist's world first of all, which may challenge our world because of the novelty or the "truth" of its disclosure. (Think of Picasso's Christ crucified on a glass cross and suspended forward in midair, or any other deliberate artistic distortion to invite a new way of thinking about an event.) But at the same time we would be unable to receive this new world were we not in some way already predisposed to it because of the structures of self-understanding that we share with the artist. The artist has transformed his or her experience of being into an art form that mediates to us an experience of being that is not merely foreign but a coming home—a seeing of "our" truth as if for the first time. And because being has been expressed in a work, the encounter with it is repeatable for succeeding generations.

Gadamer's insight becomes helpful when looking at biblical narratives. One way of looking at them is as works of art, which indeed they are. Indeed before questions of historicity or doctrine are asked of a narrative, one needs to allow the narrative to speak as art, as narrative art, as a disclosure of being in art form. Take, for example, the parable of the lost sons (I say *sons* in the plural, because part of the indirectly expressed irony is that the second son is more lost than the first). Of course there is a value in knowing Jews' repugnance for pigs, in knowing that if the father was wearing a full-length robe he willingly made himself look ridiculous running toward his homecoming son, in knowing that Jesus told this parable to those who condemned him for associating with sinners. And there may even be value in trying to determine whether this parable was original with Jesus or whether it came from the early community. But these questions can even distract from the being, the truth, the experience, being mediated by the story. The work of art speaks for itself, opening up a world for every reader/listener. In a very real sense, a narrative, like a joke, loses its force if it has to be explained.

More important for biblical interpretation is Gadamer's understanding of history. Following Heidegger, he insists that we come to every encounter with preconceptions, our own "world" through which we see. There is thus no purely objective science. This is true of all science, but it is especially true of history. We cannot see the past at all without reference to the present. Nor can we see the present without reference to the future, because our very existence is a call to being what we are not yet. Nor, for the same reason, can we see the future without reference to the present. Past, present, and future are all interfused in understanding. If such is the case, then, Gadamer's paradigm is very helpful in understanding how the events and their interpretation in the Bible have an ineluctable past, present, and future dimension. The past is always being seen through the lens of the present, and the present experience calls for and points to a future fulfillment. This is not only true of the Bible, it is true of all human experience. And for Gadamer as well as Heidegger, language is all part of this process, for language is the "house of being." It is the container and the medium of the tradition. Language is for humankind what water is for fish. In it we live and move and have our being.

Gadamer's paradigm is liberating in yet another way. The Enlightenment and Romanticism considered tradition and authority to be the enemies of free, that is, supposedly presuppositionless, research. But if the interpreter stands inevitably in a stream of tradition that makes up the large part of his world, then he cannot fail to look at the text from that perspective, though indeed he may find his world challenged or broadened by what he sees. For Gadamer, tradition and prejudice are not the enemy of understanding. They are the condition of it. For without them there is no understanding possible. He does not mean to say that all prejudices are equally valid. He believes that some are more valid than others. But it is self-deceiving to attempt to eliminate tradition and authority, for "understanding is not to be thought of so much as an action of one's subjectivity, but as the placing of oneself within a process of tradition, in which past and present are constantly fused."[23] In confronting the past, hermeneutics stands at the frontier between the foreign and the familiar. Temporal distance need not make understanding impossible; quite the contrary, it can lend greater understanding, for the truth of being that the author was expressing will stand out and survive the attrition of the contextual historical circumstances, just as aesthetic distance gives a greater appreciation of a work of art. And it is here that tradition (and tradition's "authority") have reaffirmed the lasting life-value the author was expressing. Who better understands the genius of Shakespeare's plays—the original performers or those who experience their immortal value in the context of the world today? For Gadamer a classical text is not a fixed star but a comet speeding through the sky of history bearing its light on ever new worlds.

It is not the author that one wishes to understand but the text—the text, though, not so much as a restoration of the past as an integration of the text's meaning in the present. That is why there is no real understanding of a text without its application to the present. Gadamer does not mean that the subject should uncritically surrender to the text or the tradition but that he should be open to "being" that confronts him in the text, so that there is a balance between the demands of the "other" and the demands of the self. The process is truly dialectical. On the one hand, the interpreter questions the text, but not so much to find the text as answer as to discover what the question was that called forth the text. This keeps the text as text from being taken mechanically and applied unrealistically—for example, John's negative use of the word *Jews* is his response to the question about membership in the Christian community. On the other hand, the text in turn questions the interpreter. The medium that makes possible the "fusion of horizons" between interpreter and text is language. As human beings we belong to a community of language that, despite the distance of time and culture, makes understanding possible. And when a text, expressive of being in an earlier time, meets the later interpreter, a world is opened up and in fact a new world is created, so that Gadamer can call the hermeneutical experience a "word event." It is not that I have come to understand what the author of an old text wanted to say. It is that the world which that text opens up now impinges upon my world, and the encounter is a new being-event. There is a "fusion of horizons."

In conclusion, Gadamer has contributed much to modern hermeneutical theory. His concept of "effective history," his critique of the subject/object dichotomy, his analysis of the experience of art, his exalted notion of language as the "house of being," his critique of presuppositionless interpretation, his insight into the past-present-future character of every human experience—for much of this he is indebted to Heidegger, whose philosophy he develops. What Gadamer especially brings to Heidegger, who already identified understanding as an ontological function, is the dialectical nature of it. Man is not totally passive in his response to being but interactive. There is a bit of a move toward Hegel here, one that gives more account to the subject's role without surrendering to the subjectism Heidegger strenuously contested. Still, as we come to the end of our summary of Gadamer's thought, there are questions. Palmer asks, "Is man simply to live in a kind of responsive surrender to the call of being?...How does the operation of language in understanding take into account the functions of will and desire in man?"[24] Does Gadamer give sufficient role to the critical function of the interpreter in face of the wave of "being" that washes over him? While his approach is a refreshing relief to the monotony of facticity or the analysis of a text until it yields something *else* that is then considered its meaning, Gadamer has been criticized for being too accepting of the tradition (or the object) without providing sufficient room for a critical assessment of it. While the positivists would like to put the fish under the microscope, as someone has said, Gadamer might be accused of wanting to swallow the fish whole and uncleaned. And does Gadamer's exalting of language to the ontological level adequately account for the fact that language can also be used for domination? This is the critique Jürgen Habermas makes, for the political stance of the writer or interpreter must itself be evaluated on ethical grounds.[25]

A critique of Gadamer has been made by E. D. Hirsch Jr.[26] He distinguishes between *meaning,* which is what the author intended as recoverable from the text, and *significance,* which is what the text means to subsequent readers. Looking for validity in interpretation (as the title of his book suggests), Hirsch insists that the meaning of the text is what the author meant, a meaning that is attainable and objective, and that an indefinite number of possible meanings would have no grounds for validation. Subsequent interpretations are affirmations of the significance of the text for a new situation (an operation that Hirsch accepts and legitimate and necessary). Meaning does not change, significance does. Is this a valid critique, or simply a preference for a different term? Is not the ground for validation of later meanings their continuity with the text's original meaning? What can be retained from his critique is that meaning does not pour into the reader the way sunlight hits grass, for the reader/listener retains the ability to discern that to which he or she is responding.

In summary we can say that for Dilthey as for Kant, the subject dominates the object. For Heidegger and Gadamer, properly understood, the object has priority over the subject. There is another theorist of hermeneutics who has had profound influence on the contemporary practice of the discipline. To him we now turn.

Paul Ricoeur:
Metaphor and the Surplus of Meaning

Paul Ricoeur (1913–) finds neither the interpersonal psychologizing of Schleiermacher and Dilthey nor the structuralist (text only) model (which we discuss further on) satisfactory. He also refines and sharpens some of the insights of Gadamer. Discourse, he says, refers both backward to a speaker and forward to a world. In oral discourse, Ricoeur maintains, there is an overlap between what the speaker means and what his discourse means. But in written discourse, the author's intention and the meaning of the text cease to coincide. There is a thus a difference between what the author meant and what the text means. "The text's career escapes the finite horizon lived by its author. What the text means now matters more than what the author meant when he wrote it."[27] Unlike Plato, Rousseau, Bergson, and others who distrusted discourse when put in writing (think of Francis of Assisi only with great reluctance writing a rule), Ricoeur sees the written discourse liberated both from the author's meaning and from the narrowness of the face-to-face situation. Hence this opens up the possibility of an indefinite number of readers and therefore interpretations.[28] The text, because it transcends the original audience, can open a world to the later reader whose own world is confronted and changed by it. Like a painting that, although "less" in some respects than the living person portrayed, yet in another way yields more by capturing an insight or a universe, thus presenting something new, the transformation of a universe, so the written text possesses "iconic augmentation." Iconicity is the revelation of a real more real than ordinary reality. It is the rewriting of reality, the transformation of reality. Literary works, unlike scientific works, involve metaphor and symbol. And in these works there is a surplus of meaning that goes beyond the linguistic sign. This surplus of meaning is "the residue of the literal interpretation."[29] Symbols, much more than concepts, give rise to endless exegesis because their meaning is never exhausted. Though closely related, there is a difference between metaphor and symbol. In metaphor there is already an activity of the mind or reason seeing a double meaning. Symbol is more primitive, closer to life itself, and for this reason an inexhaustible source of interpretation. Or, to put it another way, metaphor brings to the linguistic surface the more primitive depths of symbol.

Key to Ricoeur's hermeneutical theory is his insistence that once a discourse is put in writing, the text floats free of the author's intention. It takes on its own meaning because it has carved out a space in language that is now available to anyone anywhere any time. The meaning of a text comes to life in the reading of it, and this involves the subject's world. Is there no control then on the multiplicity of possible interpretations? Yes, because the text is not a cipher or a meaningless blot on the paper. It is rather like a musical score that the musician must follow but may also express in his own way. Thus Ricoeur does not hold that one interpretation is as good as another, for "the text presents a limited field of possible constructions."[30]

Ricoeur does not deny a limited validity to the structural approach to texts, but he does maintain that it is only one of several possible approaches to interpretation and, implicitly, insufficient of itself. He considers it to be one stage between a naive interpretation and a critical one, between a surface interpretation and a depth interpretation. This "depth semantics" means the opening of a world, the world of the text, whether or not it has an ostensive reference.

> *The sense of a text is not behind the text but in front of it* [emphasis mine]. It is not something hidden but something disclosed. What has to be understood is not the initial situation of discourse, but what points toward a

possible world, thanks to the non-ostensive reference of the text. Understanding has less than ever to do with the author and his situation. It seeks to grasp the world-propositions opened up by the reference of the text. To understand a text is to follow its movement from sense to reference: from what it says, to what it talks about. In this process the mediating role played by structural analysis[31] constitutes both the justification of the objective approach and the rectification of the subjective approach to the text. We are definitely enjoined from identifying understanding with some kind of intuitive grasping of the intention underlying the text. What we have said about the depth semantics that structural analysis yields rather invites us to think of the sense of the text as an injunction coming from the text, as a new way of looking at things, as an injunction to think in a certain manner.

This is the reference borne by the depth semantics. The text speaks of a possible world and of a possible way of orientating oneself within it. The dimensions of this world are properly opened up and disclosed by the text. Discourse is the equivalent for written language of ostensive reference for spoken language. It goes beyond the mere function of pointing out and showing what already exists and, in this sense, transcends the function of the ostensive reference linked to spoken language. Here showing is at the same time creating a new mode of being.[32]

In his conclusion to *Interpretation Theory* Ricoeur sums up:

Not the intention of the author, which is supposed to be hidden behind the text; not the historical situation common to the author and his original readers; not the expectations or feelings of these original readers; not even their understanding of themselves as historical and cultural phenomena. What has to be appropriated is the meaning of the text itself, conceived in a dynamic way as the direction of thought opened up by the text.

In other words, what has to be appropriated is nothing other than the power of disclosing a world that constitutes the reference of the text. In this way we are as far as possible from the Romanticist ideal of coinciding with a foreign psyche. If we may be said to coincide with anything, it is not the inner life of another ego, but the disclosure of a possible way of looking at things, which is the genuine referential power of the text.[33]

In this Ricoeur coincides with what Gadamer calls "the fusion of horizons." He anticipates the accusation that this might be simply a subjective projection of any meaning upon the text. Quite the contrary, interpretation is the process by which disclosure of new modes of being (à la Wittgenstein or Heidegger) gives to the subject a new capacity for knowing himself. "If the reference of the text is the project of a world, then it is not the reader who primarily projects himself. The reader rather is enlarged in his capacity of self-projection by receiving a new mode of being from the text itself."[34] If the narcissistic ego precedes the encounter with the text, the text helps the ego become the self. Is there a danger here that the intention of the text may get lost in favor of its therapeutic effect on the reader? Ricoeur might be free of this pitfall, but would others? This question will exercise us in the next chapter, on critical realist hermeneutics.

Ricoeur has had a profound influence on subsequent hermeneutical theorists. In particular, his position about the world that the text opens up *in front of the text* will engage us in various ways, especially in reader-response and advocacy hermeneutics.

EIGHT

Bernard Lonergan and Critical Realist Hermeneutics

It should be evident from the various approaches to hermeneutics studied thus far that a basic philosophical question underlies all attempts to discover meaning in a text: Is meaning something that washes over us like a tidal wave (total objectivity), or is it a construct of the mind (total subjectivity)? This is a question of crucial importance, for it involves the very meaning of truth. One of the contemporary thinkers who has wrestled with this question most extensively is Bernard Lonergan. His first major treatment of interpretation appears in his monumental book *Insight*. He takes it up later in *Method in Theology*.[1] What follows is a digest and explanation of Lonergan's salient ideas, though the student is reminded that no commentary can possibly replace Lonergan's original texts and should not be an excuse for ignoring them.

To understand his hermeneutical theory we must first explore some of its presuppositions.

Lonergan takes subjectivity seriously. In fully human knowing we arrive at objectivity not by suppressing subjectivity but by pursuing its functions fully in accord with the human drive to reality. And we can arrive at objectivity with reliability if we do not somewhere along the line scuttle the process. In other words, it is through authentic subjectivity that we reach objectivity. And authentic subjectivity involves several functions.

Wonder and Insight

The first thing we do in approaching a text is to wonder and question: What does it mean? What is the text saying? Then we search for an answer. We consider various possibilities and we construe what to us seems the most probable meaning. We come up with an hypothesis or *insight*. But then we continue to ask ourselves questions: Is this insight accurate? We find in ourselves a drive to "check it out" perhaps by further research, by sharing our understanding with others for their feedback, and so on, and this leads to the phase of *judgment*. Insight comes between wonder and judgment. In regard to scriptural interpretation, it suffices to do a minimum of reading in the scholarly literature today to see the plethora of insights or hypotheses offered. It's what keeps the exegetes in business. Read any scholarly commentary on any New Testament book and you will see that various options of meaning have, in the course of history, been offered for almost every text. Ben F. Meyer has illustrated the kinds of insights available under three headings: linguistic insights (What does the original Greek and the frequently underlying Aramaic substrate suggest as to the possible meaning of this text?), literary insights (What does the literary structure and context of a passage tell us about its possible meaning?), and historical insights (for example, what was the most probable original event or meaning that Jesus had in mind?).[2]

Even at this very early stage we can see that arriving at a moment of authentic insight (to say nothing about judgment of the truth of the insight) requires a lot of work. Although this should not make us distrust most commonsense reading of good translations, it does mean that, whatever value *lectio divina* may have for our prayer, it cannot replace serious study of the text. Without study we are probably not even aware of the possible alternative options of meaning in a text.

Judgment

The drive to know is universal. It is also insatiable. It means that there is something within us that constantly impels us onward. And what we are driven toward is not some subjective state of consciousness or withdrawal. We want to touch and to know what's *there*, what is real. People who make illusion their world we call psychotics. This push toward the real also inspires the need to check out our insights to see if they are supported by evidence.[3] Which of possible alternatives has the best supporting case? If we cannot reach absolute certitude, we can at least, on the basis of available evidence, come to the most probable conclusion.

Judgment is both personal and impersonal. It is personal in the sense that the knowing subject is the locus of truth. But it is impersonal in the sense that the objective reality is there whether I commit myself to it or not (and incidentally, this is why pure subjectivism cannot be a source of human community). For judgment to be possible, one must know the conditions under which the proposition can stand and then know that indeed these conditions have been met. It is possible, of course, that we have overlooked some conditions or misread how these conditions are met; hence there is the possibility of personal or collective fallibility. Our knowledge may be corrected by further information. There is the further complication of human frailty. For whatever reason, we may not care to admit the evidence. But assuming the search for evidence has not been flawed, and the evidence presents itself as "virtually unconditioned," we judge that the *hypothesis is true,* and this adds to our knowledge because our intelligence now corresponds to its object. Meyer illustrates this process in regard to determining the central core of the New Testament, which he "judges" to be the *kerygma.*[4] He illustrates how he comes to this "virtually unconditioned" conclusion by the preponderant evidence in its favor over against other hypotheses.

Applied to Hermeneutics

Lonergan's hermeneutical theory stands between the extreme of pure receptivity of the object on the one hand and pure projection or subjectivity on the other. In his theory of critical realist interpretation, the interpreter indeed brings to the text his world with all its resources, but he does so on the basis of warrants available in the text. There is, in other words, a control on unbridled subjectivity, however exciting and novel its expression might be.

Lonergan agrees with the "objectivists" that a knowledge of the original context is helpful, often crucial, to determining the text's meaning. He would also agree with the theorists of subjectivity that the richer the experience and the wholeness of the interpreter the better the reading will be. But, unlike Northrop Frye, who describes reading as a "picnic to which the writer brings the words and the reader the meaning," Lonergan maintains that authentic reading and interpretation is controlled by the warrants of the text. In other words, his theory is neither flight from subjectivity nor license for unlimited expressions of creativity for which the text is only the occasion. Rather, it is, in the radical sense of the term, *responsible*.

Thus, there are three steps to the procedure: (1) the interpreter works out an understanding of the intended sense of the text; (2) he then proceeds, on the basis of available evidence, to judge whether his understanding is accurate; and (3) finally he states what he considers to be the probable accurate understanding of the text.

This process may seem to be nothing more than common sense. In fact it is. But the process is also one that can bring about surprises and even personal transformation if it is done well. The first two steps involve a series of three hermeneutical circles:

1. *The circle of the whole and the parts* (as we described in the previous chapter in treating Schleiermacher, Gadamer, and subsequent theorists).
2. *The circle of things and words.* If I have no independent understanding of the things the words refer to, I will have a hard time understanding the words. As a deaf person will have a hard time understanding the word *tone* or a blind person *color,* so if I have no independent understanding of *trust* I will have a hard time understanding Jesus' exhortation to trust the Father—or if I have never had a significant experience of "the miraculous," even if it is only something extraordinarily wonderful in the natural order, or if I am still bound by a Newtonian mechanistic view of the laws of the universe, I may have a hard

time accepting the reality of miracles in the Gospels. If I do not have some, at least tangential, experience of the demonic (however analogous such experiences can be), I will tend to dismiss or interpret reductively Jesus' exorcisms in the Gospels.

3. *The circle of reader and text.* Understanding the text and understanding myself go hand in hand. "I understand the text in virtue of understanding myself; I understand myself in virtue of understanding the text." This raises the question of the "horizons" of text and reader. As a person with racial prejudice will dismiss out of hand initiatives to provide equal opportunities for the victims of racial prejudice, so a person may have a blind spot in regard to interpreting a text. Meyer notes that Walter Savage Lando characterized the *Inferno* as "the most immoral and impious book that was ever written" and Dante "the great master of the disgusting."[5] To interpret any text one needs at least an initial empathy with it, or at least an openness to the horizon of the text.[6]

Interpretation, then, is a matter of coming to understand *the intended sense of the text.* This is not simply "the intention of the author," which may or may not be encoded with perfect success in the text. It is the sense that is encoded in the text. To understand that, we need to know whether the sense is proper, figurative, or symbolic. We also need to know the tone and the overtones and nuances of the text, and for this literary form is important. In other words, the message is incarnated in a particular manner and that incarnation is part of the sense of the text.

Finally, what have traditionally been called the "auxiliary sciences" must not be substituted for interpretation. Lexicography, archaeology, geography, psychology, sociopolitical sciences, and the rest are analytical services that precede and prepare, or follow upon, but they do not substitute for interpretation. Though these sciences may provide harmonies, they are not the tune.

Interpretation allows the author of another world to speak to us in his own voice.

In passing, we can note how some of the other interpretative methods look to the critical realist. While appreciating the highlighting of subjectivity in reader-response criticism, critical realism notes that this method cares little about the function of *judgment*—that is, of testing out its "response" to see if it coheres with the intention of the text, in other words to see whether its interpretation is not just "interesting" but "right."

Does this mean that for Lonergan there is only one possible meaning to a text? What would he think of Ricoeur's *world in front of the text,* which can lend itself to multiple possible meanings? It is not clear how acquainted Lonergan is with Ricoeur (he cites only one of his works, *On Evil*), but the two are not really that far apart. Remember that for Ricoeur the text was not simply the *occasion* for launching the reader (or listener) on his or her unguided interpretation, but rather it set certain limits on the possible interpretations. Lonergan knows that as the text passes through the trajectory of history further meanings adhere to the text as it confronts new cultures, new crises, new historical developments. But these meanings cannot be alien to the original meaning (the authorial intention as known from the text) but must be its organic development, much like the oak contained in the acorn.

And what about Gadamer's "effective history of the text"? According to Gadamer, the history of the influence of the text should be considered part of the meaning of the text. In discussing the issue earlier, we asked whether the misuse of the text should also be considered part of the "meaning." In Lonergan's view, such a misuse should be attributed not to the text but to a faulty reception or judgment as to the text's meaning. This is an important corrective of Gadamer, for it introduces the factor of human judgment in the application of the text, with the possibility also of self-correction of faulty or inadequate interpretations.

As for the various methods studied under historical criticism, while giving full credit to the contributions of the method, Lonergan notes that the more the interpreter can identify with the reality to which the text points, the better he will understand it. This provides room for faith, grace, and the role of the Holy Spirit in leading beyond a merely rational approach to the text, as we explore next.

Subjectivity and Interpreting the Text as the Word of God

To return to the question of subjectivity: If one's capacity to interpret is measured not by "the empty head" (that is, presumably coming at the text without any prior viewpoint) but by the wealth of resources available within the interpreter (which, negatively, involves renunciation of egoism and all other dehumanizing vices and, positively, the highest appetite for the good and the true—what the saints would call "purity of heart and mind"), then to approach the scriptures precisely as *the word of God* moves us to an even higher register.[7] The Bible is no longer at best a piece of the great religious literature of the world, with meaning for the well-disposed nonbeliever. For the believer it is a divinely inspired text. It is the word of God. That means the light in which the word is read is the light of faith. And this faith is an ecclesial, communitarian thing. So it was when the text issued from the womb of the early church. So can it only be in the one who would fully understand the text. In this sense only the interpreter inspired by faith can interpret scripture as the word of God. A theologian without faith is a misnomer; he or she may be a social scientist or a student of world religions, but not a theologian. Faith of itself, of course, does not assure competence in the exegetical tools required to come up with plausible insights. As always, the critical realist will look for evidence that will lead him to the "virtually unconditioned." But as the text itself is an expression of faith, so only the one who shares the same faith will have access to the fullness of meaning encoded in the text. This also raises the question of the role of the Holy Spirit in interpretation, an issue we return to in a later chapter.

What we have seen in Part 1 is both a sketch of the history of biblical hermeneutics and some of the chief theories of the discipline, what the Pontifical Biblical Commission calls "philosophical hermeneutics." This history and especially the theories of hermeneutics provide alternative presuppositions to the various methods of interpretation that we explore in Part 2.

Part 2

THE ROAD BEFORE US

NINE

The World of the Text

A helpful way of organizing the maze of hermeneutical methods is to consider them from the following viewpoints: the world of the text, the world behind the text, the world around the text, and the world in front of the text. The logic of this simple classification should be obvious. We can study the text as it lies before us prior to any question about its prehistory or its posthistory, the way we might read a novel or a short story. But then questions arise: Who wrote this? When was it written? Did the author compose this himself or did he use previous texts or traditions? How much of this is historical? Questions such as these lead us to explore the world behind the text. But the text was addressed to readers (or listeners when it was read publicly). What about the effect of this text upon its readers, then and now? Does that contribute to the meaning of the text? Then the biblical text was incorporated into the canon that the church accepted as the word of God. Did this incorporation affect the meaning of the text? Does that contribute to the meaning of the text? The reader will soon discover, of course, that some of these methods overlap. Hence the structure offered here is not a rigid one, only, one hopes, a help to situate the different approaches in some kind of order.

The philosophical underpinnings of these different methods have been explored in the previous chapters, but it will be necessary at times to recall them briefly, or even to supply comments that were not made earlier. There are several subsets to the study of the world of the text.[1]

Textual Criticism: The Old Testament

A question that immediately arises when we confront an ancient text, especially one that preceded the printing press, is this: Is this the original text? With practically no ancient text do we have the original, only copies that have survived the attrition of decades, even centuries. At Qumran manuscripts survived for two thousand years, but we are not sure that any of them are originals, as the scribes there were prodigious copiers. That should not make us cynics, for the ancient copyists were for the most part scrupulous in their care to copy accurately. But even a well-intentioned scribe can be distracted, can at times jump from one "and" to the next, or even, confronted with a text that seems inaccurate or incomprehensible, offer his correction. And we know that in the first century there were extant versions of the Old Testament that sometimes varied widely. How then do we arrive at the most accurate text possible? That is the work of *textual criticism*. It consists of comparing extant manuscripts or fragments with one another, determining what family of texts they belong to, where that is possible (for example, several New Testament manuscripts can be traced back to an earlier parent manuscript), and eventually making a judgment as to what is the most likely original reading or intent of the author. Given the turbulent times through which biblical manuscripts had to pass (for example, the Arab invasion of Palestine), given the fragility of manuscripts, especially papyri, given the effect of climate, it is amazing how much agreement there is in the manuscripts of the Hebrew Old Testament and the Greek New Testament.

Today many translations of the Old Testament follow the Masoretic text, worked out by Jewish scribes from the ninth century onward. But in the first century that text was not considered authoritative by everyone. In fact there are significant variants not only in the Septuagint (LXX) but in the Samaritan Pentateuch and in the Qumran manuscripts. Many of these variants correspond to the LXX where it differs from the Masoretic text. Hence this heightens the possibility that the LXX actually represents an earlier form of the Hebrew text. Not all modern translations take these variants into consideration. The *New American Bible (NAB),* however, to its credit, does in its textual notes.

Origen was one of the first Christian scholars to be concerned to have an accurate text. Only with such a text could he successfully dialogue with the Jews (since the Christians were using the Septuagint). He created his famous Hexapla, listing in six parallel columns the Hebrew text, a Greek transliteration, the version of Aquila, the version of Symmachus, the Septuagint, and the version of Theodotion. This was an enormous undertaking, for which unfortunately we have only scraps left.

Textual Criticism: The New Testament

For the New Testament,[2] we have two kinds of manuscripts: uncials written in capital letters and minuscules written in lower case. Some manuscripts are on parchment, others on papyri, many of which are fragments. The most complete and helpful manuscripts are the Vaticanus, the Alexandrinus, and the Sinaiticus, dating from the fourth and fifth centuries. But there are fragments that go back to the first part of the second century (a fragment from Jesus' trial before Pilate in John's Gospel has been so dated).

The majority of variants are not significant, but some are. For example, the King James Version of 1 John 5:7–8 reads, "For there are three that bear record *in heaven, the Father, the Word, and the Holy Ghost: and these three are one. And there are three that bear witness in the earth,* the spirit, the water, and the blood: and these three agree in one." Yet all modern translations omit the italicized words, leaving only: "There are three that testify, the Spirit, the water and the blood, and the three are of one accord" *(NAB).* How do we explain this? The King James Version is based on the Textus Receptus published in 1633, but textual criticism has discovered that these words were added by some later hand. The passage is missing from every extant Greek manuscript except four, and these date from the eleventh to the sixteenth centuries, and of the four, two have the extra words written in the margin by a later hand. The words are never mentioned by the

Greek fathers embroiled in the trinitarian controversies of the fourth and fifth centuries, and they would surely have used them had they known them. They are missing from the earliest form of the Latin Vulgate translation by Jerome. Furthermore, if the words were original, there is no plausible reason why they would have been omitted in the earlier manuscripts.

This example of how the textual critics go about their work is rather clear-cut. Other judgments, however, are not so easy. Thus, in Bruce Metzger's *A Textual Commentary on the Greek New Testament*,[3] important divergences are rated on a scale of probability from A to D, A being the most probable and D the least. To save space on precious parchment, words were run together without separation. In most cases the division would be obvious, but not always (is it "manslaughter" or "man's laughter"?) In cases of divergence, the more difficult reading would normally be preferred, on the assumption that a later hand would make the reading clearer and would not make a clear reading more obscure.

Overall, thanks to the painstaking work of the textual critics, we can be confident that most of our modern translations have followed the most accurate version of the original.

Narrative Criticism

Once the integral text has been determined, the next question that naturally arises (or should) is what kind of document do we have before us? What is its literary form? If it is a letter of Paul, the answer is obvious. If it is a Gospel, what we have is a narrative.[4] Strangely, this realization is a Johnny-come-lately in the field of hermeneutics. Earlier scholars, as we saw in chapter 5, were more interested in what lay behind the text as written or oral sources, or proving or disproving the historicity of the accounts, or in studying how earlier parts were put together. But these methods progressively led to a dissatisfaction with their results, particularly in the study of the Gospels. The realization eventually dawned that the dicing of the Gospels into parts and tracing their development diachronically did not really correspond to the nature of their literary form, which was narrative. The Gospels are not a compilation of units to be analyzed for what lay outside them, be it historical facts or general ideas, or even the intention of the author (for the work often means more than its author was aware of meaning). Rather they are the story of Jesus, to be read from beginning to end, much as any other narrative is meant to be read. And the narrative has its own meaning-effect beyond the sum of its parts. Although it was admitted that the Gospels are a different type of narrative from imaginative fiction, much could be learned by studying them with the canons prevailing in the study of other narratives, ancient and modern.

And so, from the secular field of literary criticism a number of terms began to appear in scholars' study of the Gospels: implied author, implied reader, point of view, plot, character, setting, and so on. In 1977 a young bible scholar named David Rhoads invited a colleague from the English department of his institution to collaborate in a narrative study of Mark's Gospel, issuing eventually in a book, *Mark as Story: An Introduction to the Narrative of a Gospel.*[5] More works quickly followed suit.

Although a fine distinction is sometimes made between literary criticism and narrative criticism, in practice the two terms often overlap. M. A. Powell notes the following differences between literary criticism and historical criticism:

1. *Literary criticism focuses on the finished form of the text, not on how the text came about.*
2. *Literary criticism emphasizes the unity of the text as a whole.*
3. *Literary criticism views the text as an end in itself.* Historical criticism sees the text as a means to find out something else. Thus the latter is compared to a window through which we see the historical or cultural world of the text, whereas the former is compared to a mirror in which the text itself reflects a world that impacts us as a reader.[6] Literary criticism concerns the poetic function, while historical criticism deals with the referential function (that is, what "really" happened). The literary critic as literary

critic is not concerned, for example, whether an angel "actually" appeared to Mary at the annunciation but rather on the function of this episode in the development of the entire gospel. It is not that he doesn't care about the historical basis. He admits the proper role of historical criticism and may even have an interest in it himself. But as a narrative critic he brackets out the historical question in order to focus on the literary development.

4. *Literary criticism is based on communication models of speech-act theory.* Basically there are three elements to this. Every communication involves a sender, a message, and a receiver—which in written discourse means an author, a text, and a reader.

Though we treat other methods in detail following, it is helpful to focus on how narrative criticism differs. Like structuralism, narrative criticism is a text-centered method, but its rules are much less rigid and elaborate, and it tends to pay more attention to the story line than to other elements internal to the discourse. Like rhetorical criticism, narrative criticism is interested in the effect the work has on the reader and why it has this effect. But narrative criticism is more text centered than rhetorical criticism because it is not concerned with determining the original situation that evoked the work. It views the work rather from the perspective of the implied reader, the ideal reader to whom the text is addressed. Like reader-response criticism, which we examine in chapter 11, narrative criticism is interested in the reader, but not as the one who determines the meaning of the text. Rather it is the text that orients the reader's response.

Narrative criticism is very interested in the *implied reader*—not in the actual readers to whom the original work was addressed (the interest of rhetorical criticism), nor in the actual reader today (reader-response criticism), but in the reader whose world can be deduced from the text alone. The implied reader may know more than today's actual reader (for example, the implied reader of Matthew's Gospel knows that to touch a leper is to incur ritual defilement, whereas a modern reader might not know this). Or today's actual reader might know more than the implied reader (he knows, for example, the three other Gospels, the life of Paul, and much more). For the sake of experiencing the intended effect of the text, the actual reader must bracket out most information he has from outside the text at hand lest this spoil the story.

Similarly, narrative criticism is interested not in the *actual author* but in the *implied author*. The actual author of a book or passage is a real historical person like ourselves, with a different persona depending on the different situations in which the person finds himself or herself. For example, we act one way in the leisure of our home, a different way when we are addressing a crowd, or relating with our employer, or attending church or a social for a VIP. No one of these "personae" gives us a comprehensive picture of the person. Similarly, the text cannot reveal to us the real author in that person's existential fullness, only the persona through which he or she composed the text. It is the latter that we call the implied author, that is, the author as known, and known only, from the evidence of the text. This can be shown to be true especially in the case of different works by the same author. Though the actual author of *Treasure Island* and *Dr. Jekyll and Mr. Hyde* is Robert Louis Stevenson, the implied author of the two works is different. In a discourse like a gospel there is the *meaning-effect* that the implied author wishes to convey to the implied reader. This is not the meaning of the text in an abstract sense but the change, the conversion, the new point of view that the author wishes to effect in the reader—which is ordinarily the implied author's point of view.

Point of view is one of several other elements, including symbolism, irony, narrative patterns and techniques, plot, characters, setting, that space prohibits our elaborating here. For case studies in how each of these elements is applied, see Powell, *What Is Narrative Criticism?*, noted earlier.[7]

Objections have been raised against applying the canons of literary criticism to the Bible and to the Gospels in particular. The Gospels are for the most part collections of different materials, not a coherent narrative. The first part may be granted, but nothing prevents a gospel writer from incorporating previous materials, narrative or discourse, into a coherent narrative, which the Gospels obviously are. Another objection is that narrative criticism uses methods derived from the study of fiction, whereas the Gospels are meant to be taken as grounded in historical fact. The response to this objection is simply the fact that narrative criticism does not intend to deny the historicity of the gospel accounts; the exploration of that issue belongs to another, undisputed discipline.[8] Biblical history is certainly not value free; it is written from a perspective of faith. In this it shares with fictional and nonfictional narrative a subjective viewpoint. But it also claims to have been birthed by the experience of historical facts and events, and to pass these on in a faithful interpretation. Narrative criticism does not deny this. What the narrative critic tries to discover is the narrative development and impact of the work as a whole, its message and intended effect on the implied reader. This is very helpful in *experiencing* the gospel in the reading of it from beginning to end. In fact, it would seem that this should be precisely the *first* step in the study of the Gospels, for it respects the story-voice of the storyteller without interrupting with secondary questions.

Rhetorical Criticism

It is clear that much of the Bible is meant not simply to inform but to convince, persuade, reinforce convictions, impel to action. The ancients knew this, and so did the fathers of the church, as we saw. And periodically interpreters like Calvin elaborated a hermeneutical theory that could be called rhetorical.[9] However, in recent times there has been a rebirth of interest in studying the Bible as rhetoric, accompanied by an attempt to elaborate a method for such study. But on the latter point there is presently no consensus. The ticket to the enthronement of rhetoric among the methods of biblical hermeneutics is based on the obvious fact that most of the Bible, the New Testament in particular, aims at transforming the audience. Thus beyond message- or content-oriented reading of scripture we are led to a reading that evokes and strengthens personal, social, and cultural values. It takes into account the practical, the political, the powerful, the playful, and the delightful aspects of the biblical texts.[10] Although some rhetorical critics look at the Bible's rhetoric from the viewpoint of its original audience, the same appeal is ordinarily felt by the contemporary audience or reader. And so it lands us in a synchronic relationship with the texts, which appeal to the emotions and the imagination as well as to the cognitive faculties. In this it is close to reader-response criticism (which we treat in chapter 11, "The World in Front of the Text"), but it looks at the text itself as calling for a response and is less concerned about how future readers might actually respond to the text.

Aristotle divided rhetoric into three species: (1) *judicial* seeks to accuse or defend; (2) *deliberative* gives advice; (3) *epideictic* praises or blames. These three types are also found in the Bible.

How does the rhetorical critic go about his analysis? The renowned classics scholar G. A. Kennedy[11] has isolated five steps in the study of a rhetorical text:

1. One must first define a rhetorical unit, that is, determine where it begins and where it ends. A unit can be as small as a metaphor or as large as the canon itself.
2. Then one must identify the rhetorical situation. What was the situation or condition that evoked the utterance?
3. One must identify the rhetorical disposition or arrangement—what subdivisions a text falls into, what the persuasive effect of these parts seems to be, and how they work together, or perhaps fail to do so, to some unified purpose in meeting the rhetorical situation.
4. Next, one must identify the rhetorical techniques or style.
5. Finally, one must review the whole, which should be more than its constituent parts.

Wilhelm Wuellner applies these steps to an analysis of 1 Corinthians 9, which he classifies as epideictic rhetoric.[12] Among the rhetorical devices Paul uses in this section, rhetorical questions are most salient, for there are more of them in this chapter than in any other chapter of the New Testament. One cannot miss the affective quality of this stylistic device. Paul aims at praising what has been experienced and arousing shame at what has been neglected, an aim that is essentially formational. Inasmuch as rhetorical criticism aims at transformation, it comes close to the thesis of Walter Wink as described in his book, *The Bible in Human Transformation.*[13]

Some rhetorical critics rightly point out that the Jewish scriptures have their own methods of effectively communicating—parallelism, inclusion, and symmetrical arrangement, for example. Inclusion of familiar liturgical texts is another way of moving beyond content to the emotional appeal. Matthew not only includes the Lord's Prayer, familiar to his audience from daily usage, but he constructs the entire Sermon on the Mount around it as the centerpiece. Paul frequently quotes from hymns already in usage in his communities. It is the appeal of the familiar, which in religious contexts is generally more welcome than the unexpected. Ads often appeal to local loyalties for the same reason. In Texas, Lone Star Beer was touted as "the national beer of Texas."

Since rhetorical criticism focuses more on form than on content, it cannot suffice of itself as a method of textual analysis. But it does reinforce the truth that much of the Bible is both beautiful in form and powerful in persuasion.

Structuralism

In the 1960s and '70s a number of interpreters reacted against the historical or genetic method and against the pursuit of the author's intention. The seeds of this new method, called *structuralism*, had been sown earlier in the century by the Swiss linguist Ferdinand de Saussure,[14] but other linguistic schools (Russian, Czech, French) had their influence as well. While structuralists generally do not deny the validity of other methods, their concern to find meaning in a text does not lie in its history, written or oral, nor in the intention of the author, nor in the ideas it might express. The meaning is entirely and sufficiently contained in the text itself, in the interrelation of its structural elements. The reference is then to the "reservoir of meaning possibilities envisioned by the text."[15] Meaning is to be found *synchronically* (that is, text and reader are in the same time frame) rather than *diachronically* (text and reader are separated in time, and the approach is to go "through time," genetically). It is the text rather than the author's intention that holds meaning.

One of the reasons for this rejection of "the author's intention" is that it is so difficult to determine the original context of the author. The text itself, and even the context of the whole work, is insufficient to do so, for unlike oral communication between two subjects who are present to each other, one lacks the tone of voice, the emphasis, the facial expression, which makes the speaker's meaning intelligible. If, for example, I say, "Joe is on the top of the world," do I mean that Joe has climbed Mount Everest? Or do I mean that Joe is well off? Or that he is chief executive officer of a company? Or that he is feeling great? Even in oral discourse we often fail to understand. How much more in written discourse!

Words, therefore, according to the structuralists, are not clear pictures of nature or the world; they have only a relational meaning. That is, each word or statement fits into a pattern of binary oppositions, contraries, and contradictories. And it is this structure, inherent in the text, that renders meaning. The component structures can, of course, be of different types—linguistic, literary, narrative, discursive, rhetorical, or thematic. The example is often used of a musical score. The performer must read it not only from left to right but up and down; for example, notes may be paired with each other to make a harmony. Similarly in a literary work certain opposites will reveal underlying convictions: for example, Daniel Patté used the opposition of "saying" and "doing" in Matthew's Gospel to elucidate the evangelist's underlying theology. Ultimately, the structuralists try to determine certain "codes" that all discourses follow and then, below the linguistic codes the "deep structures" that reveal the author's unconscious convictions he has buried in the text.

In order to orient correctly one's research, it may be helpful to ask the question: "What happens in the text?" Not in the life setting or time of its composition...not in the mind or subconscious of the author... not in the rest of his work...but in the specific section of text under examination.[16]

In structuralism the elements of the text are examined to see how they interact to convey the text's meaning-effect. With these distinctions in mind, Daniel Patté introduces structural exegesis inductively by using the example of John 3:1–21. He distinguishes and then elaborates six steps:

1. Identify a complete discourse unit and its theme.
2. Identify the explicit oppositions of actions in the unit.
3. Identify the qualifications by which the characters that perform the opposed actions are contrasted.
4. Identify the effects upon the receivers (the persons or things affected by the actions) through which the opposed actions are contrasted.
5. Draw conclusions regarding the basic characteristics of the author's faith expressed in the unit.
6. Elucidate the specific features of the unit—that is, how the author expresses his convictions to the implied readers.

It suffices to read the development of this last section in his book (pages 65–72) to see to what conclusions this method can lead.[17] At times the methods of structuralism seem more complicated than their results warrant, but what the structuralists have alerted us to is that the text itself, independent of external considerations, has an inherent meaning that it addresses to the reader.

It is this last point that raises an additional critique of structuralism. Its weakness is precisely its limitation to the relations within the text itself, like a word game. Although texts are autonomous in a way that oral expressions are not, still no text can stand totally independent of an extratextual world. For texts build on pre-texts (something has indeed <u>preceded them, <u>even if it is oral</u></u>), and a text is meaningless until someone reads it and interprets it, and that means it is related to the reader's world as well.[18] Structuralism has also been criticized for emphasizing that words are mere conventions, arbitrary signs, an emphasis that leads to relativism.

Deconstruction

Jacques Derrida (1930–), a French philosopher, has pushed structuralism even farther.[19] Enunciations tend to self-destruct. For example, in the *Phaedrus* Plato has Socrates speak about the superiority of oral communication over writing because the speaker has control over where, how, by whom, and to whom his philosophy is taught, whereas the written text is open to misunderstanding or abuse. But the contradiction is that Plato has *written* this; and that Socrates has used metaphors from writing to discuss oral delivery—for example, speech is the word written in the mind of the speaker or is writing inscribed in the soul. In the Bible too, there is a preference for the spoken word (the very act of creation is God speaking), and yet the account of this is written. So the very text cancels itself out, or at least shows that one is not superior to the other. This confirms structuralism's tenet that words are relational. But it also leads Derrida to what he calls *différance,* the French word Derrida coined to indicate that the meaning of any utterance is indefinitely *deferred,* never completely captured and defined. To be more precise, the text provides an unlimited series of linguistic signifiers without ever leaving the world of the text. The text is never transcended. In one of his later essays Derrida uses the example of the Apocalypse to illustrate this constant deferring of meaning: the scrolls open the trumpets, which open the unnumbered visions, which open the visions of the seven bowls, and at the end the seer is told not to seal the book. Derrida understands this to illustrate the constant relay of meaning to other signifiers.

The ghost of Okham hovers over A. K. M. Adam's suggestion for entering the world of deconstruction: "We need to suspend our assumption that our words refer to things, that our expressions mean things, that there are, in fact, 'things' at all—including ourselves."[20]

Derrida's theory also latches on to the generally recognized phenomenon that every interpreter comes to the text with a set of prejudices and assumptions that will color his or her interpretation. But, along with postmodernists like Richard Rorty and J.-F. Lyotard, he maintains that discourse cannot transcend its own prejudices and thus is political rhetoric of deceit, manipulation, or at least "interests." Given such suspicion regarding every text, interpretation becomes an interplay of interests and thus, as Vincent B. Leitch, a deconstructionist, comments, the author's intention is of no more value in interpretation than any other:

> The author, according to deconstruction, may visit his text as a guest only: this celebrated "death of the author" not only decenters the text, but defers the conclusion. A text cannot be located or stopped at the author, for the inscription of the author is neither paternal nor privileged but ludic. An author can only wonder what guest roles he plays in his text. As a reader, a voyeur, he delimits textual play: his conclusions about the text rank in potential value with any other reader's.[21]

This theory, proposed for general hermeneutics, raises particularly serious questions for biblical interpretation, where the text is assumed to have a certain authority. While it might appear to free up a narrow positivist approach to the text, one wonders what place historical study and tradition, especially early tradition closer in time to the text, might have, and how the method (or lack of it) could avoid a rampant subjectivism.

Deconstructionists find that even the use of such binary opposites as transcendent/immanent, necessary/contingent, masculine/feminine, white/black, identity/difference reveals an oppressive hierarchy that privileges the first member of the pair over the second. This is a further illustration of the political nature of all discourse, and that interpretation is a power play. One of deconstruction's professed goals is to unmask the powers, that is, to level all superior/inferior or hierarchical relationships.

What is to be said of this analysis? Pushed to its ultimate, it could mean the dissolving of truth into a relativistic process. Its critics also accuse it of self-reversing contradictions.[22] Paul Ricoeur's critique of structuralism in general fits deconstruction as well:

> Language no longer appears as a mediation between minds and things. It constitutes a world of its own, within which each item only refers to other items of the same system, thanks to the interplay of oppositions and differences constitutive of the system. In a word, language is no longer treated as a "form of life," as Wittgenstein would call it, but as a self-sufficient system of inner relationships. At this extreme point language as discourse has disappeared.[23]

Thus discourse becomes a closed system, and signifiers only refer to other signifiers in an endless chain never referring to the extratextual world. In that case, language refers to, or means, nothing, and deconstruction undercuts its own claim to truth.[24] As for the political thrust of discourse (and hence, of interpretation), there is certainly no interpreter who comes to the text without presuppositions, even prejudices. But if the suspicion of political self-interest takes over the center of the discussion so that the interchange is seen as nothing but a power play, a colliding of billiard balls, all hope of arriving at self-transcending truth vanishes, and interpretation becomes a kind of linguistic Marxism, a struggle to level all distinctions linguistically, or at least to say that one interpretation is as good as another. If the modern period is identified with the Enlightenment and its rationalistic approach to the Bible, the postmodern period is identified with a decentered relativism, a new kind of agnosticism, of which deconstruction is one example.[25] Nevertheless, some interpreters have taken cues from deconstruction to propose novel insights into biblical texts.[26] The results appear to be mixed, and one may be permitted to wonder with the deconstructive method, as with structuralism, whether the insights gained might not just as easily have been arrived at by other less radical methods of exegesis and interpretation. Robert

Price's *Deconstructing Jesus* shows to what untenable conclusions the deconstructive method can lead: Judas Iscariot is Judas the Zealot, Simon Peter is Simon the Zealot, and it was the disciples who conspired to kill Jesus. And maybe Jesus didn't exist at all.[27]

Derrida toys with, without committing himself to, the apophatic or negative theology of the Christian tradition.[28] We know that every human utterance both expresses and conceals its reference—that is, the utterance expresses being and truth but never the entire being or truth of the object, not because of intentional deceit but because of the inherent limitation of language. In speaking of God, who transcends infinitely the categories of human discourse, it is easier to say what God is *not* than to say what God *is*. But this is quite different from the philosophical and linguistic nihilism of Derrida.

TEN

The World behind the Text

Every text builds on some pre-text, even if that text was oral. Texts do not drop out of heaven. They come from human authors, who use words shaped by their lived experience, building on previous usage in discourse and the cultural codes that language reflects. No matter how original and creative a discourse is, it is incomprehensible if it does not relate to the lived experience of someone. Biblical texts in particular present themselves as relating events that have gone before them, and the language they use often betrays the influence of previous texts. The Apocalypse, for example, can hardly be understood without a good knowledge of the Old Testament, because, while never citing texts explicitly, the language constantly evokes Old Testament events or texts.

Thus we come to discuss the world behind the text. Several historical and literary disciplines contribute here, such as archeology, philology, anthropology, epigraphy, lexicography, among others. We can group most of these "auxiliary sciences" under the heading of "the historical-critical" method.

The Historical-Critical Method in Textual Analysis

Unlike the synchronic methods of the previous chapter, the historical-critical method[1] is diachronic; that is, it takes seriously that the text belongs to a different age, and then it seeks to trace the development of the text from its earliest form to its present one (*dia,* "through," *chronos,* "time"). It explores the possibility of written sources the author used, the particular literary genre or form and the social milieu out of which such a text might have come, and even attempts to trace the development of the text.

Tradition criticism strives to look at the text as emerging in the flow of a tradition, and it seeks to map that flow. Common to all these approaches is the commitment to strictly scientific methods, studying the text as one would study any other ancient document, religious or secular. The value of such study, to the extent it is successful, is ultimately to determine what the final author meant in the light of the reconstruction of the text's prehistory. On the other hand, it is sometimes used to reconstruct a history of the community, either of Israel or the early church, which has its advantages and problems, as we will see following.

Most notable among these diachronic methods is that of form criticism.[2] Though begun by Hermann Gunkel in studying the Old Testament, its initiators in New Testament study were Bultmann and Dibelius, whom we discussed from the philosophical viewpoint in chapter 6. Here we simply recall that as a method it seeks to get behind the sources to describe what was happening as the tradition was handed on orally about Jesus from person to person and community to community. It is the oral form that distinguishes this method from source criticism, which is concerned with written documents. As can be seen from their writings, the form critics are interested primarily in the individual units, in classifying them and tracing their oral history. (The German *Formgeschichte* is more precise than the English "form criticism." It means the history of the forms.) The early form critics tended to view the Gospels as primarily creations of the early communities rather than factual reports of the deeds and sayings of Jesus, the historicity of which they were skeptical. Though this extreme position has now been balanced by other studies, the lasting contribution of the form critics is the attention they drew to the influence of the ongoing life of the community in the development of the gospel tradition.

But What "Really" Happened?:
The Modern Historian's Quest

If the historical-critical method is primarily interested in tracing the history of the text up to its final form and then the literal meaning of the text itself, it inevitably raises the question of the events behind the text. One of the effects of the Enlightenment, as we saw earlier, was to focus on the world behind the text in such a way that historical meaning, that is, whether the events narrated really happened or not, was taken to be the only meaning relevant to the modern mind. While there were those who fought to prove the historicity of the biblical accounts of miracles, others explained them away as the glorification of natural phenomena, or as deceptions, or as religious or moral truths in story form, or flatly as myths, and the latter either because it was the intention of the authors to write the stories as myths or that the writers were so captive of the ancient mythological worldview that they had no choice but to tell the stories mythologically. In any case, it was the question, "History or not?" that fired the debate. Though biblical interpretation has moved beyond that question, it is still a relevant one, since Christianity, like Judaism, claims a historical foundation for its faith. Consequently, remembering the limitations of historical research, we must once again ask the question.

The Old Testament

The Bible purports to narrate history. It is clearly not history in our modern understanding of the discipline. Historical novels aside, our modern approach to history-critical as opposed to precritical history—purports to get beyond the sources' "interest" or their conviction of the relevance of the events narrated, in order to reach to the "bare facts" from which the historian can then reconstruct his or her own understanding of the order of the events and their relevance. We also know, of course, that the past in its full existential reality is not retrievable (that's the meaning of past), and so the historian is dependent upon reports or other kinds of evidence, which are weighed, cross-checked, and otherwise refined. The result is a reconstruction, an approximation of the original reality. Nonspecialists depend on the consensus of historians' judgments, which are always subject to being subverted by new discoveries.

From a modern historian's point of view, biblical history is precritical. That does not mean it is false. It means rather that what it narrates is at the service of a different goal, and it is embedded in literary forms foreign to modern historiography. The interest of the Bible is primarily theological, and it is this theological interest that governs its narrating of events. It is also in many parts poetic and liturgical, and texts for festive celebrations tend to use figurative, dramatic language, even embroidering the narrative core to give the story greater impact on the audience that is celebrating the event at a distance of decades, even centuries. Nevertheless, the Bible insists that the events that brought about Israel's existence as a people not only happened but that they continue to provide authoritative directives for the community's life.

Contemporary interpreters of the Old Testament fall either at or between two extremes.[3] There are those who take the Bible with absolute historical literalism in all its details. Reading Genesis through 2 Kings thus places the creation of the world some six thousand years ago. Apparent conflicts between different passages of the Bible and extrabiblical sources are forced into harmonization or explained away. At the other extreme are those who give up any hope—or at least any interest—in the historical relevance of the Bible and approach it from a purely literary point of view, noting that even from that point of view the Bible can be meaningful to the modern reader.

Most scholarly interpreters today fall somewhere between these two extremes. The Bible is a complex book, incorporating many different voices and different literary forms from different eras and historical contexts. History is there, though it is overlaid, intentionally, with religious and theological rhetoric (taking rhetoric in its best sense, as literature aimed to ground and promote the people's faith). "The historian's task is to separate the authentic historical memory from its highly theological and often legendary context."[4] By the middle of the nineteenth century scholars were beginning to put the Old Testament under the microscope of serious historical study. H. G. A. Ewald's source analysis of the Pentateuch was followed by Julius Wellhausen's now famous documentary hypothesis, as a result of which he doubted that any valid historical picture could be reconstructed prior to the monarchy.

Martin Noth held that the exodus and the conquest of Canaan were not historical events, the latter being a retrojection of what really happened only with the expansion of the monarchy under David. W. F. Albright, a pioneer in Palestinian archeology, on the other hand, brought some significant correlations between archeology and the Bible,[5] and John Bright followed this pattern of giving the Bible the benefit of the doubt.[6]

One can get a feel for the contemporary scene by reading the transcript of a debate, published in the *Biblical Archeological Review* in 1997, among Niels Peter Lemche and Thomas Thompson, both of the University of Copenhagen, William Dever of the University of Arizona, and P. Kyle McCarter of Johns Hopkins University in Baltimore.[7] It was followed in 2000 by articles by Philip Davies and William Dever expressing contrasting viewpoints.[8] The strongest pitch for the fictional character of the Old Testament has been given by Thompson.[9] What Thompson calls the "New Israel" existed only in the postexilic period and was not fully developed until the time of the Maccabees. The biblical stories prior to the exile describe an Israel that never existed.[10] Thompson's views have met with sharp criticism from William Dever and reviewers.[11] His concern to read the Bible only theologically apparently puts much of it in the category of myth and certainly goes against the claim of the Bible itself to be historically grounded.

What, finally, can be said about the historical value of the Old Testament? It is a mixture of history and theology. Scholars debate the relative percentages of the mix. At times archeology and epigraphy provide suggestive correspondences to the biblical witness (an Egyptian inscription of the thirteenth century BC is the earliest mention of Israel); at other times they conflict with it. There seems to be a growing consensus today that in the status of today's research history cannot be securely constructed from the biblical accounts prior to the monarchy. For the sixth-century Deuteronomist historians and the fifth-century redactors of the Pentateuch, the further back in time they looked, the more their theological interest overshadowed the fewer and fewer recoverable historical sources (compare the rather sober, though particularist, memoirs of Nehemiah with the primitive history of Genesis

1–11). That should not be surprising, since at least prior to the monarchy Israel's traditions would have been largely oral, and when it came to narrating the story of Israel's origins, the concern would have been to provide the rationale for contemporary law and worship. No archeological trace has so far showed up for the exodus, yet it is the foundation of Israel's most important feast, Passover. The historian does not necessarily say that the events never happened (absence of evidence is not evidence of absence), though some would make that claim. The responsible historian says that the events cannot be independently verified and that other religious and even political interests suggest a writing or rewriting of history to meet those interests.

The New Testament

When we turn to the New Testament, we must immediately note an important chronological difference. Whereas the Old Testament literature was gathered over a period of centuries, the Gospels of the New Testament represent a development of only at most seventy years. Jesus died around the year 30, and the Gospel of John, the latest, appeared around the end of the century. This means that the historian has a much tighter control on his sources than is the case with Old Testament historiography. By the same token, however, the Gospels were not written according to the norms of modern historiography. They are proclamations of the "good news of Jesus Christ." And they reflect the ongoing concerns of the early Christian communities, their catechetical, liturgical, doctrinal, even polemical interests, which have heavily influenced the redaction of the accounts. What can the historian find there?[12]

Rudolf Bultmann no longer sought to find any historical basis for the gospel accounts. For him they were simple proclamations in response to which one could find meaning in terms of existentialism. Some of his disciples reacted to that extreme and felt that indeed a historical core could be found, and that one might relate to such a rehabilitated Jesus, but this conclusion, too, was reached at the expense of bypassing the literary and kerygmatic appeal of the Gospels.

The reaction of the Catholic Church authorities to the academy's historical skepticism was only in part a reaffirmation of the historical basis of the Bible. It was primarily a reaction to the philosophical assumptions that undergirded the methods used. When the literary critics came on the scene, influenced by the contribution that the analysis of secular literature could make to the biblical narratives, interest in the historicity of the accounts waned, and great strides were made in seeing the biblical narratives as whole works of art that could and should be appreciated on their own terms. They thus revealed, as portraits do, a particular author's interpretation of his subject and thus his theology. Whether the events and persons portrayed actually existed, or existed as portrayed, was not the concern of narrative criticism.[13]

But the question remains. Christianity, like Judaism, claims to be a historical religion. It emerged not simply from some mystic's spiritual experience, nor even from a community's corporate spiritual experience. It professes in its creed that Jesus "was crucified under Pontius Pilate," and it bases its entire cause on the claim that he rose from the dead: "If Christ has not been raised, then vain too is our preaching; vain, too, your faith" (1 Cor 15:14). It is therefore of crucial interest even to the believer to know whether one's faith is grounded in history, to know whether the events narrated really happened or not.

The problem, of course, is that the sources were not written according to the canons of modern historical research. The Gospels, to speak only of them, were not supplied with footnotes, and none of the authors was assuming the persona of a presumably neutral observer. On the contrary, they were passionate believers in their message—even to the point of giving their lives. And the response they were seeking from their audience was nothing less than conversion and a similar commitment. Although such an investment may enhance the credibility of their message, it does not guarantee that the events they describe happened exactly in the way they are narrated, and this for at least two reasons.

In the first place, the Gospels in their present form were written forty to seventy years after the events they narrate, and while they relate what Jesus said and did, they do so on the basis of oral memory and a growing tradition about Jesus. According to the testimony of the Gospels themselves, Jesus never wrote anything (except the scribbling on the ground when people brought to him the woman taken in adultery, John 8:6), nor did he command his disciples to write anything. He sent them forth to preach and to form other disciples (Mark 16:15; Matt 28:19). Although Old Testament prophets had disciples who wrote down their words (for example, Baruch to Jeremiah, Jer 36:4, 32), there is no evidence that in the lifetime of Jesus any of his disciples did so. And after his death, the imminence of his second coming was so strong in the consciousness of the disciples that they felt no immediate need to record the message in writing.

But this did not last long. And this leads to the second reason. The demise of the original witnesses, either because of mission to foreign lands or death, and the ongoing needs of the community occasioned a development that was both conservative and creative. Conservative in the sense that the orally conveyed stories and sayings of Jesus were eventually written down. Many scholars think that the shorter sayings of Jesus, particularly the rhythmic and rhetorical ones, are likely to have been preserved as Jesus spoke them (though in Greek equivalence), since they could easily be memorized. Paul also knows the difference between a "word of the Lord" and his own word (1 Cor 7:10–12). But the development was also creative in the sense that there was need to adapt the tradition to the developing needs of the community: preaching outlines, liturgical settings, new pastoral situations unforeseen by the teachings of Jesus,[14] and conflicts with the Jewish authorities, especially the Pharisees who, after the fall of the temple, competed with the Christians for spiritual leadership of the decimated Jewish community. The Gospels then envisage a particular audience challenged by a particular environment, which in many cases was different from the original life situation of Jesus.

While the church considers the final edition of the tradition, the Gospels as we have them, to hold the inspired and authoritative meaning, the historian will seek to identify the earliest layer of the tradition and distinguish it from later accretions. Is this possible? It is a delicate work, surely, and scholars have generally agreed on three criteria for telling whether a recorded saying or event originated with Jesus:

1. *The criterion of multiple attestation.* If a given event or saying is narrated in two or more sources, this enhances the probability of its being early and original.

2. *The criterion of embarrassment.* If a saying or event evokes a detectible discomfort in the gospel tradition, it has likely not been invented by the Christian community. Jesus' baptism by John is frequently cited in this category, since a community bent on exalting the holiness of its hero would not have invented his submission to a baptism of repentance.

3. *The criterion of dissimilarity.* If an event or saying contrasts with what is known of contemporary Jewish or Hellenistic thinking and cannot be ascribed to later Christian tradition, thus pointing to the uniqueness of the saying or event, then this enhances the probability of its being original. The serious limitation of this criterion is that the Jesus it comes up with is not Jewish, Hellenistic, nor Christian. N. T. Wright, a chief protagonist in the current debate over the historical Jesus, balances this last criterion with another, that of similarity, or better, dissimilarity within similarity.[15] Jesus was a Jew, and his disciples could not have so radically misunderstood him as to invent a totally different worldview.[16] What Wright means is that if a word or action of Jesus shows a dissimilarity within a Jewish similarity, this enhances the likelihood of its being original.

Given the resistance of the texts to perfect clarity in this area, it is not surprising that scholars, using the same texts, have come up with radically different reconstructions of Jesus. For Burton Mack, Jesus was a great teacher that Mark transformed into a divine figure who worked miracles.[17] The Jesus Seminar, a collaborative work of several biblical scholars, has also portrayed Jesus as a teacher who was remembered for his pithy and challenging sayings. Mack and the seminar have been criticized for failing to explain how such a person could have merited crucifixion. For Richard Horsley, Jesus was a social prophet,[18] for Geza Vermes a charismatic Jew,[19] for Morton Smith a magician,[20] for Ben Witherington III a Jewish sage,[21] for F. Gerald Downing a Cynic philosopher.[22] For Dominic Crossan, Jesus was a Galilean peasant become wandering Cynic social reformer.[23] Marcus Borg is in the same furrow, though he has a more comprehensive view of Jesus: as a Spirit-filled person, as a healer, and as an initiator of a new social movement.[24] Common to all these is a rejection of Jesus as an apocalyptic prophet proclaiming the imminent inbreaking of the kingdom (and the judgment) of God, the view held a century earlier by Albert Schweitzer. E. P. Sanders, on the other hand, sees Jesus as an eschatological prophet who thought of himself as the last messenger before the inbreaking of God's kingdom. Like several of the other New Testament historians, he comes up with a list of "almost indisputable facts about Jesus."[25] Norman Perrin has a rather extensive list of sayings of Jesus that are an "irreducible minimum," that is, sayings whose authenticity most historians would affirm.[26]

John P. Meier makes a distinction between the "real Jesus" and the "historical Jesus."[27] The former is the totality of who Jesus is. We do not know and never will know Jesus completely in that sense. In fact, we don't know anyone in that way, as the totality of the person escapes comprehension. By the "historical Jesus" Meier means those facts about Jesus that historical research can uncover. This is obviously more limited than the former, but the distinction is helpful in that it is a candid admission even before the research begins that such research is limited and will never adequately present the "real Jesus." Meier agrees with Sanders that Jesus saw himself as an eschatological prophet anticipating the divine restoration of Israel and the inclusion of the gentiles. He also has a list of facts about Jesus that can be determined by historical science. N. T. Wright takes the gospel accounts to be basically reliable. Like Sanders and Meier he holds Jesus to be a prophet who announces and inaugurates the kingdom. He believes himself to be the Messiah and that the kingdom would be brought about by means of his own death.[28] He followed his earlier book on the public ministry and death of Jesus with another eight-hundred-page historical study on the resurrection.[29] Is the resurrection of Jesus merely a matter of faith, not of history? Was it a "transhistorical" event going so beyond human experience that it escapes any kind of historical control? Are the resurrection accounts mere legends? Theories abound, and after evaluating the major ones, Wright presents his own step-by-step argument that the apostolic witness could only be grounded in a real-time experience of the bodily resurrection of Jesus.

The names mentioned here do not exhaust the number of eminent scholars who have studied Jesus as a historical figure. These persons have devoted their lives to this endeavor and deserve respect, especially from the nonspecialists. However, the fact that such academicians using the same evidence come up with radically different conclusions cautions us not to be hasty to jump on anyone's bandwagon.[30] One thing, of course, that they do agree on is that there is a historical core behind the Gospels as we have them. This would seem to be simple common sense. It took some powerful impetus to launch the Christian movement, and that movement itself said it was Jesus. Was Jesus just a sage, a wandering Cynic? Was Jesus an eschatological prophet hailing the imminent reign of God? Or could he have been both—and more? The best hypothesis, as N. T. Wright has observed, is that which accounts for all the evidence. The problem comes with dating the evidence and the sources: How much is from Jesus, how much from the early church? And what weight is to be given to the noncanonical Gospel of Thomas? In the view of some scholars, it provides a key to the "real Jesus." Yet, while possibly containing sayings that go back to Jesus, it dates from the middle of the second century and reflects a gnostic milieu, which can hardly be the milieu of the historical Jesus.[31] In the view of this author, the retrievable historical evidence shows Jesus primarily as an eschatological figure, a prophet with an urgent agenda, with his wisdom sayings being incorporated into his vision of the kingdom that is both coming and is here. If his precursor, John the Baptist, was an eschatological prophet, and the disciples of Jesus continued an eschatological expectation, then the greatest historical probability is that the bridge between the two, Jesus, was also in the eschatological mold.

Faith and History

For believers who take Jesus as the Son of God and commit their lives to that faith, these results may seem minimal and disappointing, perhaps even the reduction of conflicting positions to the lowest common denominator.[32] Christians believe they can contact "the real Jesus" directly by faith and even experience the power of the Holy Spirit given by the risen Lord ("to know him and the power of his resurrection and the fellowship of his sufferings," Phil 3:10). They take the Gospels as the inspired word of God and thus are inclined to think of the events narrated as historical because they have in some way experienced that "what happened then is happening now." For them the fact that miracles happen today confirms the reality of the miracles that happened then, especially healings that replicate those narrated in the Gospels. Believers will thus be inclined to wonder what kind of a world the scholars are living in, that so differs from the world of their experience. And historians who exclude the possibility of supernatural or otherwise inexplicable intrusions into human history have predetermined their own conclusions.

Will these worlds never meet? Are historians and believers destined to dismiss each other as irrelevant? That would be tragic, for both can learn from each other. John P. Meier's distinction between the "real Jesus" and the "historical Jesus" may be helpful here. The real Jesus, as noted previously, refers to the totality of Jesus' being. The historical Jesus refers to the limited knowledge available through the canons of scientific research. Historians and enlightened believers alike understand the Gospels to be witnesses of the faith of early Christian communities, enriched by the ongoing experience of those communities that mined the tradition and developed it to meet their practical needs. That there is a historical core to the Gospels is indisputable. Believers should take heart that historians, who fall on a spectrum from disbelief to full belief, have been able to establish a solid core of "indisputable facts" of the life of Jesus. But faith in Jesus is not the mere capitulation of the rational mind before "the facts." The act of faith is the surrender of the self to the movement of divine grace, a supernatural light that is a revelation of the selfhood of God in Jesus Christ. It is a different way of knowing. The gift of the Holy Spirit, which accompanies faith in Christ, empowers the Christian to know Jesus as Lord and God as "Abba" (1 Cor 12:3; Rom 8:15; 10:9; Gal 4:6). The believer has no doubt that he has met "the real Jesus," though obviously in an obscurity that awaits the full light of glory in the next life. Part of that faith is the conviction that God has entered human history in Jesus Christ, who "suffered under Pontius Pilate," and he is reassured that his faith has historical precedents. These historical precedents do not compel his faith, but they do mean that his faith is not irrational. It "makes sense."

Those historical precedents, however, are not just the "indisputable facts" that historians have reached. The immediate historical precedent is the witness of the apostolic church revealed in the New Testament. In fact, when a person comes to believe in Jesus Christ as Lord, he does so by first encountering the faith and the witness of those who knew him in his public life and in his resurrected state as Lord. The believer trusts the apostolic witness, which he takes as the witness given by the Holy Spirit. And that trust enables him to make the same act of faith that the witnesses have made. The enlightened believer knows that witness is not a detached, neutral relaying of information but a passionate appeal coming from persons and communities who have been transformed by the message. Their voice is convinced and urgent. Who could possibly be dispassionate in proclaiming that a fire is about to engulf a sleeping family? And the fact that the witness proclaims the relevance of Jesus for a community's life seventy years later by developing the tradition leaves the believer with only one question: "Well, what else would you expect?" The believer expects continuity with Jesus, not archival replication. Development need not be deviation.

To the person of faith, that continuity with Jesus and development into the future is provided by the Holy Spirit, who "will lead you into all truth" (John 16:13), who will "receive of what is mine and declare it to you" (John 16:14–15), who will reveal

157

"the deep things of God" (1 Cor 2:10). But that Spirit is known by its bearing witness to Jesus (Rev 19:10; 1 Cor 12:1–3). It is not another Jesus the Spirit reveals but only the riches of the same Jesus. To say with Paul that "if we once knew Christ according to the flesh, yet we now know him so no longer" (1 Cor 5:16) is not to deny the relevance of what we can know of Jesus through historical research. Quite the contrary: the early church soon had to fight the docetists and gnostics who debunked the human reality of Jesus. It simply means that knowing Jesus in a merely human way is inadequate and incomparable to knowing him in the revelation of the Spirit.

But will this faith prejudice objective historical research? Is a believing historian a contradiction in terms? The answer is, Every historian is a believing historian. There are no presuppositionless methods of inquiry. Everyone approaches reality through the lens of one's own history, culture, language, and prejudices—in a broad sense, one's faith. It is better to admit this at the start than to pretend to a complete, disinterested, neutral objectivity, which is a prejudice of its own. The key is to become as aware as possible of one's lens, to distrust the tendency to project onto the evidence conclusions that the evidence does not support. At the same time, however, one's faith stance and experience may give a clearer insight into the evidence than that of the nonbeliever, as the previous example of contemporary miracles attests.[33] Believing and researching, after all, coexist in the same subject, and there is no reason why honesty about both cannot lead to objectivity. That basically is what Pope John Paul II was trying to say in *Fides et Ratio*. N. T. Wright puts it this way:

> History, then, prevents faith becoming fantasy. Faith prevents history becoming mere antiquarianism. Historical research, being always provisional, cannot ultimately veto faith, though it can pose hard questions that faith, in order to retain its integrity precisely as Christian faith, must struggle to answer, and may well grow strong through answering. Faith, being subject to the vagaries of personality and culture, cannot veto the historical enterprise (it can't simply say "I don't like the

Jesus you write about, so you must be wrong"), but it can put hard questions to history, not least on the large topic of the origins of Christianity, and history may be all the better for trying to answer them.[34]

Source, Form, and Redaction Criticism

The historical critics make use of several tools of criticism. Source criticism looks at the possible written sources that an author has used. Mark and Q are thus considered the written sources used by Matthew and Luke, though there is some dispute as to how much of these were written, how much oral.

Form criticism, as we noted in chapter 6, is concerned with the oral prehistory of the text, and it studies the life setting out of which this text may have emerged.

Redaction criticism grew out of a dissatisfaction with the results of form criticism. Scholars began to turn their attention to the editorial work of the evangelists. This was easier to do in view of the consensus that Mark was the first Gospel, that Q could be isolated, and that Matthew and Luke used both Mark and Q in their works. By studying how the writers put together their sources, arranged them, curtailed or expanded them, the critic could arrive at the "theology" of a given writer. And since an individual passage must be interpreted in the light of the whole book, this procedure became very helpful in bringing to light the different portraits of Jesus and other perspectives of early Christian theology. This method was applied to the books of the Old Testament as well. The method opened up a deeper spiritual meaning to the texts than had been available by the positivist approach of the preceding century. This method has been called "redaction criticism," or occasionally "composition criticism." This latter term runs the risk of confusing redaction criticism with literary or narrative criticism. Though redaction critics were not interested in recovering the "Jesus of history," their method was nevertheless historical in the sense that they understood the meaning of the text to depend on its genesis, that is, the history of the text itself, as well as the intention of the author. Norman Perrin describes the method this way:

> The redaction critic investigates how smaller units—both simple and composite—from the oral tradition or from written sources were put together to form larger complexes, and he is especially interested in the formation of the Gospels as finished products. Redaction criticism is concerned with the interaction between an inherited tradition and a later interpretive point of view. Its goals are to understand why the items from the tradition were modified and connected as they were, to identify the theological motifs that were at work in composing a finished Gospel, and to elucidate the theological point of view which is expressed in and through the composition. Although redaction criticism has been most closely associated with the Gospels, there is no reason why it could not be used—and actually it is being used—to illuminate the relationship between tradition and interpretation in other New Testament books.[35]

A good example of redaction criticism is chapter 18 of Matthew. It is called the "Community Discourse" because he has assembled sayings of Jesus scattered elsewhere in Mark and Q, plus his own source (M) and arranged them topically around the theme of community relationships. What happens when individual sayings are given a new topical context is that the meaning of the individual pericopes is moved to a new register. For example, the saying of Jesus about receiving a little child, which in Mark 9:36–37 is not clearly connected with the preceding verses about humility and service, now means not only accepting the kingdom in a childlike way, but also relating to fellow community members with similar openness (Matt 18:2–5). And the cutting off of members, which in Mark 9:42–48 meant the avoidance of personal occasions of sin at any cost, in Matthew legitimates the exclusion of destructive members from the community (18:6–9). Similarly, placing the figure of the shepherd seeking the lost sheep (vv. 12–13) in the center of the chapter and framing it with the counsel not to despise the little ones for whom the Father cares (v. 10), and with the Father's will that none of them perish (v. 14), suggests that the community must take on the shepherd's heart, and, however much the community has standards of membership, it needs to reach out to the straying lest they perish.

Sociocultural Studies

In recent decades the social sciences have contributed considerably to our understanding of the world in which the Bible took shape. This is really an expansion of the historical-critical method. It focuses on values, social structures, and conventions common in the culture in which the biblical author lived.[36] To get an idea of how this method works, it suffices to look at the table of contents of one example of it, *The Social World of Luke-Acts: Models for Interpretation*, ed. Jerome Neyrey.[37] The various contributors study the influence of honor and shame as values of the ancient Mediterranean world, the collective rather than the individualistic personality, labeling and deviance as boundary markers, urban social relations in the preindustrial city in Luke-Acts, the countryside, sickness and healing, temple versus household, patron-client relations, meals and table fellowship, the social location of the implied author.[38] Studies such as these have been very helpful in clarifying the historical and cultural matrix of the Bible. Perhaps the most significant difference between modern Western culture and the culture of biblical times is the dominance of tribal identity over personal identity (what the social scientists sometimes call "the dyadic personality"). The practitioners of these methods must be careful, of course, not to assume that all the contemporaneous cultures were identical, lest they project onto the biblical texts values or ideas that belonged to a different, albeit contemporary, culture. Likewise one must be careful not to apply categories derived from today's social science on the assumption that they will automatically fit the ancient world. This is particularly questionable when modern psychological categories are used to interpret biblical texts.[39] But with those caveats, the contributions of the social sciences have been quite helpful.

Conclusion

The importance of the historical-critical method must neither be under- nor overestimated. It makes an important contribution in seeking to establish the original meaning of an individual text and, in redaction criticism, the meaning that comes from the assembling of individual units. At the same time, taken alone, it frequently leaves the modern reader with little help in finding a contemporary application of the text. That is why for a complete interpretation it needs to be completed by other methods. This is the point made by the Pontifical Biblical Commission, when it states that "exegesis is truly faithful to the intention of biblical texts when it goes not only to the heart of their formulation to find the reality of faith there expressed but also seeks to link this reality to the experience of faith in our present world."[40]

ELEVEN

The World in Front of the Text: Reader Response

The biblical writers were not recording events or discourses for archival purposes. Just as the oral word was addressed to a live and present audience, the written word was inscribed both for oral proclamation and for the edification of whoever might read it privately.[1] If we think of communication as involving a sender, a message, and a recipient, then the focus of this chapter is on the recipient. There are two kinds of recipients. One is the recipient envisaged by the writer as we can decode it from the text. This is sometimes called the "ideal reader" or the "implied reader." We know, for example, that the Gospel of Luke was addressed to a certain Theophilus, whether he was Luke's benefactor or a type of "one who loves God" (the meaning of *Theophilus*). In this case the addressee is explicit. But most often the audience is only implied. Even Luke certainly meant his Gospel to reach more than Theophilus. Matthew, Mark, and John do not mention to whom their works are addressed, but it is relatively easy to discern the kind of audience each has in mind. Each assumes his readers (or hearers) know *something* already, the "in-house" language that they would understand (for example, the meaning of *Messiah* in the Jewish communities). They build on this foundation to further instruct, encourage, and challenge.

There is, second, the *actual reader*, the one like you or me, who either picks up the book and reads it or listens to it being read. The actual readers never coincide perfectly with the ideal or implied reader, but the closer they come to him or her, the better they will understand the text. Among actual readers there are some who are interested in the Bible for what it can tell them to support certain causes, and these we call "advocacy readers." Let us look at each of these in turn.

The Implied (Ideal) Reader

As mentioned, the implied or ideal reader is the reader to whom the author addresses his text. This can be twofold. The author may have in mind a specific historical target group for which the gospel is written. Mark, for example, is usually credited with addressing the community in Rome that has experienced persecution. Some even think the gospel was written to be read at a single sitting to baptismal candidates just before they received the sacrament. But, inasmuch as the text is written, it is also available, and intended, for anyone well disposed who might read or hear the gospel. We can thus distinguish between the immediately intended audience and the broader or universal one, like the difference between the initial plunge of a stone in a pond and the ripples that follow. Although the Pastoral Letters are addressed to the individuals Timothy and Titus, it is clear that the author expects them also to be read publicly, for the concluding line in Titus and 2 Timothy is "Grace be with you all."

In any case, communication is not like sending my checks through a vacuum tube to a teller in a drive-through bank. I select something to communicate, I shape it so it will fit into a pipeline (language), and I send it to the receiver, who unpacks it and stores it in his mental box. What makes this image simplistic, as Walter Ong points out,[2] is that it ignores what really happens in human communication. The sender is already aware of the receiver, and the sender's communication is shaped by the receiver before it is sent. For example, if I am speaking to a child I will shape my message differently from the way I would shape it for an adult. Hence, there is an effect produced by the receiver (whether the actual audience or the implied audience) already in the sender. This is more obvious in oral communication than in written, but the author of a text also has an audience in mind, even if it is imaginary. (The biblical writers invariably had a real audience in mind, the community of believers to which the text was addressed.) Now this process can also be looked at from the viewpoint of the receiver, for a text comes to life only as it is received and enfleshed in the receiver. As Saint Thomas would say, "Everything that is received is received in the mode of the receiver." Every reader in some way rewrites the book he or she is reading, as we can see when we pick up a book that has been highlighted by someone else. The highlighter may well have given importance to something in the text that to the author was secondary or incidental, or he or she may have skipped what to the author was primary.

In many respects reader-response theory is nothing new. The fathers were quite aware of it. Saint Ephrem writes:

Lord, who can comprehend even one of your words? We lose more of it than we grasp, like those who drink from a living spring. For God's word offers different facets according to the capacity of the listener, and the Lord has portrayed his message in many colors, so that whoever gazes upon it can see in it what suits him. Within it he has buried manifold treasures, so that each of us might grow rich in seeking them out.

The word of God is a tree of life that offers us blessed fruit from each of its branches. It is like that rock which was struck open in the wilderness, from which all were offered spiritual drink....

And so whenever anyone discovers some part of the treasure, he should not think that he has exhausted God's word. Instead he should feel that this is all that he was able to find of the wealth contained in it. Nor should he say that the word is weak and sterile or look down on it simply because this portion was all that he happened to find. But precisely because he could not capture it all he should give thanks for its riches.

Be glad then that you are overwhelmed, and do not be saddened because he has overcome you. A thirsty man is happy when he is drinking, and he is not depressed because he cannot exhaust the spring. So let this spring quench your thirst, and not your thirst the spring. For if you can satisfy your thirst without exhausting the spring, then when you thirst again you can drink from it once more; but if when your thirst is sated the spring is also dried up, then your victory would turn to your own harm.

Be thankful then for what you have received, and do not be saddened at all that such an abundance still remains. What you have received and attained is your present share, while what is left will be your heritage. For what you could not take at one time because of your weakness, you will be able to grasp at another if you only persevere. So do not foolishly try to drain in one draught what cannot be consumed all at once, and do not cease out of faintheartedness from what you will be able to absorb as time goes on.[3]

Ephrem's concern for the reader/listener, however, does not suggest that for him the meaning is something that the reader *brings* to the text. Rather, whatever the reader authentically discovers is already there in the text, waiting to be drawn upon according to the capacities of the reader.

The appeal to the reader/listener can be well illustrated by a section of Matthew's Gospel. Chapter 11 begins with the appearance of John the Baptist's disciples, who ask whether Jesus is the one to come, "or shall we look for another?" They would not have asked that question had Jesus' perfectly fit the kind of "coming one" John had described. This "mightier one" was to bring the cleansing fire of judgment upon the unrepentant (Matt 3:7–12; Luke 3:7–17). But Jesus instead was the face of God's mercy, forgiveness, and healing. Though Jesus praises John, it is obvious that John's disciples, if not John himself, have an inadequate understanding and response to Jesus. This is followed by Jesus' reproaches to the towns of Corazin, Bethsaida, and Capernaum, obviously for their negative response to Jesus and his message. But then the chapter climaxes with a praise of God for the positive response of the disciples. And finally, Jesus as it were steps out of the pages of the text to address his appeal to the reader: "Come to me, all you who labor and are burdened, and I will give you rest. Take my yoke upon you and learn from me, for I am meek and humble of heart; and you will find rest for yourselves. For my yoke is easy, and my burden light" (Matt 11:28–30).

The use of *yoke* indicates an address to particular Jewish contemporaries whom Jesus sees as burdened by the complicated legalism of the scribes and Pharisees. Instead, echoing the image of Sirach 51:23, 26, he offers his wisdom as a light yoke, since it is found in the person of Jesus. Here we can discern the immediate audience Matthew is envisioning, the implied reader or listener. Our example could also be used as an example of rhetorical criticism.

But, as Ricoeur has said, the text now floats free both of Matthew's control and of his immediate audience, and that raises the issue of the response of anyone who encounters the text. It is this latter understanding of reader-response that interests contemporary theorists. They fall on a spectrum depending on whether meaning is determined by reader over the text or text over the reader. Powell lines up these theories as follows:[4]

I. Reader *over* the Text

1. *Deconstruction.* Powell inserts a question mark here because this method may or may not fit here.

2. *Transactive Criticism.* Norman Holland is the originator of this system. Interpretation is largely determined by the defenses, expectations and wish-fulfilling fantasies of the reader. The content of the text is read, even transformed, according to one's own personality. It has no universal or correct meaning. This is reader-response's most extreme form. Is there no control whatever on the interpretation one might give to the text? This leads to the next category, an attempt to bring some control to the reader-centered "transactive criticism."

3. *Interpretive Communities.* Although agreeing that no single reading of a given text is the "right" one, the later Stanley Fish proposes that a community may agree on a reading strategy that accepts only those meanings that are in accord with its accepted strategy.[5] What do you see as the strengths and weaknesses of this method?

II. Reader *with* the Text

These methods give dominance neither to the text nor to the reader but see the interpretive process as a dialectical one between reader and text.

1. *Affective Stylistics.* The early Fish had proposed this model. As the reader moves through the text, he begins to get an idea of what it is about and some expectation of what is to come. As he moves through the text, his interpretation is either confirmed or corrected.

2. *Phenomenological Criticism.* Wolfgang Iser's method is similar to the preceding. He sees the reader's expectations constrained by his or her desire to find consistency in the work as a whole. These expectations cannot be absolute, however, since the narrative will usually contain various gaps that the reader must fill in according to his own creativity.[6]

There is, doubtless, an activity of the reader in the communication process. For example, not only the writer but also the reader is involved in the development of character in a narrative. When we first meet a character we respond to the initial clue given by the text; we form an idea or an image of the character. But then, as the narrative proceeds, our original image is either affirmed or corrected, in any case enriched, by further clues. It is in precisely this way that the author via his text intends to involve the reader. "Reading is a temporal process of making and revising meaning— the reader develops expectations along the way, and finds them fulfilled, disappointed, or revised as reading continues."[7]

Comparing these methods with the others studied, we can say that both structuralism and narrative criticism see the reader in the text, not over it or with it, as in the reader-response theories. In the former, it is the text that configures or determines the reader's response; in the latter the reader is more in control. Structuralism insists that reading, like writing, is bound by certain codes in the text itself. Narrative criticism presupposes that the reader is in the text—the implied reader certainly.

Advocacy Criticism

This is a category closely aligned with reader-response theory but including a host of approaches, all characterized by the promotion of certain causes or concerns in society. There are feminist hermeneutics, liberation hermeneutics, black hermeneutics[8]—to mention only a few. Liberation theologians, the first significant group to appear, began to reread the scriptures through the lens of the oppressed peoples of the world, beginning with Latin America. Suddenly certain biblical themes stood out on the horizon of their hermeneutics—especially the exodus in the Old Testament, and Mary's Magnificat, read as a song of liberation, in the New. Martin Luther King Jr. preached with powerful rhetoric from some of those texts. Feminists began rereading the Bible with the lens of the texts' interest, disinterest, or opposition even to the uplift of women. In one current of feminism, texts showing the role of women were gleaned and highlighted, and in some cases significant new insights were gained. Feminists further on the spectrum began to find the Bible so patriarchal and androcentric that they abandoned it altogether, even abandoning the Christian faith.[9]

The danger, of course, in advocacy hermeneutics is that the practitioners may become very selective of texts, or may be inclined to read them in only a certain way. I remember hearing one liberation theologian say, in a public discussion, "I am interested in the Bible only insofar as it relates to the liberation of my people." Some promoters of liberation have taken a wholly Marxist interpretation of the Bible, an approach that most people would dismiss as reductionist, that is, a deformation of the Bible into an unrecognizable counterfeit.[10] However, inasmuch as traditional exegesis and hermeneutics often themselves reflect bias or unquestioned presuppositions, these new approaches can be very helpful in alerting the academy to neglected aspects of biblical research. New experiences in the church and in the world can lead to new questions and sometimes to discovering a new relevance of certain biblical data neglected in the past. For example, the charismatic renewal has occasioned scholars to look much more carefully at the portions of the New Testament that deal with the Holy Spirit and the charisms, neglected for centuries because there was not a widespread *experience* of the modalities of the Spirit's action resembling those in the New Testament.

In advocacy criticism much more attention is paid to the *real* readers of the text, not to the ideal reader or the encoded constraints of the text. The real readers live in a real world, and if this world is oppressive then they will turn for help to any source, and the Bible is one of those sources. It is understandable that their *interest* is what makes the Bible meaningful for them. They will tend to see and hear very strongly those passages that address their situation; and they will tend to mute those passages that do not, or that tend to balance their urgent concerns with wider perspectives. The value of their reading is not perhaps so much for themselves as for those of opposing views, who need to hear what they, in turn, may have muted in the Bible. The point is that the Bible is meant to address all cultures, and if the Christian community embraces all cultures and ethnic groups, then it is a meeting ground where conflicting interpretations can, one hopes, interact and move toward mutual understanding and resolution.

When such conflicting interpretations do meet, can they find any help to move from the isolation of one's own world to that of the other? However strong one's convictions, it is healthy to realize the limits of reader-response criticism. Certainly anyone interested in praying the scriptures, or sharing them in a Bible study group, or preaching or catechizing from them, will be very interested in his or her own personal response as well as the response of any group to whom he or she tries to communicate the meaning of the text. Response of the reader/listener needs to be evoked if meaning is to be found at all, for meaning assumes communication and reception. However, without controls, reader-response can become totally subjective and can be used for unhealthy political, myopic, egoistic, even oppressive ends. In assigning meaning to a text, one needs to check to see if one's judgment is correct. Here Lonergan's paradigm is helpful. Meeting a conflicting interpretation can alert us to our prejudices or be the occasion of confirming our understanding.

What tools do we have to check the validity of our judgments? First of all, there is the text itself. Though the text, in Ricoeur's words, opens up a world in front of the text, this can hardly be in utter discontinuity with the literal meaning of the text as it expresses its world. Interpretations totally contrary to the meaning of the text (taken in terms of the entire biblical witness) have cut from under themselves any grounding.[11] The genetic methods (historical-critical, and so on) need to be respected and used in the measure that they are helpful. While giving due voice to contemporary experience, a further check is, indeed, tradition, for the particular text has a history of interpretation in the living community of the church (in this we would be in partial agreement with the later Stanley Fish's theory of the interpretive community). That community is both the vertical one of the past and the horizontal "community of communities" of the present. Vatican II wrestled with this question, for which the solution is not simple. It stated, as we shall see, that there is a sense in which the word of God is above the church, creates the church, feeds the church, and judges the church. In that sense the word of God is *over* not only the individual reader but the entire church as well. But in another sense, the church *discerns* the word by which it is created, fed, and judged. This assumes a stance of faith that believes that the Holy Spirit guides the judgment of the church concerning the word she hears as she listens to the ancient text. This leads to the question of canonical criticism, the concern of the next chapter. Before we do so, though, there is one other dimension of reader-response criticism that must be addressed.

Effective History of the Text

Up to this point we have presented reader-response criticism as an encounter between an ancient text and a contemporary reader. However, the reality is that the biblical text has been affecting readers and listeners already for thousands of years, and the human responses to what people believed to be the word of God certainly must tell us something about the meaning of the words. Even though the meaning they sometimes saw was incorrect or even disastrous, the positive effect of the word on world history and on transformed human lives certainly may tell us more than an interpretation that ignores its historical trajectory.

This is what Gadamer called the "effective history" of the text. The sun may be studied as something in itself—its size, weight, degrees of heat, its solar flares. But one does not really comprehend the sun unless one studies the effects it has as its rays traverse millions of miles, pass through our atmosphere, and create and sustain life on Earth. Similarly, the *effect* of the word as it comes to us has passed through generations who have found meaning in it. That handed-down meaning is part of the world we live in. It affects us prior even to our reflecting on it.

If the pages of Christian history are splotched by interpretations that would blame and persecute the Jewish people for killing Jesus, or deny human rights and due process to anyone, the word has also made innumerable saints, built cathedrals, inspired magnificent works of art and drama, succored the poor, and provided moral grounding for governments. In the Gospel of Mark, Jesus describes the word of God as seed that immediately becomes people, developing according to the response each gives (Mark 4:14–20). The Sermon on the Mount concludes by warning that the word must be lived if it is to survive, which suggests that the teaching of Jesus is more like a recipe, the proof of which is in the living. That proof is not with those who mouth religious formulas but with those who *do* the will of the Father (Matt 7:21–27). Or, as someone once said, "You are the only Bible some people will ever read." It has been said that the saints are the footnotes of the gospel. If so, then if you would know what Jesus meant in his description of the Last Judgment, when he said that what is done to the "least" is done to him, then look at Saints Martin de Pores, Elizabeth of Hungary, Francis of Assisi, Peter Claver who spent his life ministering to slaves in their wretchedness, Vincent de Paul, who said to a co-worker who complained about the ingratitude of the poor, "Be grateful if the poor forgive you for the bread that you give them." Or Mother Teresa of Calcutta. To name a few. Note that we classify the effective history of the text under reader response, because it is the readers'/listeners' response that carries the word through history. That response may not always be within the parameters set by the text, as history shows. False or inadequate interpretations can lead to misguided, even disastrous consequences. But that should be attributed to the inadequacy of the receiver rather than to the text.

Legal Hermeneutics for Comparison

In the light of what the reader now knows of biblical herme-neutics, and as a lead into canonical criticism, it will be enlight-ening and clarifying to compare what we have learned with legal hermeneutics. Law obviously presupposes a community consti-tuted by a foundational agreement, which in the United States we call the Constitution.

There are basically three methods employed in constitutional interpretation: (1) What the actual *words* meant *then*. What did the words mean in 1787 or 1789 or 1866 (when Congress sent the Fourteenth Amendment to the states for ratification)? Usually dictionaries from those time periods are consulted to determine what the authors really meant. (2) The framers' *intentions:* for example, what was Madison's intention as the original author? What was the intention of Congress that passed it? For example, what did the First Amendment ("Congress shall make no law respecting an establishment of religion, or prohibiting the free exercise thereof") mean, considering that Congress authorized a day of Thanksgiving or the practice of opening Congress with a prayer? Here it is actual practice rather than words that indicates intention. And what was the intention of the state legislatures in ratifying the Constitution? (3) The text applied to *current or changed conditions*. Some Justices, such as Justice William Brennan, have interpreted the text of the Constitution as a "living Constitution." Although the language used by the framers of the Constitution had not been altered, it was applied in the 1960s to events and conditions no framer could have predicted. Because the words are written in capacious, broad language, the Court may interpret the language in light of a broader level of general-ity than was previously used. For example, the particular justifi-cation for the Fourteenth Amendment after the Civil War was to protect newly freed blacks. But its language regarding due process and equal protection of the laws is not limited to the former slaves, but may be asserted of any person. Or the principle "All men are created equal" was extended to emancipation of slaves (though Jefferson had slaves). Clearly, in the legal realm, the country and the courts have to ask themselves what the

173

Constitution means in the new social situation. It will not do to simply repeat the text; the text must be interpreted. That may cause a tension between what the words meant to the framers and its applicability to the new situation, as several constitutional cases show.[12] As a result of decisions made by the courts, there arises inevitably a tradition of interpretation that aids further decisions. In fact, there is really no reversal of any previous decision unless it can be shown that the new case is really different from the old *(stare decisis)*. There is also an ultimate authority, the Supreme Court, as the final arbiter of what the Constitution means *now*. If the Constitution were left to individual interpretation, there would be chaos and ultimately no nation. Of course, many in the nation may not agree with a given decision, and they may use legitimate means to overturn it. But in the case of the Supreme Court's judgment on the application of the Constitution, their judgment is the final recourse. As Justice Robert H. Jackson said, "We are not final because we are infallible, but we are infallible only because we are final."[13]

The parallels with biblical interpretation should be obvious. We highlight some of them, leaving the reader to pursue possible others. The historical-critical method corresponds to the first stage, the effort to determine what the words meant at the time they were written, and, with the help of auxiliary sciences, to determine the intention of the biblical author (stage 2). But then the horizon of the contemporary world meets the horizon of the text, and the much more difficult question is to determine what the text means in the world today. The tradition of interpretation must be given its due place, as well as the history of the influence of the text. The Bible is not exactly the "constitution" of the church, though some "Bible only" churches may consider it so. It is a *witness* to revelation, the essence of which has been condensed into the formulas of the Creed. The latter would be closer to a constitution for the church of Christ. More important, if indeed the church is a community committed to the Bible and the Creed, the final authoritative decision as to their meaning for the life of the church today cannot depend on each individual's private interpretation. The very nature of a community in a changing world demands a final arbiter, infallible or not. That leads us to the next chapter.

TWELVE

The World around the Text: Community and Canon

A good number of the methods analyzed in the previous chapters seem to assume an individual reader and an individual text, at times almost as if they found each other in a hermetically sealed environment. That biblical interpretation should take this route was almost an inevitable consequence of the individualism that flowered at the time of the Reformation and the "priesthood of all believers" that encouraged increased literacy and at times the notion of every person as his own interpreter. And eventually the Bible was moved from the church's lap to the professor's lectern. Thus "professional interpretation" became the preserve of the academy—or, where an ecclesial community was involved, the *sola scriptura* principle became "scripture alone *as interpreted in our tradition.*" Western thinking, which became more and more individualized and less and less open to any external authority, lost its moorings in the broader *koinonia,* the community of faith, the very matrix out of which scripture emerged in the first place. For the advantages it brought, it was a high price to pay.[1]

The Roman Catholic Church, in reaction, tended to insist on the role of authority in the final determination of the meaning of the scripture, although this was based on a strong sense of tradition going back to the patristic period. The Eastern churches also maintained a strong sense of tradition and found in the liturgy scripture's best hermeneutic.[2] This fact was impressed on me at an ecumenical theological discussion in which I participated a number of years ago. We spent a great deal of time discussing Bultmann and the post-Bultmannians, the New Criticism—all very much wrestling with the philosophical basis for scriptural interpretation. In the group was a Greek Orthodox priest who had listened intently to all the discussion but had not said a word. When finally we highly cognitive theologians paused for a moment, it occurred to someone in the group to ask the Orthodox priest how all of this struck him. He had a simple answer: "In our tradition it is the liturgy that interprets the word."

His response was a refreshing reminder that for centuries the church has found meaning in the scriptures by ritualizing them. Even broader than the liturgy, sacred art, drama (the morality and passion plays), song, dance, and other media expressed the word in nonverbal ways. While there were certainly deviations, this nonverbal expression was indeed a hermeneutic, and it continues to be so in less rationalistic cultures. It is a hermeneutic no more prone to misinterpretation than the proliferation of verbal interpretations that followed the invention of the printing press and more widespread literacy.

Oral and Written Transmission

To understand the role of the community both in the formation and the interpretation of scripture, it is necessary first to become aware of how much our own presuppositions about interpretation are dictated by the literate (writing and print) culture that is ours. Though the Bible is a written text, it emerged in an oral culture, a culture that was only minimally changed by the consigning of oral tradition to writing.[3] Writing the scriptures was only an aid to the oral or even nonverbal communication of the tradition, which in some cultures has continued to our day. The earliest Christians, like the Pharisees before them and unlike the scribes, prized oral tradition and considered the teacher to be more important than the text. Papias in the early second century put more trust in the living witnesses to whom he listened than in written texts that were circulating about Jesus. And yet the text eventually came to have its own authority. Thus understanding the relation between orality and text is essential to grasp what happened when books became canonized. Let us begin by looking at the dynamics of preliterate communication.

Virtually all scriptures of the literate world religions emerged either in cultures without writing at all or in cultures where writing was intimately connected, both before and after, with oral-performative traditions. Books were not the contribution of individual minds to the pool of world literature; rather they were the consigning to writing of orally mediated tradition. The scarcity of books encouraged readers to memorize the books in the process of reading and the act of reading was most often a public performance, thus forming the center of a social event. While the distilling of meaning was important in the performance of the texts of the Puranas, the Bhagavad Gita, the Tantric texts and others in the Hindu tradition, the Vedas, which circulated orally for centuries (maybe millennia), were memorized as syllabic texts by people who did not understand the language of the texts themselves, convinced that the sacred sounds (rather than their semantic meaning) were to be preserved and sent forth to penetrate the cosmos. It was thus not the text that was scripture; the sounds were. They did not need to be understood or interpreted.[4] Is there possibly an analogy here with what happened in the Catholic Church when liturgy moved from Latin to the vernacular? Even though they did not understand Latin, many Catholics felt the loss of something sacred, as if the language they did not understand conveyed better the <u>sense of transcendent mystery</u>. And is it any wonder that shortly after the vernacular became widespread, many Catholics in the charismatic movement began praying in the unintelligible syllables of tongues?

The non-Vedic texts, like those of the Hebrew scriptures, were to be understood and interpreted, but even there it was, in the earliest times, oral performance that actuated the word, and, since the context was most often social, called for an interpretative commentary. The written text was simply an aid for oral performance.[5] Even the letters of Paul show the kind of oral patterning of dictation in composition, with a view to being read aloud to the audience.[6]

Recent studies have illuminated many of the dynamics in oral cultures and shown how different they are from our own. Walter Ong has assembled from these studies several characteristics of transmission in oral cultures.[7] From his list of traits I have selected those I think most relevant to biblical interpretation and recast them in my own terms.

1. *Compound rather than complex.* In the Hebrew Bible nearly every sentence begins with what is called the *waw conversivum,* meaning "and." Older English translations like the Douay account of the creation account in Genesis retain this "and," but modern translations try to avoid the monotony of successive "ands" by using subordinate clauses. The "ands" are a relic or oral transmission.

2. *Repetitive.* Repetition and redundancy are characteristic of oral speech to keep the listener on track but also to fill in the gaps while the speaker is thinking of the next thought. It also helps reinforce what was said and perhaps not attended to by some in the audience, since in oral discourse it is impossible to "reread" what has been communicated. The story is told that a very successful preacher in a rural community was once asked by a reporter the secret of his success. He replied, "First of all I tells 'em what I'm gonna tell 'em. Then I tells 'em. Then I tells 'em what I told 'em." Ezekiel is very repetitive, uselessly so from a literate point of view.

3. *Traditional.* Because knowledge is accumulated at considerable human investment and texts are not available to retrieve it, repetition of what is known becomes very important lest it be lost. And those who know and can repeat the wisdom of the past are highly revered. Writing tends to downgrade the oral authority and, since the wisdom of the past is now preserved in texts, it favors the younger discoverers of something new. In India and Nepal I lived with people of a largely oral culture. Education did not mean training people to think for themselves, to reason things out; it meant a faithful repetition of traditional formulas—with much more emphasis on memory.

4. *Tinged with conflict.* Interaction is often associated with name-calling or "put-down" speeches, such as that between David and Goliath; but this is balanced by encomiums of praise. In a society where survival is a priority, life forces tend to be polarized into white-or-black categories. There are heroes and villains, good and evil, virtue and vice, devils, witches, and saints. When the Ayatollah Khomeini called the older George Bush "Satan," this was the residual sound of an oral culture. This conflictual atmosphere is part of a larger entity called by sociologists

"antilanguage," language that is particular to a group and helps define the group's boundaries over against the "others."

5. *Involving the listener.* The listeners are assumed to be involved in the story as participants, at least vicariously. The written text, on the other hand, objectifies the story so that one can be more of a detached spectator. Plato excluded poets from his *Republic* because people tend to get emotionally involved with the characters like Achilles or Odysseus. Sound tends to involve the listener more than visual reading does the reader, because it reaches further into the interior. This is important for understanding the Bible, for although the text is written, it was meant to be proclaimed, preached, relived as if there had been no text at all. Communication was a game in which the listener was a crucial player. The African American practice of preaching, in which the audience is expected to respond spontaneously with outcries of "Amen" or other supportive exclamations throughout the sermon, is an obvious carryover of an oral culture.

6. *Through the lens of the present.* Only those memories of the past are preserved that have some relevance to the present. There were no dictionaries in oral societies, so the context of meaning was given by facial expressions, gestures, voice inflections, and the real setting in which communication occurred. Studies on the handing on of genealogies in oral cultures have shown that the genealogies are revised to adjust to the new political situation. "The present imposed its own economy on past remembrances."[8] We have seen how a number of stories in Genesis are told from the viewpoint of the relation of Israel to the surrounding peoples (for example, the role of Esau, eponymous ancestor of the Edomites). In the Gospels it seems perfectly logical that the past story of Jesus would be interpreted from the viewpoint of its relevance to the present existential situation of the author and his community. As theologian Vincent Taylor long ago said, there were certainly many things Jesus did and said that would have been of intense interest to us today but they just dropped out of memory because they did not serve the ongoing needs of the community. The things that were remembered were those that continued to minister to the life of the community.

179

Rhetorical training in the Roman world encouraged two types of memorization of texts: the memorization of words *(memoria verborum)* and the remembering of the principal topics, the understanding and recollection of the realities *(memoria rerum)*. Memorization of the realities

> compels the recollector to actively shape up material for an occasion, whether as composer or viewer or reader, and thus is ethically more valuable, consistent with the moral emphasis given to rhetoric by Cicero, Quintillian himself, Augustine, and the tradition of monastic prayer. Especially in composition, memory for things is preferred to rote iteration, even when the speaker has accurate command of the original words.[9]

The degree of memory in the transmission of the words and deeds of Jesus has been much disputed, but it is obvious from the Gospels that the topics have been adapted to the perceived needs of the audience, and this must have happened already at the oral period.

7. *Concrete rather than abstract.* Biblical peoples did not think abstractly. Instead of describing peace as the "absence of hostilities" or even "the abundance of good things," Isaiah would say the wolf would lie down with the lamb, and the child would put his hand unharmed over the adder's lair (Isa 11:6–8).[10] Concrete experience is better than concepts. In India the story is told of a tourist trekker who passed through a village on his way to another. He asked someone in the village how long it would take him to walk to the other village. The other did not respond but joined him in walking for a short time. Finally he said, "At the rate you're going, it will take two hours."

Orality and Community

In tribal communities the individual thinks of his identity only in the context of community. Asked what sort of person he was, a peasant responded, "What can I say about my heart?...Ask others; they can tell you about me."[11] In Nepal, where I was direc-tor of novices for our Indian candidates, we once received a letter that went something like this:

> My name is Santosh. My father is a farmer, in good health. My mother is a housewife, in good health. My oldest brother is in the army; my next oldest brother works in the post office; my sister is studying to be a nurse; my little brother is in the third standard at school. *Now that you know all about me,* I hope you will let me enter your order.

A résumé quite different from our Western emphasis on edu-cation, work experience, and recommendations! Identity comes from relationships, from the family situation in which one finds oneself. Father John Kavanaugh, SJ, relates his experience of teach-ing the philosophy of Descartes to Africans. After he had explained the mathematician-philosopher's dictum, "I think, therefore I am," a member of the class responded, "In Africa we would rather say, 'We exist, therefore I am.'" That is why a violation of the tribal social order has severe consequences. Understanding this world-view is very helpful when we approach the Bible. In this dyadic per-sonality, as today's social scientists call it, one does not think of individual rights but of family rights and of tribal survival and growth.

I would add to this list of characteristics a few observations from my experience with tribal peoples of India and Nepal, where, despite schools and books, the thinking pattern is still very much that of a primary oral culture. In teaching, I found the stu-dents bored with abstractions, even with outlines of carefully structured material. But give them a symbol or a story and they were "all ears." And let them put the matter in a song or dance or work of art or some form of celebration, and their creative energy was inexhaustible. Now this is the way the faith of the Bible was transmitted for centuries even among people who could read the scriptures. Not that the scriptures were despised. On the contrary, they were expounded by preachers and argued from by the fathers of the church. But the tradition was carried on also, perhaps primarily, by art, drama, poetry, hymns, liturgies, pilgrimages, and other forms. Behind this thinking was the idea that the written text was more like a script for a play. It came to life only when either vocalized in the living setting of the worshiping community or in some art form involving human creativity.

An important consequence of this is the effect that oral communication has on community. Oral communication favors community building in a way that writing does not. Writing and reading are private activities. Oral communication is always *inter vivos*. Even when the interaction is agonistic, it brings people together. In primary societies a question is ordinarily taken not as a request for information but as a challenge to one's personal turf. In Ireland one will often find one's question answered with a question. While traveling in Ireland a priest friend of mine asked one of the locals, "Why do you Irish always answer a question with a question?" "Oh, do we now?" came the reply. This helps us understand why in the Gospels, Jesus' argumentation with his enemies is more a battle of wits than a search for abstract truth. When Jesus was asked by what authority he did these things, he riposted with a question in return, "Tell me, was the authority of John from God or from men?" That stopped his enemies cold by hanging them on the horns of a dilemma.

Another example comes from the world of commerce. As Ong says, in primary oral societies even business is not business; it is rhetoric. In purchasing something in the market, one does not just pay and be gone (as nowadays in our supermarkets prices are precalculated by code and read by machine). One haggles, maneuvers, enters a battle of wits, till finally the two settle on a price. "'Bad, bad!' says the buyer; but once he has gone his way, he boasts" (Prov 20:14). Business, like questioning, is a personal interaction.

Oral communication enables a group to feel together, as every teacher knows. As long as the teacher is speaking he or she has an audience. Once the teacher passes a handout and the students begin reading, the audience has dissolved into a group of individuals. We can already anticipate the cataclysmic effect that the printing press would have on society in general but on biblical interpretation in particular.

Transmission in Oral Societies

Studies of oral transmission have shown that the one who hears and later transmits the discourse rarely does it verbatim, except where a poetic formula is short and firm. He will tend rather to transmit the story in forms and rhythms that he has learned.[12] This is true even of ritual texts, though perhaps less so. The words of the narrative of the institution of the Eucharist vary from one Gospel to the next. While Birger Gerhardssohn has tried to show that memorization patterns in oral transmission enhance the likelihood of having the *ipsissima verba* of Jesus,[13] and surely the respect for the Master would have favored such a tendency, the evidence of the Gospels seems to indicate that the transmitters were not memorizers, at least of narrative. Rather, they interiorized the story and recast it in their own words with a view of making the passage meaningful to their particular audience, a practice, which we saw earlier, was completely in keeping with the rhetorical practices of the day.

With due respect to the scholars who have published a color-coded version of the "Five Gospels," if their underlying assumption is that the words they felt could be with moral certainty assigned to Jesus (a process arrived at by vote!) had greater authority than the words of transmitters who applied the teaching of Jesus to later situations, this effort is really misguided, for it does not respect the flexibility that all oral transmission supposes. The issue is not where the greater authority lies but whether the transmitters, however they expressed themselves, were in continuity with the tradition. *They* certainly claimed to be.

The Text as Score

In speaking of the *word* of God, the Bible does not use the image of the written word but the spoken word. God does not write. He speaks. The Hebrew word *dabar* comes from a root meaning "to get behind and push," which is exactly what breath does. The word goes forth from the mouth and has a power of its own. Isaac, tricked into blessing Jacob by mistake, could not withdraw the blessing; he could only send out a second-rate blessing on Esau to neutralize somewhat the effects of the first. The power of the spoken word explains why ancient peoples took seriously both blessing and curse, why oral cultures have ways of delivering persons from a curse thought to be a real incubus on the victim.

This sense of the power of the oral word was not lost when the biblical traditions were committed to writing. It was not merely that only a few educated persons could read and thus reading was essentially what some select people would do "into the ears" of the listeners (2 Kgs 23:2; 2 Chr 34:30; Neh 8:2–3; Jer 29:29; 36:6, 10, 13–21). It was rather that the script was only an aid to oral presentation, which retained its prestige as the communication of life and power. Today we are so accustomed to "reading for ourselves" in presumed divorce from the sounding of the words (think of speed reading courses where even internal "sounding" is suppressed) that it is difficult for us to recapture the vitality of the oral experience. In the early church it was assumed that whenever a scripture passage was read in the assembly, it was "fulfilled in your hearing" (Luke 4:21); that is, the old event was becoming a new event in the present experience of the community. This was particularly true when the word proclaimed was part of the Eucharist, for the Christ that came into the midst of the community in the Eucharist was understood to come clothed in the word just proclaimed from the scriptures. This view of things was already the underlying assumption of Luke's Emmaus story (Luke 24:13–32), where Jesus comes veiled in the word that he interprets and then comes to full revelation in the breaking of the bread. In this sense Ricoeur's statement is valid for the church's experience: the text opens up a world *in front of the text*. This assumes, though, that the scripture read is only like the score for oral performance (which is already an interpretation), and that preaching follows that shows exactly how "this Scripture is fulfilled in your hearing."[14] When the vernacular liturgy was introduced in the United States, the reader was told to conclude the first reading by stating, "This is the word of the Lord." Sometimes a fervent reader would even hold up the book, as if to say, "Look, here is the written word of God from which I have just read." However, in more recent years, this rubric was changed to read simply, "The word of the Lord." What was the intention of that change? It signaled a preference for the oral communication over the written, that is, the sense is not "The text that I have just read is God's word," but rather, "What I've just *proclaimed* and you have just *heard* is God's word." The ideal form of such communication would be the memorization and delivery of the word without the written text. Today TV newscasters attempt to avoid the distantiation that reading their text involves by looking directly into the camera, as if looking the (imagined) audience in the face, though we all know that, with the aid of the "teleprompter," they are reading a text.

The Effect of Writing, Printing, and Electronics

Walter Ong has shown how the diffusion of writing, and even more so of printing and the electronic media, has actually transformed human consciousness. As is obvious from the previous discussion, the written word cuts the reader off from the living voice, placing before him only a text that cannot respond to questioning. In this sense the text is "dead," though it is often written to allow the message to survive the death of its author. It moves the message from the aural to the visual. It allows a much more analytic approach even to time, which is now thought of in terms of space on a calendar. Oral people will often be unable to tell you when they were born, but literate people know the exact day and celebrate it. With the advent of printing, the word was even more reified; it became part of the industrial or manufacturing process, something to be sold and bought. Orally based rhetoric was no longer the center of education. Now that words were more than sounds, technicians began to fret over correct spelling. (Think of the careless way the names of immigrants were written in the passenger lists of the ships arriving in this country in the 1800s—a relic of orality.) Written texts are also viewed more as providing information, whereas oral messages were more performance oriented. The epic, characterized by individual stories loosely joined often by the journey motif, gives way to the novel and the detective story, where the author has a tight control of every element of the plot and hones his material in view of that specific end. The written and printed text gives a sense of closure in a way that orality did not. Most important for our purposes, the written and printed text promoted the sense of personal privacy and interiority in a way unthought of before.

At the same time, the written text stands over against the reader, sometimes as an authority, sometimes as an object of criticism. When an early version of Deuteronomy was found in the temple, King Josiah trembled before it and made it the blueprint for his reforms. God's word was now in an authoritative text. But texts could also allow the tradition to be questioned in ways that oral transmission could not. "Literacy encouraged, at the very same time, criticism and commentary on the one hand, and the orthodoxy of the text on the other."[15] But Jeremiah protests the scribes' claim of the authority of their written text (the Torah) over against the authority of the oral word *(dabar)* of the prophet (Jer 8:7–9).

> In Christian teaching orality-literacy polarities are particularly acute, probably more than in any other religious tradition, even the Hebrew. For in Christian teaching the Second Person of the One Godhead, who redeemed mankind from sin, is known not only as the Son but also as the Word of God. In this teaching, God the Father utters or speaks His Word, his Son. He does not inscribe him. The very Person of the Son is constituted as the Word of the Father. Yet Christian teaching also presents at its core the written word of God, the Bible, which, back of its human authors, has God as author as no other writing does.[16]

The age of electronics, radio, television, and computers, has brought another dimension to the orality-literacy development. While radio and television appear to be a return to orality, there is an obvious difference, because the distantiation effected by writing continues. The visual is emphasized (children spend more time watching television nowadays than reading), but the isolation of the writing mode continues to dominate. The performer has no idea who is listening; he or she must imagine the audience beyond the microphone or camera. There is no interaction, save in the call-in shows, and in those cases there is tight control over what is allowed in and what not. For this reason, many TV shows are performed before a live audience to assist both performer and viewer/listener to have a sense of interactive communication. But the interaction with the viewing audience is illusory. On the receiving end, if there happens to be a group watching the television program, interaction among the viewers tends to be minimal, reserved largely to commercial time, and many viewers dislike distracting conversational comments while the program is in progress.

A further result is that the media (which now include computers and the Internet), as well as rapid transportation, have made the world a global village, so that one is in immediate contact with events around the world, and yet at the same time the distance and the complexity of political structures intensifies the frustration of having no control or interactive possibility with the event witnessed. This tends to foster a psychic and emotional numbness that easily gets transferred into the real world, for example, when persons witness a rape but do nothing about it.

An important result of the electronic explosion is the fact that information and even performance-oriented communication (think of advertisements) pour into the individual with a massiveness and persuasiveness with which the weekly sermon (for those who attend) struggles to compete. And the sense of belonging to a faith community orchestrated by a teaching authority is regularly assaulted by very different values.

These factors provide a context for returning to the more specifically biblical issue of the text and the community.

The Canon: Books Accepted for Oral Proclamation

We turn now to *canonical* criticism. The "canon," of course, means the list of books considered authoritative for the community, whether Jewish or Christian (from the Greek *kanon*, meaning "measure" or "rule" or "list"). Although the word *canon* for these books was first used only by Athanasius (293–373), the process of selection was at work from the very beginning. It was not an instantaneous event. A list did not fall from heaven one day, signed by the Holy Spirit and enumerating books that God had inspired. It was rather a developing consciousness in the church, over a period of centuries. Naturally, the only scriptures that the apostles knew were the books of the Old Testament, and this meant that the early church saw those books as key to understanding the mystery of Christ. But what books belonged to the Old Testament? One cannot really speak of a canon as a closed list of books, either in Hebrew or Greek, until the rabbis, beginning at the end of the first century, but not ending there, began to feel the need to distinguish "their" scriptures from those of the Christians. Prior to that, Greek-speaking Jews were using the Septuagint (LXX) both in Palestine and the diaspora, with its larger number of books than would eventually be recognized by the rabbis as the Hebrew canon. Christians took over the longer canon of the Septuagint. Although a number of the fathers of the church, under the influence of Jerome (who had spent time with the rabbis in Palestine), opted for the Hebrew canon, they generally did not object to the extra books being read in church "for edification." Already in the West the Councils of Hippo in (AD 393) and Carthage (397 and 419) determined that the Christian canon would include the extra books (with the exception of 1–2 Esdras and the Prayer of Manasseh). The decision of these local councils was reaffirmed by the general council of Trent (1546), which held that the deuterocanonicals (Tobit, Judith, Wisdom, Sirach [Ecclesiasticus], Baruch with the Letter of Jeremiah, 1 and 2 Maccabees, Additions to Daniel and Esther) are to be accepted "with equal devotion and reverence."[17] Luther did not consider them canonical but retained them, placing them between the Old and the New Testaments. The first English edition in which they were dropped appeared only in 1835 by the British and Foreign Bible Society. The fact that they had not belonged to the Hebrew Bible was not the only reason for excluding them from the Protestant canon. Catholics had used 2 Maccabees to support the doctrine of purgatory and Tobit had been used to support the importance of works.

The formation of the New Testament canon also followed a sifting process. Although there was early agreement on the core, variations occurred on the fringes. The fourth-century Codex Sinaiticus, for example, contains the Epistle of Barnabas and most of the Shepherd of Hermas, books that eventually dropped out of the canon. For some time there was hesitation about the Epistle to the Hebrews and the Apocalypse. Of course, there had been general agreement for centuries on most of the books.[18]

The issue for Trent was that the books of the wider canon had been read for centuries in the worshiping church. This was a touchstone for determining canonicity: books "accepted" by the early and later Christian communities for public, liturgical reading. The texts of course were not printed; they were manuscripts precious because of their rarity. And the written text was only as it were a script to be enacted in the public proclamation. The word of God was not thought of as a thing on a page but as brought to life in the oral proclamation. The living word was not ink on a page but breath and sound from a living voice.

The books that were accepted in this fashion for public reading were taken as having divine authority. The criteria were three:

1. *Apostolic authority*—that is, the tradition they witnessed could be traced back to the apostles. That did not mean that a book would have to be *written* by an apostle (Mark and Luke were not one of the Twelve). It does not even exclude the possibility that the church erred historically in assuming that a book was apostolic because it bore an apostle's name (though the church did reject the apostolic claims of many documents that it judged as spurious and thus excluded them from the canon).

2. *Orthodoxy.* This meant that the early communities gradually sifted out works that did not express what they understood to be the authentic tradition. This process began early but it was intensified by the rise of gnostic and other writings considered suspect or even condemned.

Did this mean that the church considered itself above the scriptures? No, but it was convinced it could discern that which fed its life with divine nourishment and that which did not. If I may be permitted another personal illustration: in one of our communities there was an aquarium with guppies. One of the brothers was responsible for maintaining the aquarium and regularly feeding the guppies. He did so with properly prepared fish food. One day I found myself watching the guppies as I ate a hot dog. I wondered how the guppies might like to share my lunch. So I peeled off a mite of the hot dog and dropped it in the water. Sure enough the guppies rushed toward it. One of them snatched it, but no sooner had he tasted it than he blew it out of his mouth with utter disdain. That guppy knew it was not food fit for a fish. There was something similar in the consciousness of the early church. It is true that each of the sacred writings was produced from the womb of an earlier Christian community. But that particular writing was more than a community product. It was also divine food, the inspired word of God. In reading it the later community identified it as the kind of food fit for the church, the divinely inspired word. Other books did not measure up; in fact, some of them were totally distasteful and therefore rejected.

3. *Flexibility.* Besides apostolic authority and orthodoxy there was another, subordinate factor, that assisted the canonization process. It is what the canonical critics call *"flexibility."* The texts that eventually won common acceptance were those that served well for liturgical celebrations, for catechetical instruction, preaching, and application to new situations. There was already a hermeneutic at work in this selection process, and it was very community oriented. It was in part because of its narrower focus (addressed to martyr candidates) that the Apocalypse was slow to gain universal acceptance. The Gospels, on the other hand, because of their largely narrative character, could easily be transferred from one culture to the next. We must repeat, of course, that this was not the only criterion for accepting a book. Apostolic authority and orthodoxy were primary.

Canonical Criticism as a Discipline

If the Protestant canon has fewer books and the Orthodox more than the Catholic, within each confession there is a concern about what the total canon means for the interpretation of the individual books and individual passages. This "canonical criticism" or "canon criticism" involves (1) taking the final version of the text as the one to be explained; (2) seeking to explain it in light of the entire Bible; and (3) asking whether even the order of the books sheds any light on the Bible as overall narrative. We take up each of these in turn.

THE FINAL AUTHORITATIVE TEXT

In 1979 Brevard Childs in a groundbreaking book noted the difference between examining a passage as a historical critic and examining it as *scripture*.[19] One example he uses is the books of Ezra and Nehemiah. In their present form these books are confusing because the narratives they contain are not arranged in chronological order. The historical critics try to reconstruct the historical sequence in order to understand the development of the events and the issues. But the order they come up with (and even today the critics don't agree) is not the order in which these were originally placed, the order in which they were continuously copied over the centuries, the order in which they were received into the canon. So there was some kind of intended meaning to the present order, and the canonical critic is interested in discovering this. In the case of Ezra-Nehemiah the present arrangement is a theological rather than a historical one.

Or consider the psalms. If the individual psalms are inspired, what is to be said of the *order* in which they are presently arranged? Most scholars agree that Psalm 1 was meant as an introduction to the whole Psalter, all of which was then to be read as the struggle of the righteous against the wicked. And some authors note that the first two collections of psalms (1–41 and 42–72) recall the promises made to David of an eternal dynasty, while the third collection (73–89) ends with a lament that God is not keeping his promises (89:39, 49), and the fourth (90–106) answers the lament by assuring that, though there is not a king on the throne of David, God nevertheless reigns (93:1; 96:10; 97:1; 99:1). There is good reason to believe that Psalm 50, which deals with the renewal of the covenant and rebukes the people for their infidelities, and Psalm 51, the famous *Miserere* psalm of repentance, were placed in tandem to express the call to repentance and then actual repentance. The psalms gain a new meaning because of the order in which someone later placed them.

The "secular" observations and advice in Proverbs 10–31 become religious when read in the light of 1–9, indicating that they are meant to be a living out of the fear of God, the beginning of wisdom, and are part of obedience to God's Lady Wisdom against Dame Folly. The story of the woman caught in adultery in John 8:1–11 is thought by many scholars to be a Lukan tradition that circulated independently before finding a resting place in John, and for this reason some commentaries skip it completely. It is missing from the earliest and best manuscripts. Yet it was incorporated early in John, perhaps as an illustration of John 7:51 preceding, which speaks of caution in determining guilt before the law. Should it be considered when determining the overall theology of the fourth Gospel? That is the kind of question canonical criticism asks.

Hence, canonical criticism is concerned, among other things, with the *final* form of the book or the text, even if it was edited by a later scribe. For decades historical critics sought to discover the original form of the text, what lay behind the text in its present form. The assumption was often that the original form, if it could be retrieved—often with hypothetical or problematic results—would be the most authoritative. That effort had a value, certainly, but it ignored the importance of the final form, which was that which the church accepted into the canon. Canonical placement provides the last interpretative framework to the text, reflecting the latest level of historical development. This, according to the Pontifical Biblical Commission in its 1993 *The Interpretation of the Bible in the Church* also enjoys the final authority: "It is the text in its final stage, rather than in its earlier editions, which is the expression of the Word of God."[20] James A. Sanders would broaden this "final text" approach to consider the process by which the word was received in the successive biblical communities, thus setting a paradigm for all future resignifications of the text.[21] In this case, however, one would have to distinguish between the authority of the final biblical text and the secondary authority of later resignifications of it.

THE PART IN THE LIGHT OF THE WHOLE

There were two consequences to this assembling of books containing "the word of God." One was that the church decided to listen to any one passage in light of the individual work and any one book in the light of the others, with the New Testament having authority over the Old. Hence, no one passage of scripture could maintain absolute dominance if there was another passage that appeared to contradict or modify it (except in the case of a clear New Testament revision of an Old Testament passage). Each passage would have to be interpreted in the light of the rest of the particular book in which it appeared, and each book would have to be interpreted in the light of the *whole* witness of the Bible.

A practical consequence of this can be seen in the way the revised psalter of the *New American Bible* handled the word *man* in Psalm 1: "Happy *the man* who follows not the counsel of the wicked....*He* is like a tree planted near running water....Whatever *he* does prospers." The revision reads, "Happy *those* who do not follow the counsel of the wicked....*They* are like a tree planted near streams of water....Whatever *they* do prospers." Among the *Criteria* given by the American bishops to the Joint Committee on Inclusive Language (responsible for those revisions), was the following:

> Although certain uses of *he, his,* and *him* once were generic and included both women and men, in contemporary American usage these terms are often perceived to refer only to males. Their use has become ambiguous and is increasingly seen to exclude women. Therefore, these terms should not be used when the reference is meant to be generic....[22]

Was the Hebrew *enosh,* used in Psalm 1 for "man," intended to exclude women? From a strictly scholarly point of view some have argued that it was so intended (at least indirectly), since in ancient Israel only men devoted themselves to the study of the Torah (see Sir 39:1–11), and there was a Jewish saying (not recorded in the Bible) that he who teaches his daughter the law is like making her into a harlot. But Father Joseph Jensen, OSB, in commenting on the change from *he* to *they* in Psalm 1 writes:

193

When Psalm 1 is used in the Christian liturgy, we ought not to restrict its meaning to a narrowly historical understanding. Were we to do that, the "law" in question would remain simply the Torah of the Old Testament. When this psalm is used in the Christian liturgy, however, it applies to all, and the "law" includes, in addition to the richness of the Old Testament legislation, all the New Testament instruction, the Sermon on the Mount and the epistolary exhortations....The mere fact that Psalm 1 is now part of a canon that includes the Sermon on the Mount and St. Paul's dictum that "in Christ Jesus there is neither male nor female" gives it a new nuance that ought not be ruled out by a literalistic interpretation.[23]

A further effect concerned the understanding of the whole Old Testament as a narrative climaxing in the New Testament, and this despite the particular horizon and literary form of any individual book examined on its own merit. This was indeed a quantum leap, and it was equivalent to the Christian community assuming the role of author, at least to the extent that it assembled these books into some semblance of continuity, doctrinal and even narrative. The canon meant that the Bible became a book. By saying that God was the author of all these books (and God obviously had a single plan in inspiring them), the church was really saying that there is one message, one narrative overarching all the others, and the church claimed that she understood at least the essential outlines of that message.[24] The meta-narrative did not even end with the gospel fulfilling the Old, but looked forward to its consummation in the final book of the New, the Apocalypse. The church, of course, rooted her claim in the further claim that she possessed the Holy Spirit given by Jesus to lead the church into the fullness of truth (John 14:26). Postmodernists like George Aichele would claim that the overarching authority of the canon does violence to the meaning or potentiality of individual texts by imposing a foreign meaning on them, and this is one of the "oppressions" postmodernism seeks to do away with, leaving every text open to unlimited meanings, whether canonical or not.

Meaning is thus totally constructed by the reader independently of any authoritative control.[25]

What is to be said of this? If the part cannot be understood without the whole, it is also true that the whole cannot be understood without the part. It is thus eminently helpful to understand the part in its own right, which is largely the service provided by the historical critic, but then it must be seen in the topography of the whole. If the Bible is a meta-narrative, then the tensions between certain texts can be understood as steps in a progressive revelation, a pedagogy by which God takes his people where they are and gradually lead them to a purer understanding of who he is and what his expectations are. For example, 2 Kings 24:1 says the Lord incited David to take a census, while 1 Chronicles 21:1 says "a satan" did it. The earlier text wanted to affirm that whatever happens is in the Lord's control, whereas the later one wished to exempt the Lord from any question of responsibility for David's sinful decision. In the early stages of climbing a mountain one may be impressed with the enormity of a nearby crag, only to see it shrink into its relative proportion as one reaches the summit. Accepted as part of a meta-narrative, a passage or an event may appear highly significant to the people of God at the time of its occurrence or of the committing it to writing, but then takes on a different hue as it yields to later revelation and is taken up into a larger frame of meaning.

This is what James A. Sanders calls *"resignification,"* a process that takes place in both the Old and New Testaments. Israel continued to read the royal psalms, even when there was no Davidic king on the throne, understanding them as a promise of the Messiah yet to come. In using the word *disciples* Matthew is presumably referring to those who followed Jesus in his historical public ministry. But many scholars think the evangelist is also referring to the successors of those disciples who are the authoritative teachers in Matthew's community. We can say that some kind of resignification takes place every time a text is read. This happens in our secular experience every time we stand for the national anthem. That hymn does not merely signify what the poet expressed in the attack on Fort McHenry. It has also gathered unto itself the history of a nation, right up to the moment when we rise to celebrate *this* moment of our history.

In the Bible, it is especially in the psalms that this accumulation of meaning and resignification occurs. Very few psalms yield with certainty their original author or historical situation. But they were used and reused over the centuries in Jewish liturgy and piety, becoming a new event every time they were reused. Their meaning therefore does not lie in the circumstances of their original composition, however helpful it might be to know this, but rather in the experience of faith which they express and which a later generation with a new experience of faith chooses to express not by composing a new psalm but by the repetition of the old one.

But a meta-narrative or progressive revelation will not solve all the problems of textual tension. Sometimes in the same book there are tensions difficult to explain. Isaiah 43:18 says, "Remember not the former things," and 46:9 says, "Remember the former things, those long ago." These differences can be explained, of course, by different contexts, like the textual contradiction between Micah 4:3 and Isaiah 2:4, on the one hand, saying that swords will be turned into plowshares and spears into pruning hooks and, on the other, Joel 3:10 saying that plowshares will be turned into swords and pruning hooks into spears. But what about the difference between the Synoptics and John on the date of Jesus' death? Did it happen on Passover (Synoptics) or on the day before (John)? There was even a dispute between Saint Polycarp defending the Johannine date and Pope Anicetus defending the Synoptic date (both claiming apostolic authority, Polycarp for John, Anicetus for Mark-Matthew). The fact that the church decided to accept both into the "fourfold gospel" is telling. There was no attempt to reduce the difference to one or the other. Instead, respect for the apostolic tradition of both meant holding them together in a single canon. This made a problem for later historical critics but immensely enriched the theologies of the paschal mystery.

A MESSAGE IN THE ORDER OF THE BOOKS?

Although the books of the Jewish canon were preserved in scrolls and hence could be stored in any order, it is clear that from the earliest times priority was given to the Torah, the first five books, the Pentateuch. Then came the Former and Latter Prophets, and finally the "Writings," the rest of the books, an order already testified by Sirach's Greek translator in the second century BC. This meant that the Jewish community understood the Bible story from Genesis through the prophets to Ezra-Nehemiah as the history of Israel within the history of the world, from creation through the kings, the prophets, the exile, and the restoration (with its layers of reinterpretation) as one continuous story. The rest of the writings complemented the great narrative either by way of celebration (the Psalms, the Canticle of Solomon) or instruction (the Wisdom books and the rest). But 1 and 2 Chronicles, the final books, in revisiting the narrative of the kings, hailed David primarily for his work of preparing and planning the temple (even if he didn't build it), thinly suggesting perhaps that, with no descendent of David on the throne since Zerubbabel, Israel might very well get along without a Messiah if it had the temple and the priesthood, both of which were the chief legacy of David. The book concludes exhorting every Jew to go up to the temple in Jerusalem (2 Chr 36:23).[26]

As for the New Testament, it was attached to the Old, thereby indicating (against Marcion) that it was the flowering and fulfillment of the Old. The order of the Old Testament books in the earliest Christian witnesses we have varied greatly, but in both the East and the West the prophets were eventually settled at the end. In the West, both in Catholic and Protestant canons, Malachi comes last of all, prophesying the purification of the temple priesthood and the promise of the Sun of Justice, thus reasserting the primacy of the Messianic hope, a fitting introduction to the New Testament.[27]

Within the New Testament, two of the three major uncial manuscripts (Vaticanus and Alexandrinus) have the general epistles (those of James, Peter, John, and Jude) following Acts and before the Pauline epistles, unlike the order we have in our Bibles today. Could this be accidental? Or is it, as John W. Miller holds, that the pre-Constantinian church preferred to listen first to its Jewish "pillars" represented by the general epistles (Gal 2:9), thus honoring its Jewish roots. Later, as gentiles began to dominate, the letters of the "apostle of the gentiles" were moved ahead of them—a change that Miller believes is due to Eusebius at the time when he began making multiple copies of the Bible at the request of his "hero," the Christian emperor Constantine, who fostered a wholly gentile church.[28]

The Role of the Church

Commitment to the canon is indeed a reader-response position but very different from the individual reader-response theories we examined earlier, particularly the postmodern one. It is the *church* that is the reader, and while the individual can certainly be nourished by the scriptures (otherwise the church itself could not be) and even proclaim the scriptures in word and deed, the communal interpretation stands as a guard against false paths an individual (or an individual community) might take.

But who speaks for the church? The creeds and the decisions of the church councils were formulated in part as authoritative boundaries for interpreting the Bible. While leaving many of the unresolved exegetical questions to the biblical scholars, the Roman Catholic Church has reserved to its teaching magisterium (the bishops, the councils, and the popes) the role of proclaiming with final authority the meaning of any specific scriptural text. This process is never arbitrary. They too listen to the witness of the scriptures! But they also listen to the tradition of the church, which has "guarded the deposit" over the centuries. (See our study of *Dei Verbum* in chapter 14.) Doctrine may be defined, but definitive pronouncements on individual texts of the Bible are very rare. When a problem arises, as happened at Trent, the church may quote a scripture passage as authorizing a church teaching (for example, John 20:22 as supporting the forgiveness of sins in the sacrament of reconciliation), or it may say that it is not clear how a given hypothesis can be reconciled with a datum of scripture (as Pius XII did with polygenism in *Humani Generis*).

Liturgy and the Canon Today

Earlier we noted how the selection of books for the canon was determined in part by their usefulness and flexibility for proclamation and worship. It is also true that many of the books themselves contain liturgical texts. The Eastern churches, as we have also noted, consider the liturgy the place where the meaning of the scriptures come to its fullest expression. Along with the proclamation of the word, the ritual reenactment of the paschal mystery by the entire community is the ultimate unfolding of meaning. Vatican II sought to reinvigorate this understanding in the Roman Catholic Church.

The use of scripture in the liturgy involves selection of texts for given days and feasts, following the seasons and the commemoration of saints. Scripture readings are thus scattered in the lectionaries, sometimes ignoring their original contexts. And some texts are omitted altogether (for example 1 Timothy 2:11–15, "I do not permit a woman to teach..."). This is certainly an interpretive move, and it implies a pragmatic canon. Is it legitimate? On the one hand, one might say that it does violence to the biblical canon or even an individual book by slicing it up, bypassing the original contexts of some texts and eliminating others. On the other hand, with the exception of the paschal mystery interpreting the Old Testament, the Bible itself rarely makes a judgment of its own topography, leaving this in the hands of whoever might choose to use the texts. Individual readers may be nourished by their private reading of the Bible, creating their own topography, with both the impact and the perils of their personal interpretation. But the worshiping community has always been the ideal environment for scripture to have its full power as the word of God. Problematic texts that require a detailed explanation of their historical context, like the text from Timothy, are appropriate in a classroom or Bible study but would be distracting in worship. So this pragmatic "canon within a canon" cannot be faulted for continuing a tradition analogous to the early church's selective instinct. Those who made the selections for the latest Roman Catholic lectionary were not only biblical scholars;

they were also sensitive to the *sensus fidelium* in the broader Christian community.

If one of the most important questions addressed by canonical criticism is the effect of the whole Bible on its individual parts, and for Christians the final authority of the New Testament over the Old, then how does this work out in practice? In earlier chapters we studied how the fathers and the medievalists wrestled with the question. In the next chapter we return to that question in its contemporary context.

THIRTEEN

The Spiritual Sense of Scripture

"It's a weasel word." This characterization of the spiritual sense by a historical critic, who also happens to be a member of the Pontifical Biblical Commission, expresses the confusion that reigns in the uses and abuses of the term. Yet both official and unofficial documents insist on the importance of the spiritual sense and that the exegete must not neglect it. Pope Pius XII in *Divino Afflante Spiritu* and the Pontifical Biblical Commission (PBC) in *The Interpretation of the Bible in the Church (IBC)* affirm its importance. Vatican II in *Dei Verbum*, article 12, echoing Origen and Jerome, said, "Holy Scripture must be read and interpreted in the same Spirit in which it was written." This implies that there is a work of the Holy Spirit in the text—what we could call the objective sense ("in which it was written") and in the reading/interpretation—what we could call the subjective sense ("read and interpreted in the same Spirit"). The PBC offers this definition: "The spiritual sense of Sacred Scripture is the meaning expressed by the biblical texts when read under the influence of the Holy Spirit in the context of the paschal mystery and of the new life which flows from it."[1] Here again we note the subjective element ("read under the influence of the Holy Spirit") and the objective ("the meaning expressed in the biblical texts"). We must distinguish, of course, between the reading of Old Testament texts by the New Testament authors, where the spiritual sense of the old text *becomes* the literal sense of the new, and, on the other, subsequent readings either by communities or by individuals, which are not guaranteed the same authoritative inspiration. It is the latter that we look at first.

Subjective Disposition

The subjective element presupposes reading the text in the light of faith, which assumes the reader keeps in mind the centrality of Christ, the entire canon, tradition, and the magisterium of the church. These provide the boundaries for spiritual interpretation but are not intended to limit personal or communal insights into what Ephrem called "the inexhaustible spring" of the sacred word. We can think of the volumes of spiritual commentaries by the fathers, theologians, saints, and mystics over the two thousand years of the church's history (the "effective history" of the text). We can also recall the tradition from Origen down to Lonergan that the one who comes closest to personally identifying with the reality of which the text speaks will best understand it.

Objective Sense

Ignace de la Potterie writes concerning *Dei Verbum*, article 12:

> We can now conclude that the causality of the Spirit (first cause) through his action on the sacred writer (secondary cause) is equally exercised on the *actual text* of Scripture, which the ancient writer has *written*, and which believers today *read* and *interpret*. This amounts to saying that there is an indwelling of the Spirit in Scripture itself, that the text that has been written is the bearer of the Spirit, and that it must then be read and interpreted in the Spirit. *[emphasis his]*[2]

This is a striking way to put it: "There is an indwelling of the Spirit in Scripture itself." We do not ordinarily think of the Holy Spirit indwelling a text, but it follows from the analogy already used by the ancients between the incarnation of the Word in Jesus Christ and the embodiment of the word (as revelation) in the human, written word. That analogy would also imply a pneumatology, for where the Word is, the Spirit must also be. As the Holy Spirit overshadowed Mary to produce the Incarnate Word, so the

Holy Spirit overshadows the author so that the written word is also the word of God. And as the Spirit dwells in Jesus' humanity, so the Spirit dwells in the written word, waiting to disclose to the reader the hidden riches therein.

But this objective spiritual meaning of Old Testament texts, according to the PBC, is what the church sees in retrospect thanks to the event of Jesus Christ culminating in his resurrection and sending of the Holy Spirit. In the New Testament the literal sense is already focused on the paschal event, and that is where the literal sense is also the spiritual sense. To put it briefly, the spiritual sense is the christological sense. As far as the use of the Old Testament texts is concerned, the spiritual sense is a light revealing a meaning hitherto unexpected yet not wholly foreign to the original text. On the one hand, there must be continuity with the literal sense, which "remains the indispensable foundation. Otherwise one could not speak of the 'fulfillment' of Scripture. Indeed, in order that there be fulfillment, a relationship of continuity and of conformity is essential." On the other hand, the document immediately adds, "But it is also necessary that there be transition to a higher level of reality," which its later document also calls "transcendence."[3] The literal sense often lends itself to such a transformation, when, for example, certain texts speak hyperbolically of David's throne that will be established "forever" (2 Sam 7:12–13), a matter that happened only with the resurrection of Jesus. The document, using an expression of Ricoeur, speaks about the "dynamic aspect" of certain texts, by which it means a "profound element of continuity" at the same time that there is a move to a different level.

Horizontal or Vertical?

The retrospective approach rather easily identifies those Old Testament texts to which the New Testament explicitly or implicitly refers. We might call it "the horizontal approach," and it can be done even by secular scholars. But if we look at it theologically, on the principle that God is the author of the entire Bible, the interpretive key would be that God, intending to create, redeem, and draw all to himself, arranges events that are mimetic, the paradigm being the paschal mystery. The events share, ontologically, as it were, in their paradigm, the resurrection, which is first in God's intention although last in execution. In this understanding, which could be called "vertical" (or "supraspective"), it is not so much the paschal mystery that sheds light on the exodus, for example, as it is the exodus that participates mimetically in the paschal mystery.[4] The mimetic model would seem to correspond better to the image of the shadow *(skia)* used of the Old Testament happenings in Hebrews 10:1 and the way the fathers read those events, not as milestones viewed in retrospect but as the paschal mystery already hidden there by God's design.

In any case, while Christians recognize the enduring value of much of the Old Testament in itself, the revelation and the proclamation of the person and event of Jesus Christ relativizes all texts to an ancillary role. In the synagogues, the sacred texts of the Old Testament were carefully transcribed on scrolls, and the scrolls were enshrined as in a tabernacle because the written word was reverenced as God's presence among his people. This practice of reading the word only from scrolls continues in synagogues today. But Christians quickly dropped that form and popularized the codex, separate sheets bound on one side like our books today. This procedure dethroned the written word from its primacy and made it subservient to the living word about Jesus. Frances Young points out how the preference of the early church for the codex and its rapid adoption over scrolls, which even today are considered by the Jews the only liturgical form worthy of the holy word, testifies to the primacy in which Christians held the paschal mystery. The codex form, more practical for transport and used as a handbook for missionary preaching, pointed to Jesus Christ as the Word in a way which the scrolls did not. In support of this new approach she quotes from Ignatius of Antioch. In disputing with the Jews who insisted on proof of the gospel from their scriptures, their "records," Ignatius of Antioch replies that the gospel is indeed in their scriptures, but then adds, "But for my part, my records are Jesus Christ; for me the sacrosanct records are His cross and death and resurrection, and the faith that comes through Him. And it is by these, and by the help of your prayers, that I am hoping to be justified."[5] It is basically the same truth that *Dei Verbum* emphasized in saying that the Word of God is Jesus Christ, and the written word is a witness to him. In any case, Ignatius is saying what the Biblical Commission is saying: that the Old Testament is now read in the light of Jesus Christ, the paschal event of his death, resurrection, and sending of the Spirit.

The Typical Sense

Well enough for the principle. But how does it work out in practice? Are there several different spiritual senses? The most obvious connection of the New Testament with the old is prophecy, words that point forward to a fulfillment. But the New Testament sees fulfillment also in *realities,* what the fathers call prophecy of a different kind—in persons, things, events, or situations. For example, the paschal lamb is identified in the New Testament as a type of Christ. This is what tradition has identified as the *typical sense.* We identified a number of these "types" and "anti-types" in chapter 2. The New Testament text that gives the corresponding identification of the Old Testament type is the literal sense, the Old Testament the typical.

Thematic Fulfillment: Continuity and Discontinuity

Another way in which the PBC connects the Old Testament and the New is in their 2002 document, *The Jewish People and Their Scriptures in the Christian Bible.* Without calling the connection the spiritual sense, they chose nine themes, founded in the Old Testament but transcended in the New: the revelation of God; the human person: greatness and wretchedness; God as liberator and savior; the election of Israel; the covenant; the Law; prayer and cult, temple and Jerusalem; divine reproaches and condemnations; and the promises. The document shows how each of these themes develop in the Old Testament and how the New Testament sees them brought to completion and transcended.

Thus it sanctions or at least chooses to give preference to the thematic approach in situating the relation of the Old Testament to the New. From the viewpoint of progressive revelation, such thematic study can be helpful in orienting the reader to interpretations in keeping with the objective thrust of the texts.[6] It also provides a more likely bridge in ecumenical exchanges with the Jews, who would be less likely to appreciate the spiritual sense as previously described.

The Fuller Sense *(Sensus Plenior)*

In the early decades of the twentieth century Catholic biblical scholars were looking for a means to preserve the assured results of the historical-critical method, while at the same time making room for the meaning that certain texts took on in later reuse in scripture or in the ongoing history of the church, such as the teaching of the councils. Andres Fernandez in 1925 coined the term "fuller sense" *(sensus plenior)* to cover texts in which a deeper meaning is seen later either in scripture itself or in the tradition of the church, and this sense became popular among a large number of Catholic scholars. This sense presumes that God had more in mind than the original author expressed. "The fuller sense is defined as a deeper meaning of the text, intended by God but not clearly expressed by the human author."[7] This in itself would not distinguish it from the spiritual sense as described above, for there too, especially in the typical sense, God surely had more in mind than the Old Testament author expressed. The *IBC* lists it separately from the spiritual sense, suggesting that it is in a different category. They further describe it as "a meaning that a subsequent biblical author attributes to an earlier biblical text, taking it up in a context which confers upon it a new literal sense, or else it is a question of the meaning that an authentic doctrinal tradition or a conciliar definition gives to a biblical text."[8] The words *attributes* and *confers* suggests that the fuller sense lacks the continuity with the literal sense that the earlier definition required of the spiritual sense. It is attributed to the earlier text, or confers upon it a meaning that is not "clearly" in the literal sense.

The Pontifical Biblical Commission gives three examples: (1) Isaiah 7:14 referring to the *almah* who will conceive is rendered "virgin" by Matt 1:23, basing himself on the Septuagint *parthenos*. (2) The New Testament references to the Father, Son, and Holy Spirit are given more specification in the fathers and the church councils. (3) The Council of Trent gave the fuller sense of Romans 5:12–21 on the consequences of the sin of Adam for the race.

Some scholars have expressed reservations or opposition to the fuller sense. Raymond Brown, who supported the sense in his early work,[9] later questioned its usefulness, expressing the hope that the development of the new literary theory might do a better job.[10] In any case, the fuller sense is at least recognized by the PBC without criticism. It is important to note that the fuller sense does not legitimate just any meaning, for it supposes the reuse of the text either in scripture or in tradition (for example, the fathers and the councils).

Intertextuality and Unanswered Questions

When a New Testament author uses an Old Testament text explicitly or implicitly, how much of the original context might he intend to import? And what is to be said of the possibility that some New Testament texts and structures are reuses of texts or even the order of texts in the Old?[11] When the Apocalypse uses Old Testament languages and images, is this only reuse of language or is something more going on here in terms of fulfillment? The prologue of John incorporates creation and wisdom motifs from the Old Testament. Are these expansions of the spiritual sense? Archaeologists are constantly discovering how the stones of earlier buildings were reused in later ones. Something like that happens when New Testament authors reuse Old Testament motifs to develop their work. Another image might be helpful. In the physics lab elements may be floating around in a solution, but when electrolysis is applied they crystallize. This seems to be what happened in the consciousness of the early community when the electrifying event of Jesus' resurrection passed through their understanding of the Old Testament. Everything seemed to fall into place: prophecy, persons, events, scenarios, the Law, Wisdom, vocabulary. Not that it happened instantly; but the Old Testament became the disciples' book in a new, transcendent way. It became their way of thinking about and expressing what Christ meant.

And what is to be said when a New Testament author borrows an expression from the Old Testament but uses it in a sense foreign, even opposed to the original sense? In 1 Corinthians 15:44–45 Paul says that at the final resurrection, "The word that is written shall come about: 'Death is swallowed up in victory. Where, O death, is your victory? Where, O death, is your sting?'" The first part is a free rendering of Isaiah 25:8: "He will destroy death forever." The last part is taken from Hosea 13:14: "Where are your plagues, O death! Where is your sting, O nether world!" In Hosea this is part of God's threat to close his eyes to compassion for Israel because of its hardness of heart. He calls up plagues, death, and sting as punishments. But Paul uses the rhetorical question as part of his assurance of God's total victory over death. One could dismiss the difference as simply Paul's borrowing an expression that adds a flourish to his affirmations. But Paul does introduce the text as the confirmation of a fulfillment: "The word that is written shall come about." Is Paul using this in an ironic sense, that since Christ has defeated death what were threats in Hosea are now rhetorically mocked as impotent? Or is Paul dependent on the positive context of the previous sentence already given in the LXX: "I will deliver them out of the power of Hades, and will redeem them from death"?

What is clear from our discussion is that much more work needs to be done to clarify the meaning of the spiritual sense. Church documents and exegetes agree that the spiritual sense exists. But there is no consensus on exactly what is meant by the term. As of this writing, a team of members of the Catholic Biblical Association of America is addressing the issue, beginning, wisely it seems, with an inductive approach, that is, analyzing individual New Testament texts from which a list of usages can be derived and then, one hopes, a more systematic understanding of what at present is still for many a "weasel word."

As we conclude this part of the book, the reader is perhaps overwhelmed by the variety of methods of interpretation and their conflicting claims to validity. Most of these methods, however, are complementary rather than opposed, and an integral hermeneutic will take from each the enrichment it can give. Deconstruction is the exception, for it is essentially self-reversing and equivalently proclaims it has nothing to offer. And one must be cautious of methods that dispense with evidence-based judgment, lest the interpreter fall into subjectivism. With these caveats and the understanding that we now have of the methods and their underlying philosophies, we are in a position to look at the documents of the Roman Catholic Church that treat these issues.

FOURTEEN

Dei Verbum: Text and Commentary

The twentieth century witnessed a number of church documents dealing with scripture and its interpretation. The most authoritative is that issued by the Second Vatican Council in 1965 entitled *Dei Verbum: The Dogmatic Constitution on Divine Revelation*. The council approved the final draft of the document by a nearly unanimous vote. Out of 2,350 possible votes, 2,344 approved and only 6 voted "non-placet" ("no"). What follows is the translation published by the N.C.W.C. (National Catholic Welfare Conference, since renamed the United States Catholic Conference of Bishops [USCCB]). The original text contained footnotes giving references to other church documents or authors. These are reproduced with *superscript numbers* in the text below and are found at the end of the document as endnotes. The *lettered* footnotes are not part of the official text. They are commentary offered by the author of the present textbook, who assumes total responsibility for their content. Much more extensive studies of the document are available.[a]

Preface

1. Hearing the word of God with reverence and proclaiming it with faith,[b] the sacred synod takes its direction from these words

---

[a]For a thorough commentary on the development and meaning of the Constitution *Dei Verbum,* see "Dogmatic Constitution on Divine Revelation" by Joseph Ratzinger, Alois Grillmeier, and Béda Rigaux in *Commentary on the Documents of Vatican II,* vol. 3, ed. H. Vorgrimler (New York: Herder & Herder, 1968), 155–272. See also Augustin Bea, *The Word of God and Mankind* (Chicago: Franciscan Herald Press, 1967); and René Latourelle, ed., *Vatican II Assessment and Perspective Twenty-Five Years Later,* vol. 1 (Mahwah, NJ: Paulist, 1988), 123–381.

[b]When *Dei Verbum* uses the expression "the word of God" it ordinarily means more than the word as inscribed in the scriptures. It refers to the entire revelation of God. Thus,

of St. John: "We announce to you the eternal life which dwelt with the Father and was made visible to us. What we have seen and heard we announce to you, so that you may have fellowship with us and our common fellowship may be with the Father and His Son Jesus Christ" (1 John 1:2–3).ᶜ Therefore, following in the footsteps of the Council of Trent and of the First Vatican Council,ᵈ this present council wishes to set forth authentic doctrine on divine revelation and how it is handed on,ᵉ so that by hearing the message of salvation the whole world may believe, by believing it may hope, and by hoping it may love.¹ᶠ

Chapter I
Revelation Itself

2. In His goodness and wisdom God chose to reveal Himself and to make known to us the hidden purposeᵍ of his will (see Eph 1:9) by which through Christ, the Word made flesh, man might in the Holy Spirit have access to the Father and come to share in the divine nature (see Eph 2:18; 2 Peter 1:4). Through this revelation, therefore, the invisible God (see Col 1:15; 1 Tim 1:17) out of the abundance of His love speaks to men as friends (see Ex 33:11; John 15:14–15) and lives among them (see Bar 3:38),ʰ so that he

---

the church "hears" and "proclaims" rather than "reads" the word. The terms are more fitting for the entire process by which revelation was handed down and continues to be handed down in the church. But note how the church puts herself in this opening sentence *under* the word of God, as it will say later on in #10. "With faith" in the Latin is *fidenter,* which also suggests the kind of confident boldness with which the early church proclaimed the word (Acts 4:13, 29, 31; 28:31).

ᶜThe ultimate purpose of the proclamation is not the communication of ideas or even doctrines. It is communion *(koinonia)* with the triune God.

ᵈThe Council of Trent responded to the controversy over *sola scriptura*. It also settled the books recognized by the Catholic Church as canonical. Vatican Council I had important texts on revelation. Vatican II sees itself rereading those texts in the light of the present situation.

ᵉFrom the very introduction, the council wants to call attention to the importance of tradition, which it alludes to here as the process by which revelation is handed on.

ᶠThe pastoral intention of the council appears here.

ᵍ"Hidden purpose" is *sacramentum,* which might also be translated "mystery." It suggests more than the "eternal decrees of his will," the expression used by Vatican I. Thus, beyond ideas or commands, revelation is a mystery of life, as the scripture cited indicates, because ultimately it is God revealing himself.

ʰThe Latin *alloquitur et conversatur* suggests dialogue and response.

may invite and take them into fellowship with Himself. This plan of revelation is realized by deeds and words[i] having an inner unity: the deeds wrought by God in the history of salvation manifest and confirm the teaching and realities signified by the words, while the words proclaim the deeds and clarify the mystery contained in them. By this revelation then, the deepest truth about God and the salvation of man shines out for our sake in Christ, who is both the mediator and the fullness of all revelation.[2]

3. God, who through the Word creates all things (see John 1:3) and keeps them in existence, gives men an enduring witness to Himself in created realities (see Rom 1:19–20). Planning to make known the way of heavenly salvation, He went further and from the start manifested Himself to our first parents. Then after their fall[j] His promise of redemption aroused in them the hope of being saved (see Gen 3:15) and from that time on He ceaselessly kept the human race in His care, to give eternal life to those who perseveringly do good in search of salvation (see Rom 2:6–7). Then, at the time He had appointed He called Abraham in order to make of him a great nation (see Gen 12:2). Through the patriarchs, and after them through Moses and the prophets, He taught this people to acknowledge Himself the one living and true God, provident father and just judge, and to wait for the Savior promised by Him, and in this manner prepared the way for the Gospel down through the centuries.[k]

4. Then, after speaking in many and varied ways through the prophets, "now at last in these days God has spoken to us in His Son" (Heb 1:1–2). For He sent His Son, the eternal Word, who enlightens all men, so that He might dwell among men and tell them of the innermost being of God (see John 1:1–18). Jesus Christ, therefore, the Word made flesh, was sent as "a man to men."[3] He

---

[i]The council avoids the word *truths* in favor of "words and deeds" at this point, reserving "the deepest truth about God..." for later in the paragraph. God's acts in history are themselves revelatory, but the words interpret the deeds and vice versa. The historical nature of revelation is clearly affirmed here.

[j]This is one of only two references (#4) to sin in the entire document. The whole paragraph is optimistic; the sinful situation of humanity as described, for example, in Romans 1–3, is not developed, nor is Augustine's description of scripture as medicinal. Some believe the document should have given more attention to this aspect.

[k]The Old Testament is presented here as a divine pedagogy, as is developed further in chapter 4.

"speaks the words of God" (John 3:34), and completes the work of salvation which His Father gave Him to do[l] (see John 5:36; 17:4). To see Jesus is to see His Father (John 14:9). For this reason Jesus perfected revelation by fulfilling it through his whole work of making Himself present and manifesting Himself: through His words and deeds, His signs and wonders, but especially through His death and glorious resurrection from the dead and final sending of the Spirit of truth. Moreover He confirmed with divine testimony what revelation proclaimed, that God is with us to free us from the darkness of sin and death, and to raise us up to life eternal.

The Christian dispensation, therefore, as the new and definitive covenant, will never pass away and we now await no further new public revelation before the glorious manifestation of our Lord Jesus Christ (see 1 Tim 6:14 and Tit. 2:13).[m]

5. "The obedience of faith" (Rom 1:26; see 1:5; 2 Cor 10:5–6) "is to be given to God who reveals, an obedience by which man commits his whole self freely to God, offering the full submission of intellect and will to God who reveals,"[4] and freely assenting to the truth revealed by Him. To make this act of faith, the grace of God and the interior help of the Holy Spirit must precede and assist, moving the heart and turning it to God, opening the eyes of the mind and giving "joy and ease to everyone in assenting to the truth and believing it."[5n] To bring about an ever deeper understanding of revelation the same Holy Spirit constantly brings faith to completion by His gifts.[o]

---

[l]"Christ no longer speaks merely of God, but he is himself the speech of God" (J. Ratzinger).

[m]"New" signifies anything that goes beyond what has already been revealed in Jesus. It does not exclude further explicitation of the "deposit of the faith," such as the dogmatic definitions of councils and the deeper understanding the church has of that revelation as it progresses through time. Joseph Smith's revelations, for example, were proposed as new and authoritative in character and became the foundation of the Church of Jesus Christ of Latter-Day Saints (the Mormons). "Public" distinguishes the basic Christian revelation from "private revelations," such as those given to saints and mystics. Some of these private revelations have received church approval (though many have not), but such approval only means that such revelations are "worthy of pious belief"—but they do not belong to the truths that all Catholics must believe. In Jesus God has said all, because he has said himself. All future prophecy, teaching, revelation, and so on, is to be measured by Christ (1 Cor 12:1–3).

[n]Faith is both a free human act and a gift—whence the mystery.

[o]This sentence affirms the fact of growth in faith. The light of faith reaches out and touches every dimension of the believer's being. The gifts of the Holy Spirit, though not

6. Through divine revelation, God chose to show forth and communicate Himself and the eternal decisions of His will regarding the salvation of men.[p] That is to say, He chose to share with them those divine treasures which totally transcend the understanding of the human mind.[6q]

As a sacred synod has affirmed, God, the beginning and end of all things, can be known with certainty from created reality by the light of human reason (see Rom 1:20); but teaches that it is through His revelation that those religious truths which are by their nature accessible to human reason can be known by all men with ease, with solid certitude and with no trace of error, even in this present state of the human race.[r]

Chapter II
Handing on Divine Revelation

7. In His gracious goodness, God has seen to it that what He had revealed for the salvation of all nations would abide perpetually in its full integrity and be handed on to all generations.[s] Therefore Christ the Lord in whom the full revelation of the supreme God is brought to completion (see 1 Cor 1:20; 3:13;

---

specified here, would include those that give a deeper insight into the revelation received (1 Cor 2:9–16), the charismatic gifts that confirm the preaching of the gospel (1 Cor 1:5–7), and probably the fruits of the Spirit (Gal 5:22) and the "Messianic" gifts of Isaiah 11:2–3, which tradition has associated with the conferral of the Holy Spirit.

[p]Again, God communicates *himself*, hence the personal and relational nature of revelation. Note also that the scope of his revelation is what concerns human salvation. This prepares for the statement in #11 concerning the "truth for the sake of salvation," hence not an interest in scientific or historical truths for their own sake but only as oriented to salvation.

[q]Other truths knowable by human reason may be confirmed by revelation, but the primary focus of revelation is on those things that human beings cannot know by themselves, for example, the mystery of the Trinity.

[r]This is basically a repetition of the teaching of Vatican Council I. Note how this statement counters the widespread subjectivism of our times.

[s]This chapter seeks to answer the question, "How does divine revelation come down to us? How does it pass through time?" This is a serious question because, on the one hand, Christianity is a historical religion, committed to the principle, on the one hand, that God said all he had to say in a given period of history culminating with Jesus Christ, with the limitations of a particular culture, and yet, on the other hand, this revelation is meant for all times and cultures. It is especially significant that this chapter on the handing on of revelation (or "tradition") *precedes* those on the scriptures. Scripture, then, is a way, a privileged way no doubt, that revelation is handed on.

4:6), commissioned the Apostles to preach to all men that Gospel which is the source of all saving truth and moral teaching,[7] and to impart to them heavenly gifts.[t] This Gospel had been promised in former times through the prophets, and Christ Himself had fulfilled it and promulgated it with His lips.[u] This commission was faithfully fulfilled by the Apostles[v] who, by their oral preaching, by example, and by observances handed on what they had received from the lips of Christ, from living with Him, and from what He did, or what they had learned through the prompting of the Holy Spirit.[w] The commission was fulfilled, too, by those Apostles and apostolic men who under the inspiration of the same Holy Spirit committed the message of salvation to writing.[8][x]

But in order to keep the Gospel forever whole and alive within the Church, the Apostles left bishops as their successors, "handing over" to them "the authority to teach in their own place."[9][y] This sacred tradition, therefore, and Sacred Scripture of both the Old and New Testaments are like a mirror in which the

---

[t]"Gifts" is more than "truths." It would include sacraments, charisms, the gifts of authority as well as the scriptures. In saying that the gospel is the *source* of all saving truth and moral teaching, the document leaves open the possibility that some truths not explicitly stated in the gospel could nevertheless be legitimately and accurately derived from it.

[u]The gospel was not just ideas or moral truths that were reaffirmed from the Old Testament or revised. He first of all lived the gospel ("fulfilling" it) and then proclaimed what he lived. Hence the gospel is not just a law but a life, indeed the person of Jesus Christ.

[v]Despite personal weaknesses, the apostles did not fail their teaching and ministering mission. Thus they did not distort the teaching of Jesus, and the church rightfully considers their presentation of Jesus' teaching to be authentic and normative. This flies in the face of some scholars who approach the New Testament with a "hermeneutic of suspicion" and apply their own lights to uncover the "authentic" teaching of Jesus.

[w]What the apostles received from Christ was not only teaching but lived experience and practices. Moreover, what they handed on was not limited to their earthly memories of Jesus but included matters inspired by the Holy Spirit subsequent to Jesus' resurrection and ascension. For example, the decision of the Council of Jerusalem would have been unnecessary had Jesus left specific directions about the non-circumcision of gentile converts. The apostles attributed their decisions on this matter to the Holy Spirit (Acts 15:28). See also decisions of Paul that he believed were inspired by the Holy Spirit in instances where he did not have a "word of the Lord" to resolve the issue (1 Cor 7:40).

[x]"Apostolic men" leaves open the question of the authorship of the Gospels. Mark and Luke were not apostles; the final edition of Matthew and John may not be from the hand of an apostle but of a disciple formed in the tradition of those apostles.

[y]"Whole," that none of it be lost; "alive," so that it not be a museum relic, something available to the world today only through historical research. "Bishops as their successors": although the word *bishop* is not used exactly in that sense in the New Testament, Timothy and Titus have full power to legislate in Paul's name.

pilgrim Church on earth looks at God, from whom she has received everything, until she is brought finally to see Him as He is, face to face (see 1 John 3:2).[z]

8. And so the apostolic preaching, which is expressed in a special way in the inspired books, was to be preserved by an unending succession of preachers until the end of time.[aa] Therefore the Apostles, handing on what they themselves had received, warn the faithful to hold fast to the traditions which they have learned either by word of mouth or by letter (see 2 Thess 2:15), and to fight in defense of the faith handed on once and for all (see Jude 1:3).[10] Now what was handed on by the Apostles includes everything which contributes toward the holiness of life and increase in faith of the people of God; and so the Church, in her teaching, life and worship, perpetuates and hands on to all generations all that she herself is, all that she believes.[bb]

This tradition, which comes from the Apostles, develops in the Church with the help of the Holy Spirit.[11] For there is a growth in the understanding of the realities and the words that have been handed down.[cc] This happens through the contemplation and study made by believers, who treasure these things in their hearts (see Luke 2:19, 51) through a penetrating understanding of the spiritual

---

[z]The simile "mirror" suggests the imperfection of this knowledge compared to the knowledge of face-to-face vision. Without saying that scripture and tradition are one source, the fact that the document speaks of one mirror rather than two suggests the intimate interrelation of scripture and tradition.

[aa]The focus here is on the active preaching by which revelation is carried on. The inspired books are seen here as a privileged record and witness of the *preaching* of the apostles.

[bb]This concerns the content of tradition. It does not mean that everything in the church is good tradition; some traditions may need to be purified, changed. The liturgical reform sanctioned by Vatican II corrected some of the intrusions of personal devotions into the liturgy. Also note the three ways the message is passed on: *teaching* (for example, the very document we are reading), life (the lives of saints, canonized or not, communities, Christian families, living people who believe and experience the Lord) and *worship* (for example, in the Eucharist we are saying what we are as a people and "remembering" in the sense of reliving all that Jesus is and teaches). There is a hermeneutic in the life and worship of the Christian community. The latter is a hermeneutic especially treasured by the Eastern churches.

[cc]Tradition *develops (traditio proficit)*. It is not a static thing, repeating the same things over and over again mechanically but rather responding in a living way to new contexts, new cultures, new times. We see this already in the New Testament, for example the Fourth Gospel's adaptation of the early Jewish kerygma to the Hellenistic world. This growth of tradition, however, is primarily a growth in *understanding (crescit perceptio)* of what is already there in the realities and the words.

realities which they experience, and through the preaching of those who have received through episcopal succession the sure gift of truth.[dd] For as the centuries succeed one another, the Church constantly moves forward toward the fullness of divine truth until the words of God reach their complete fulfillment in her.[ee]

The words of the holy fathers[ff] witness to the presence of this living tradition, whose wealth is poured into the practice and life of the believing and praying Church. Through the same tradition the Church's full canon of the sacred books is known,[gg] and the sacred writings themselves are more profoundly understood and unceasingly made active in her,[hh] and thus God, who spoke of old, uninterruptedly converses with the bride of His beloved Son,[ii] and the Holy Spirit, through whom the living voice of the Gospel resounds in the Church, and through her, in the world, leads unto all truth those who believe and makes the word of Christ dwell abundantly in them (see Col 3:16).[jj]

[dd]It is noteworthy that the teaching office is placed last in this series and first place is given to the contemplation and study of all believers and the understanding that comes from spiritual experience. The role of the magisterium is not so much productive as critical—though one hopes bishops will also be persons who pray, contemplate, and study, as we see in the prolific output of Pope John Paul II.

[ee]Again a non-triumphalistic admission of the incompleteness of our knowledge, which leads to a desire to grow in it.

[ff]Not the popes but the writers of the first centuries: Ignatius, Clement, Hippolytus, Augustine, Chrysostom, and so on. Not that these are the only witnesses, but they are the first writing witnesses after the scriptures.

[gg]At a certain period in the church, common agreement was reached concerning which books are to be read as the word of God and which not. This touches on the relation of tradition to scripture, for without tradition we would not even know which books we should read as God's word.

[hh]Tradition keeps scripture alive. Where do the scriptures live? Not on the printed page but in the life of the church, in the lives of those to whom the word means something. Hence scripture needs tradition to live. We see this already in the parable of the sower, where the word is first of all a seed, and then it becomes people who respond to the word (Mark 4:14–20).

[ii]Note here again how tradition is seen as giving life to the word. The letter, spoken and written of old, is not read just as an object, but somehow through it *God* converses with his people. While this is true of the individual, it is primarily to the Church, the community as such that God converses. We can be sure we are hearing our bridegroom's voice only if we are the bride, that is, if we surrender our individualism (though not our uniqueness) to the body of the Church.

[jj]The Holy Spirit leads into all truth (John 16:13). The Christ event, while rooted in the limited time and history of Palestine, extends to all times through the Holy Spirit. Christ who "leaves" the church "comes again" through the Holy Spirit to "remind us" of all that happened and to proclaim the meaning of it to us now. That, in the last instance, is what is meant by *tradition.*

9. Hence there exists a close connection and communication between sacred tradition and Sacred Scripture. For both of them, flowing from the same divine wellspring, in a certain way merge into a unity and tend toward the same end. For Sacred Scripture is the word of God inasmuch as it is consigned to writing under the inspiration of the divine Spirit,[kk] while sacred tradition takes the word of God entrusted by Christ the Lord and the Holy Spirit to the Apostles, and hands it on to their successors in is full purity, so that led by the light of the Spirit of truth, they may in proclaiming it preserve this word of God faithfully, explain it, and make it more widely known.[ll] Consequently it is not from Scripture alone that the Church draws her certainty about everything which has been revealed.[mm] Therefore both sacred tradition and Sacred Scripture are to be accepted and venerated with the same sense of loyalty and reverence.[nn]

10. Sacred tradition and Sacred Scripture form one sacred deposit of the word of God, committed to the Church. Holding fast to this deposit the entire holy people united with their shepherds remain always steadfast in the teaching of the Apostles, in the common life, in the breaking of the bread and in prayers (see Acts 2:42), so that holding to, practicing and professing the heritage of the faith, it becomes on the part of the bishops and faithful a single common effort.[12][oo]

[kk]A quasi-definition of scripture: the word of God inasmuch as it is consigned to writing. Thus the word of God itself is something much more—Christ himself, his deeds, his actions, the unspoken and the unwritten as well as the written.

[ll]Tradition, unlike scripture, is not called the word of God. It is defined not by what it is but by what it does: it *hands on* the word of God. Its function is described here as *conservative*: to keep, explain, and pass on something already given. This balances the statement in #8 that tradition develops.

[mm]The text does not say that tradition provides new content but that it has an epistemological function in regard to what is revealed.

[nn]This does not mean that the word of God and tradition are the same thing. It means simply that, if tradition is the means by which we now experience, touch, hear the word of God, to reject it is also to reject the possibility of hearing God's word. To use a homely example, it would be like cutting the wires by which our friend is speaking over the phone to us. Obviously the wires are not the friend, are not as important as the friend, but they are the only way we can presently hear his voice.

[oo]The role of the faithful and therefore of the laity in tradition is here clearly stated. It is not just the hierarchy who are responsible for the handing on of the authentic revelation. All are responsible for the word of God, though in functionally different ways.

But the task of authentically interpreting the word of God, whether written or handed on,[13] has been entrusted exclusively to the living teaching office of the Church,[pp] whose authority is exercised in the name of Jesus Christ. This teaching office is not above the word of God, but serves it, teaching only what has been handed on, listening to it devoutly, guarding it scrupulously and explaining it faithfully in accord with a divine commission and with the help of the Holy Spirit, it draws from this one deposit of faith everything which it presents for belief as divinely revealed.[qq]

It is clear, therefore, that sacred tradition, Sacred Scripture and the teaching authority of the Church, in accord with God's most wise design, are so linked and joined together that one cannot stand without the others, and that all together and each in its own way under the action of the one Holy Spirit contribute effectively to the salvation of souls.

Chapter III
Sacred Scripture, Its Inspiration and Divine Interpretation[rr]

11. Those divinely revealed realities which are contained and presented in Sacred Scripture have been committed to writing

---

[pp]"Authentically interpreting" highlights the precise, critical function of the magisterium. Ordinarily, however, this is not done in isolation from what is going on in the whole church. Understanding develops through life; the official teaching clarifies and rectifies understanding. Although all Christian life is an interpretation of the scriptures, in the last analysis, it is the teaching office of the church that has the final authority. Doctrine ordinarily develops through a process: the people as a whole experience, theologians discuss, the magisterium decides.

[qq]The teaching office is not above the word of God, and therefore cannot arbitrarily say what it will or what might be politically correct at a given time; on the contrary, it is bound by the deposit of faith, to which it too, like all the faithful, must "listen devoutly" (see #21: "All preaching in the church must be nourished and regulated by Sacred Scripture"), and its critical function is a service to the whole church.

[rr]Chapter 1 dealt with revelation itself, which is broader than the Bible, chapter 2 with the handing on of revelation (also broader than scripture), and now chapter 3 deals with scripture expressly, namely the written word of God. It will also be concerned with what we mean when we say scripture is inspired. "Inspiration and its results, the inspired books, belong to the area of the *assimilation* of revelation and the saving reality of God, not of the *historical constitution* of revelation and salvation." Grillmeier, in *Commentary on the Documents of Vatican II,* vol. 3, ed. H. Vorgrimler, p. 228.

under the inspiration of the Holy Spirit. For holy mother Church, relying on the belief of the Apostles (see John 20:31; 2 Tim 3:16; 2 Peter 1:19–20; 3:15–16), holds that the books of both the Old and New Testaments in their entirety, with all their parts,[ss] are sacred and canonical because written under the inspiration of the Holy Spirit, they have God as their author and have been handed on as such to the Church herself.[14] In composing the sacred books, God chose men and while employed by Him[15] they made use of their powers and abilities, so that with Him acting in them and through them[16] they, as true authors, consigned to writing everything and only those things which He wanted.[17tt]

Therefore, since everything asserted by the inspired authors or sacred writers must be held to be asserted by the Holy Spirit, it follows that the books of Scripture must be acknowledged as teaching solidly, faithfully and without error that truth which God wanted put into sacred writings[18] for the sake of salvation.[uuu] Therefore "all

---

[ss]All their parts as accepted into the canon. Thus, though scholars question whether Mark 16:9–20 was part of the original work of the evangelist, it belongs to canonical scripture and is considered inspired. Thus also, if a disciple-editor reworked an earlier version of John, it is the present text that is considered inspired.

[tt]Note however that the document avoids the term *dictated* that had been used by Leo XIII, lest it give the impression that the human writer was not a true author or that inspiration bypassed the human activities that authorship demands. Thus, as authors, they might use sources, shaped by the faith community in which they lived, edit and organize their composition in such a way that the very selection, editing and arranging of their text reveals a theological dimension that mere collection of sources would not.

[uuu]Note the specification: not just truth in general, but that truth which God wanted put into the sacred writings for our salvation. An earlier formula, "saving truth" (*veritas salutaris*) was hotly discussed in the council. It was judged to be not theologically mature and was finally rejected in favor of the present text. It echoes Ephesians 1:13: "You also, who have heard the word of truth, the gospel of your salvation...." The scope of inspiration is therefore not just faith and morals but whatever is in the Bible, hence historical material as well, but only to the degree that it contributes to our salvation. For example, Genesis 1 speaks of God creating a "dome" over the earth (the sky). We know scientifically that the sky is not a solid bowl, but this does not diminish the "truth for salvation." If we take strict scientific or historical truth as the criterion for the inspiration of the Bible, then we are measuring it according to modern understanding of science and history (a point made already by Pius XII in *Divino Afflante Spiritu* in calling attention to the literary forms of the Bible). More important, we are equating inspiration with historical or scientific accuracy. On the floor of the council Cardinal Koenig pointed out that the scriptures themselves contain not only approximations but inaccuracies. For example, Mark 2:26 says that David entered the house of God under the high priest Abiathar. But 1 Sam 21:1ff. says it was not under Abiathar but under his father Ahimelech. Matthew 27:9 says the death of Judas fulfilled a prophecy of Jeremiah; in fact it is Zechariah 11:12–13 that is quoted. In Daniel 1:1 we read that King Nebuchadnezzar besieged Jerusalem in the third year of King Jehoiakim, that is, 607 BC, but from the authentic chronicle of King Nebuchadnezzar we

Scripture is divinely inspired and has its use for teaching the truth and refuting error, for reformation of manners and discipline in right living, so that the man who belongs to God may be efficient and equipped for good work of every kind" (2 Tim 3:16–17).

12. However, since God speaks in Sacred Scripture through men in human fashion,[19] the interpreter of Sacred Scripture, in order to see clearly what God wanted to communicate to us, should carefully investigate what meaning the sacred writers really intended, and what God wanted to manifest by means of their words.[vv]

To search out the intention of the sacred writers, attention should be given, among other things, to "literary forms."[ww] For truth is set forth and expressed differently in texts which are variously historical, prophetic, poetic, or of other forms of discourse.[xx] The interpreter must investigate what meaning the sacred writer intended to express and actually expressed in particular circumstances by using contemporary literary forms in accordance with the situation of his own time and culture.[20] For the correct understanding of what the sacred author wanted to assert, due attention must be paid to the customary and characteristic styles of feeling,

---

know the siege can only have taken place three years later. Yet, in terms of the teaching for our salvation, the passages and books in questions are in no way modified by these historical errors. The sacred authors used the historical information available to them in their days, often in sources, but they used them for a sacred purpose.

[vv]There is some tension between the first and the last part of this sentence. Critical exegesis seeks to determine the meaning of an individual text on its own terms. Here *Dei Verbum* affirms the inspiration of the literal sense, which is the intention of the author inasmuch as it is available in the text. But the placing of "and" instead of "which is" to introduce the second clause leaves open the possibility of meanings beyond the literal, which God may have had in mind. The council seems to have deliberately left this obscure and open to debate. See our chapter on the spiritual senses of scripture. In any case, as we saw in the chapter on canonical interpretation, a given passage must be interpreted in the light of the whole of scripture.

[ww]"Among other things" indicates the list given here is not exhaustive. The way is open to develop other tools. At least those given here are important to be used.

[xx]The Bible is a library, with different kinds of books and often different literary forms within a given book. Is Jonah to be classified as historical or prophetic or didactic? Even the ancients' notion of history differs greatly from ours. The period prior to Abraham is classified as "primitive history" in which the sacred author(s) used the memories of ancient peoples, often their folktales, to construct a theological interpretation of those ages lost in the distant past. The "religious history" we find in the Bible often ignores secondary agents and reduces all to God's intervention. We find a "national epic" in chapter 5 of Judges. We speak of Joshua-Judges-Samuel-Kings as "historical books," but the Jews considered them "the former Prophets."

speaking and narrating which prevailed at the time of the sacred writer, and to the patterns men normally employed at that period in their everyday dealings with one another.[21][yy]

But, since Holy Scripture must be read and interpreted in the same spirit in which it was written,[zz] no less serious attention must be given to the content and unity of the whole of Scripture, if the meaning of the sacred texts is to be correctly worked out. The living tradition of the whole Church must be taken into account along with the harmony which exists between elements of the faith.[aaa] It is the task of exegetes to work according to these rules toward a better understanding and explanation of the meaning of Sacred Scripture, so that through preparatory

---

[yy]"Feeling" here is listed before "speaking" and "narrating." This is close, if not identical, with what the theorists of understanding call "pre-understanding." For example, while Platonists might think of man as an imprisoned soul, the Israelites thought of him rather as an animated body. Or the importance of progeny in ancient societies—the more the better—differs considerably from that of today's developed world. Or the notion of the national god, defender of national interests. Or, to use examples from another culture, a tribe discovered in Mindinao (Philippines) that has evolved very little from the Stone Age had no concept of "weapon," since war was never in their experience. Or certain Indian tribes in Peru had no idea of sacrifice as part of their religion. This cultural "pre-understanding" is the medium through which one sees things, like fish in water or human beings in gravity. It is always there, unaverted to, yet it conditions everything human beings do.

[zz]The introductory "but" is not to be read in opposition but rather as completing the previous thought. It is not sufficient to use the human sciences to analyze the texts. For the Christian interpreter these texts, inspired by the Holy Spirit, demand on the part of the interpreter a corresponding enlightenment by the Holy Spirit. This does not mean the same charism of inspiration. It is rather the pre-understanding of faith, a sharing of the same faith that the author had in writing this text. This implies, as we saw in chapter 8 on Lonergan, that the reader must have some experience of the *reality* to which the text refers, or he will not understand it. As Origen already pointed out, if the Holy Spirit inspired the text, the Holy Spirit must also guide the interpreter. In an earlier draft of the text the reference to the Spirit was lacking and only the three norms of the unity of scripture, tradition, and the analogy of faith were mentioned. An Eastern bishop said that text was too timid and even legalistic, and he called for a return "to the totality of the mystery of the Church" and hence for a reference to the mission of the Holy Spirit, which was added in the final version. In the light of the expression, "what meaning the sacred writers really intended, and what *God* wanted to manifest by means of their words," it is possible to read the document as saying that there is more to the text than meets the eye of the scientific interpreter and more than may have been in the mind of the author. The document therefore seems to suggest that there is more meaning in the text when it is interpreted as *revelation* than is accessible to mere human science. This phrase is studied in an exhaustive article by Ignace de la Potterie, "Interpretation of Scripture in the Spirit in Which It Was Written (*Dei Verbum* 12c)" in Latourelle, *Vatican II*, 220–66.

[aaa]The work of the Holy Spirit in interpretation does not bypass but indeed promotes the use of three principles by which the inspired meaning of scripture is discerned: (1) The content and unity of the whole of scripture. Since the Bible is the entire book in which the

study the judgment of the Church may mature.[bbb] For all of what has been said about the way of interpreting Scripture is subject finally to the judgment of the Church, which carries out the divine commission and ministry of guarding and interpreting the word of God.[22 ccc]

13. In Sacred Scripture, therefore, while the truth and holiness of God always remains intact, the marvelous "condescension" of eternal wisdom is clearly shown, "That we may learn the gentle kindness of God, which words cannot express, and how far He has gone in adapting His language with thoughtful concern for our weak human nature."[23] For the works of God, expressed in human language, have been made like human discourse, just the Word of the eternal Father, when He took to Himself the flesh of human weakness, was in every way made like men.[ddd]

---

church listens to the word of God, it is important to hear each voice in harmony with the other voices found there. Since the whole of the Bible is the work of the same Spirit, the interpreter must listen to the whole whenever interpreting a part. Sometimes apparent contradictions between one book and another can be resolved in terms of different perspectives on the same issue. At other times one needs to take into consideration the progressive nature of revelation and the revisions the New Testament makes, for example, of the Old. Implicit in this affirmation, which stands in tension with the earlier statement that the exegete should strive to find the literal meaning of the specific text, is that a canonical reading may adjust or contextualize a specific text beyond its original literal meaning. (2) However, what is meant by "the whole of scripture"? Obviously this would involve privileging certain texts above others. But where is that judgment found? In the living tradition of the whole church. (3) The analogy ("harmony") of the faith, an echo of Romans 12:6. The elements of the faith, as embodied for example in the Creed, are parts of an integral revelation, and there should be no contradiction between them but rather a complementarity and mutual illumination.

[bbb]In the light of the preceding sentences, the role of the exegete goes beyond analysis and should provide at least an initial hermeneutic. This aspect of the exegete's task is more fully developed in the 1993 document of the Pontifical Biblical Commission, *The Interpretation of Scripture in the Church*, which we recommend as a companion text. The role of exegetes is not to proclaim doctrine but through their specific expertise to *prepare* for the mature judgment of the church through the magisterium.

[ccc]The document distinguishes between the exegetical/interpretive role of the exegetes and the "divine commission and ministry" of interpretation given to the magisterium. A process is here involved that gives the exegete freedom to research and explore the meaning of the ancient texts in the community of his fellow professionals and at the same time relieves him of the responsibility of making the final judgment of the meaning of the word of God for the church.

[ddd]We recognize the teaching of Saint John Chrysostom studied earlier. The most significant statement here is that the divine word follows the rules of human discourse, and thus this opens up all the possibilities of literary forms and study of the scriptures according to all the human sciences.

Chapter IV
The Old Testament[eee]

14. In carefully planning and preparing the salvation of the whole human race the God of infinite love, by a special dispensation, chose for Himself a people to whom He would entrust His promises. First He entered into a covenant with Abraham (see Gen 15:18) and, through Moses, with the people of Israel (see Ex 24:8). To this people which He had acquired for Himself, He so manifested Himself through words and deeds as the one true and living God that Israel came to know by experience the ways of God with men. Then too, when God Himself spoke to them through the mouths of the prophets, Israel daily gained a deeper and clearer understanding of His ways and made them more widely known among the nations (see Ps 21:29; 95:1–3; Is. 2:1–5; Jer 3:17). The plan of salvation foretold by the sacred authors, recounted and explained by them, is found as the true word of God in the books of the Old Testament: these books, therefore, written under divine inspiration, remain permanently valuable. "For all that was written for our instruction, so that by steadfastness and the encouragement of the Scriptures we might have hope" (Rom 15:4).

15. The principal purpose to which the plan of the old covenant was directed was to prepare for the coming of Christ, the redeemer of all, and of the messianic kingdom, to announce this coming by prophecy (see Luke 24:44; John 5:39; 1 Peter 1:10), and to indicate its meaning through various types (see 1 Cor 10:12).[fff] Now the books of the Old Testament, in accordance with the state of mankind before the time of salvation established by Christ, reveal to all men the knowledge of God and of man and the ways in which God, just and merciful, deals with men. These

---

[eee]See Stanislas Lyonnet, "A Word on Chapters IV and VI of *Dei Verbum*: The Amazing Journey Involved in the Process of Drafting the Conciliar Text," in Latourelle, *Vatican II,* 157–207.

[fff]"The principal purpose" indicates that this was not the only purpose. The Ten Commandments, for example, the warning of the prophets, the teaching of the wisdom literature, would have value even had there been no New Testament. It is this value that Jews and Christians share today. But Christians read the Old Testament primarily as a document illustrating God's preparatory pedagogy that finds its completion in the New.

books, though they also contain some things which are incomplete and temporary, nevertheless show us true divine pedagogy.[24] These same books, then, give expression to a lively sense of God, contain a store of sublime teachings about God, sound wisdom about human life, and a wonderful treasury of prayers, and in them the mystery of our salvation is present in a hidden way. Christians should receive them with reverence.

16. God, the inspirer and author of both Testaments, wisely arranged that the New Testament be hidden in the Old and the Old be made manifest in the New.[25] For, though Christ established the new covenant in His blood (see Luke 22:20; 1 Cor 11:25), still the books of the Old Testament with all their parts, caught up into the proclamation of the Gospel,[26] acquire and show forth their full meaning in the New Testament (see Matt 5:17; Luke 24:27; Rom 16:25–26; 2 Cor 14:16) and in turn shed light on it and explain it.[ggg]

Chapter V
The New Testament

17. The word of God, which is the power of God for the salvation of all who believe (see Rom 1:16), is set forth and shows its power in a most excellent way in the writings of the New Testament. For when the fullness of time arrived (see Gal 4:4), the Word was made flesh and dwelt among us in His fullness of grace and truth (see John 1:14). Christ established the kingdom of God on earth, manifested His Father and Himself by deeds and words, and completed His work by His death, resurrection and glorious Ascension and by the sending of the Holy Spirit. Having been lifted up from the earth, He draws all men to Himself (see John 12:32), He who alone has the words of eternal life (see John 6:68). This mystery had not been manifested to other generations as it was now revealed to His holy Apostles and prophets in the Holy Spirit (see Eph 3:4–6), so that they might preach the Gospel,

---

[ggg]Origen would probably have been very comfortable with this formulation, which echoes his seeing the New Testament in every passage of the Old (as we saw in chapter 2), although today his unabashed use of the allegorical method has been abandoned.

stir up faith in Jesus, Christ and Lord, and gather together the Church. Now the writings of the New Testament stand as a perpetual and divine witness to these realities.[hhh]

18. It is common knowledge that among all the Scriptures, even those of the New Testament, the Gospels have a special pre-eminence, and rightly so, for they are the principal witness for the life and teaching of the incarnate Word, our savior.

The Church has always and everywhere held and continues to hold that the four Gospels are of apostolic origin. For what the Apostles preached in fulfillment of the commission of Christ, afterwards they themselves and apostolic men,[iii] under the inspiration of the divine Spirit, handed on to us in writing: the foundation of faith, namely, the fourfold Gospel, according to Matthew, Mark, Luke and John.[27]

19. Holy Mother Church has firmly and with absolute constancy held, and continues to hold, that the four Gospels just named, whose historical character the Church unhesitatingly asserts,[iii] faithfully hand on what Jesus Christ, while living among men, really did and taught for their eternal salvation until the day He was taken up into heaven (see Acts 1:1).[kkk] Indeed, after the Ascension of the Lord the Apostles handed on to their hearers what He had said and done. This they did with that clearer understanding which they enjoyed[28] after they had been instructed by

---

[hhh]Note how the New Testament is placed in the category of witness. This is an exceedingly rich concept, which lends itself to much further exploration and also to possible abuse. See Sandra M. Schneiders, *The Revelatory Text* (San Francisco: HarperSanFrancisco, 1991), 132–56.

[iii]As mentioned earlier, "apostolic men" covers the fact that two of the authors of the Gospels at least (Mark, Luke) were not members of the Twelve, and it also leaves open the possibility that disciples of the apostles were involved in the composition of the other two (Matthew and John).

[iii]See José Caba, "Historicity of the Gospels (*Dei Verbum* 19): Genesis and Fruits of the Conciliar Text," in Latourelle, *Vatican II*, 299–320.

[kkk]The important word here is *faithfully*. Fidelity to "what Jesus really did and taught" did not demand a mechanical repetition of his deeds or words, though there is no reason to doubt that we do have in the Gospels sayings that go back to Jesus. But we must remember that Jesus for the most part spoke Aramaic, and the Gospels are written in Greek—a process that in itself demanded a judgment of the authors as to what words in the new language would best translate the *meaning* of the original. Furthermore, as the sequence of this article will specify, both in the preaching during the oral period and in the writing there was a concern to pass on the tradition in a living way so that it would be meaningful in the new and often different circumstances and cultures into which it was being planted.

the glorious events of Christ's life and taught by the light of the Spirit of truth.[29] The sacred authors wrote the four Gospels, selecting some things from the many which had been handed on by word of mouth or in writing, reducing some of them to a synthesis, explaining some things in view of the situation of their churches, and preserving the form of proclamation but always in such fashion that they told us the honest truth about Jesus.[30] For their intention in writing was that either from their own memory and recollections, or from the witness of those who "themselves from the beginning were eye-witnesses and ministers of the Word" we might know "the truth" concerning those matters about which we have been instructed (see Luke 1:2–4).

20. Besides the four Gospels, the canon of the New Testament also contains the epistles of St. Paul and other apostolic writings, composed under the inspiration of the Holy Spirit, by which, according to the wise plan of God, those matters which concern Christ the Lord are confirmed, His true teaching is more and more fully stated, the saving power of the divine work of Christ is preached, the story is told of the beginnings of the Church and its marvelous growth, and its glorious fulfillment is foretold.

For the Lord Jesus was with His apostles as He had promised (see Matt 28:29) and sent them the advocate Spirit who would lead them into the fulness of truth (see John 16:13).

Chapter VI
Sacred Scripture in the Life of the Church[III]

21. The Church has always venerated the divine Scriptures just as she venerates the body of the Lord, since, especially in the sacred liturgy, she unceasingly receives and offers to the faithful the bread of life from the table both of God's word and of Christ's body. She has always maintained them, and continues to do so, together with sacred tradition, as the supreme rule of faith, since,

---

[III]For further reflections on this section see James Swetnam, "The Word of God and Pastoral Theology in the Contemporary Church," in Latourelle, *Vatican II,* 364–81.

as inspired by God and committed once for all to writing, they impart the word of God Himself without change, and make the voice of the Holy Spirit resound in the words of the prophets and Apostles. Therefore, like the Christian religion itself, all the preaching of the Church must be nourished and regulated by Sacred Scripture. For in the sacred books, the Father who is in heaven meets His children with great love and speaks with them; and the force and power in the word of God is so great that it stands as the support and energy of the Church, the strength of faith for her sons, the food of the soul, the pure and everlasting source of spiritual life. Consequently these words are perfectly applicable to Sacred Scripture: "For the word of God is living and active" (Heb 4:12) and "it has power to build you up and give you heritage among all those who are sanctified" (Acts 20:32; see 1 Thess 2:13).

22. Easy access to Sacred Scripture should be provided for all the Christian faithful. That is why the Church from the very beginning accepted as her own that very ancient Greek translation of the Old Testament which is called the Septuagint; and she has always given a place of honor to other Eastern translations and Latin ones, especially the Latin translation known as the Vulgate. But since the word of God should be accessible at all times, the Church by her authority and with maternal concern sees to it that suitable and correct translations are made into different languages, especially from the original texts of the sacred books. And should the opportunity arise and the Church authorities approve, if these translations are produced in cooperation with the separated brethren as well, all Christians will be able to use them.

23. The bride of the incarnate Word, the Church taught by the Holy Spirit, is concerned to move ahead toward a deeper understanding of the Sacred Scriptures so that she may increasingly feed her sons with the divine words. Therefore, she also encourages the study of the holy Fathers of both East and West and of sacred liturgies. Catholic exegetes then and other students of sacred theology, working diligently together and using appropriate means, should devote their energies, under the watchful care of the sacred teaching office of the Church, to an exploration and exposition of the divine writings. This should be so done that

as many ministers of the divine word as possible will be able effectively to provide the nourishment of the Scriptures for the people of God, to enlighten their minds, strengthen their wills, and set men's hearts on fire with the love of God.[31] The sacred synod encourages the sons of the Church and Biblical scholars to continue energetically, following the mind of the Church, with the work they have so well begun, with a constant renewal of vigor.[32]

24. Sacred theology rests on the written word of God, together with sacred tradition, as its primary and perpetual foundation. By scrutinizing in the light of faith all truth stored up in the mystery of Christ, theology is most powerfully strengthened and constantly rejuvenated by that word. For the Sacred Scriptures contain the word of God and since they are inspired really are the word of God; and so the study of the sacred page is, as it were, the soul of sacred theology.[33] By the same word of Scripture the ministry of the word also, that is, pastoral preaching, catechetics and all Christian instruction, in which the liturgical homily must hold the foremost place, is nourished in a healthy way and flourishes in a holy way.

25. Therefore, all the clergy must hold fast to the Sacred Scriptures through diligent sacred reading and careful study, especially the priests of Christ and others, such as deacons and catechists who are legitimately active in the ministry of the word. This is to be done so that none of them will become "an empty preacher of the word of God outwardly, who is not a listener to it inwardly,"[34] since they must share the abundant wealth of the divine word with the faithful committed to them, especially in the sacred liturgy. The sacred synod also earnestly and especially urges all the Christian faithful, especially Religious, to learn by frequent reading of the divine Scriptures the "excellent knowledge of Jesus Christ" (Phil 3:8). "For ignorance of the Scriptures is ignorance of Christ."[35] Therefore, they should gladly put themselves in touch with the sacred text itself, whether it be through the liturgy, rich in the divine word, or through devotional reading, or through instructions suitable for the purpose and other aids which, in our time, with approval and active support of the shepherds of the Church, are commendably spread everywhere. And let them remember that prayer should accompany the reading of Sacred Scripture, so that

God and man may talk together; for "we speak to Him when we pray; we hear Him when we read the divine saying."[36]

It devolves on sacred bishops "who have the apostolic teaching"[37] to give the faithful entrusted to them suitable instruction in the right use of the divine books, especially the New Testament and above all the Gospels. This can be done through translations of the sacred texts, which are to be provided with the necessary and really adequate explanations so that the children of the Church may safely and profitably become conversant with the Sacred Scriptures and be penetrated with their spirit.

Furthermore, editions of the Sacred Scriptures, provided with suitable footnotes, should be prepared also for the use of non-Christians and adapted to their situation. Both pastors of souls and Christians generally should see to the wise distribution of these in one way or another.

26. In this way, therefore, through the reading and study of the sacred books "the word of God may spread rapidly and be glorified" (2 Thess 3:1) and the treasure of revelation, entrusted to the Church, may more and more fill the hearts of men. Just as the life of the Church is strengthened through the more frequent celebration of the Eucharistic mystery, similarly we may hope for a new stimulus for the life of the Spirit from a growing reverence for the word of God, which "lasts forever" (Is 40:8; see 1 Peter 1:23–25).

Original Notes to Dei Verbum

1. Cf. St. Augustine, *De Catechizandis Rudibus,* C. IV 8: PL 40, 316.

2. Cf. Matt 11:27; John 1:14 and 17; 14:6; 17:1–3; 2 Cor 3:16 and 4:6; Eph 1:3–14.

3. *Epistle to Diognetus,* c. VII, 4; Funk, Apostolic Fathers, I, p. 403.

4. First Vatican Council, *Dogmatic Constitution on the Catholic Faith,* Chap. 3, "On Faith": Denzinger 1789 (3008).

5. Second Council of Orange, Canon 7: Denzinger 180 (377); First Vatican Council, loc. cit.: Denzinger 1791 (3010).

6. First Vatican Council, *Dogmatic Constitution on the Catholic Faith*, Chap. 2, "On Revelation": Denzinger 1786 (3005).

7. Cf. Matt 28:19–20 and Mark 16:15; Council of Trent, session IV, *Decree on Scriptural Canons:* Denzinger 783 (1501).

8. Cf. Council of Trent, loc. cit; First Vatican Council, session III, *Dogmatic Constitution on the Catholic Faith*, Chap. 2, "On Revelation": Denzinger 187 (3005).

9. St. Irenaeus, *Against Heretics* III, 3, 1: PG 7, 848; Harvey 2, p. 9.

10. Cf. Second Council of Nicea: Denzinger 303 (602); Fourth Council of Constance, session X, Canon 1: Denzinger 336 (650–652).

11. First Vatican Council, *Dogmatic Constitution on the Catholic Faith*, Chap. 4, "On Faith and Reason": Denzinger 1800 (3020).

12. Cf. Pius XII, Apostolic Constitution, *Munificentissimus Deus*, Nov. 1, 1950: AAS 42 (1950), p. 756; *Collected Writings of St. Cyprian*, Letter 66:8: Hartel, III, B, p. 733: "The Church [is] people united with the priest and the pastor together with his flock."

13. Cf. First Vatican Council, *Dogmatic Constitution on the Catholic Faith*, Chap. 3, "On Faith": Denzinger 1792 (3001).

14. Cf. First Vatican Council, *Dogmatic Constitution on the Catholic Faith*, Chap. 2, "On Revelation": Denzinger 1787 [3006]; Biblical Commission, Decree of June 18, 1915: Denzinger 2180 [3629]: EB 420; Holy Office, Epistle of Dec. 22, 1923: EB 499.

15. Cf. Pius XII, encyclical *Divino Afflante Spiritu*, Sept. 30, 1943: AAS 35 [1943] p. 314; EB 556.

16. "In" and "for" man: cf. Heb 1 and 4:7; ("in"): 2 Sm 23:2; Matt 1:212 and various places; ("for"): First Vatican Council, *Schema on Catholic Doctrine,* note 9: Coll. Lac. VII, 522.

17. Leo XIII, encyclical *Providentissimus Deus*, Nov. 18, 1893: Denzinger 1952 (3293); EB 125.

18. Cf. St. Augustine, "Gen ad Litt." 2, 9, 20; PL 34, 270–271; Epistle 82, 3: PL 33, 277: CSEL 34, 2, p. 354; St. Thomas, "On Truth," Q. 12, A. 2, C.; Council of Trent, session IV, Scriptural Canons: Denzinger 783 (1501); Leo XIII, encyclical *Providentissimus Deus:* EB 121, 124, 126–127; Pius XII, encyclical "Divino Afflante Spiritu": EB 539.

19. St. Augustine, *City of God*, XVII, 6, 2: PL 41, 537: CSEL, XL 2, 228.

20. St. Augustine, *On Christian Doctrine* III, 18, 26; PL 34, 75–76.

21. Pius XII, loc. cit. Denzinger 2294 (3829–3830); EB 557–562.

22. Cf. First Vatican Council, *Dogmatic Constitution on the Catholic Faith,* Chapter 2, "On Revelation": Denzinger 1788 (3007).

23. St. John Chrysostom, *In Genesis* 3, 8 (Homily 17, 1): PG 53, 134; "Attemperatio" [in English "Suitable adjustment"]. in Greek *synkatabasis.*

24. Pius XI, encyclical *Mit Brennender Sorge,* March 14, 1937: AAS 29 (1937), p. 51.

25. St. Augustine, *Quest. in Hept.* 2, 73: PL 34, 623.

26. St. Irenaeus, *Against Heretics,* III, 21, 3: PG 7, 950; (Same as 25, 1: Harvey 2, p. 115). St. Cyril of Jerusalem, *Catech.* 4,35; PG 33, 497. Theodore of Mopsuestia, *In Soph.* 1, 4–6: PG 66, 452D–453A.

27. Cf. St. Irenaeus, *Against Heretics,* III, 11, 8: PG 7, 885, Sagnard Edition, p. 194.

28. John 2:22; 12:16; cf. 14:26; 16:12–13; 7:39.

29. Cf. John 14:26; 16:13.

30. Cf. instruction *Holy Mother Church* edited by Pontifical Consilium for Promotion of Bible Studies; AAS 56 (1964), p. 715.

31. Cf. Pius XII, encyclical *Divino Afflante Spiritu:* EB 551, 553, 567.

32. Cf. Pius XII, ibid.: EB 569.

33. Cf. Leo XIII, encyclical *Providentissimus Deus:* EB 114; Benedict XV, encyclical *Spiritus Paraclitus:* EB 483.

34. St. Augustine, *Sermons,* 179,1: PL 38, 966.

35. St. Jerome, *Commentary on Isaiah,* Prol.: PL 24, 17.

36. St. Ambrose, *On the Duties of Ministers* I, 20, 88: PL 16, 50.

37. St. Irenaeus, *Against Heretics,* IV, 32, 1: PG 7, 1071; (Same as 49, 2) Harvey, 2, p. 255.

FIFTEEN

A Study Guide to
The Interpretation of the Bible in the Church
(Pontifical Biblical Commission, April 15, 1993)
Questions for Comprehension, Reflection, Discussion[a]

The Address of Pope John Paul II

1. Compare and contrast the emphasis on *Providentissimus Deus* with *Divino Afflante Spiritu*. (#3–#5) What is the role of exegesis relating to the spiritual sense?

2. What consequences flow from the analogy of Catholic exegesis and the mystery of the incarnation? (#6–#8)

3. What practical elements of the exegete's life should help his or her understanding and teaching of the word? (#9)

4. What characteristics of the new document does the pope note? (#13–#15)

---

[a]If the student wishes to pursue a study of the document beyond what is presented here, see Joseph A. Fitzmyer, SJ, *The Biblical Commission's Document "The Interpretation of the Bible in the Church": Text and Commentary* (Subsidia Biblica 18; Rome: Biblical Institute Press, 1995), xvi and 212; and the helpful study by Peter J. Williamson, *Catholic Principles for Interpreting Scripture: A Study of the Pontifical Biblical Commission's* The Interpretation of the Bible in the Church (Rome: Biblical Institute Press, 2001). A Vatican-sponsored symposium was held in Rome in 1999, the results of which were published as *L'interpretazione della Bibbia nella Chiesa: Atti del simposio promosso dalla Congregazione per la Dottrina della Fede* (Libreria Editrice Vaticana, 2001), 342 pp. Papers that are not in English are provided with an English summary.

The Document

(Page numbers refer to the edition by Pauline Books and Media, 1993.)

5. How does the document describe the state of the question of interpretation today? (30–33)

6. What is the limited scope of the document, and what does it intend *not* to adopt a position on? (33–34)

7. What is the document's attitude toward the historical-critical method? (35)

8. With what names and methods is development of historical criticism of the Old Testament (OT) associated? (35–37)

9. With what names and methods is the development of historical criticism of the New Testament associated? (37–38)

10. What do the terms *historical* and *critical* mean? (38)

11. What is the meaning of *textual criticism, literary criticism, genre criticism, tradition criticism, redaction criticism*? (39)

12. What are the contributions and the limitations of the historical-critical method? (40–41) How does the document understand the proper relation between the diachronic and the synchronic methods? (42)

13. What are the three kinds of rhetorical analysis? (43–44)

14. What are the strengths and weaknesses of rhetorical analysis? (45)

15. What is narrative analysis? (46)

16. What is meant by *real author, real reader, implied author, implied reader,* and *narrative world*? (46–47)

17. Explain: "A text will continue to have influence in the degree to which the real readers can identify with the implied reader." (47)

18. What are the usefulness and the limitations of narrative analysis? (48)

19. What is meant by *semiotic analysis* (or *structuralism*)? (49) What are the advantages and disadvantages of this method? (51)

20. What difficulties with the historical-critical method gave rise to "canonical criticism"? (52)

21. What questions remain to be answered in the canonical process? (54–55)

22. In the use of Jewish traditions of interpretation, what distinction of approaches must be kept in mind by the Christian interpreter? (57)

23. What two principles guide the approach of the History of the Influence of the text (*Wirkungsgeschichte*, or "effective history")? (57)? What are the fruits and the pitfalls of this method? (58–59)

24. What is the sociological approach—as applied to the Old Testament? (60) As applied to the New Testament? (61) What are some of the risks involved? (61)

25. What other aspects beyond the sociological does the cultural anthropology approach bring? (62) What are the contributions and the cautions about the use of this method? (63)

26. What are the contributions of psychological and psychoanalytical studies to biblical interpretation? (64) What are their limits? (65)

27. What are the main principles guiding the liberationist approach to hermeneutics? (This is stated very well and concisely on 67–68)

28. What are the values of this liberationist reading of the scriptures? (68) And the risks? (68)

29. What two criteria does feminist hermeneutics add to the historical-critical approach? (70)

30. What have been the benefits of feminist hermeneutics? (71) What cautions are in order about the methods it sometimes uses? (71–72)

31. How would you describe fundamentalism? (72–73)

32. What is the major critique of fundamentalism? (73) What is the problem with its interpretation of the Gospels? (74) What are the dangers of fundamentalism? (75)

33. Identify the positions of Bultmann, Gadamer, Ricoeur (77–78). What is meant by *distantiation?*

34. What contributions have modern hermeneutical theories made to exegesis? (79)

35. What critique does the document make of these theories? (80)

36. What is the literal sense of scripture? (Be precise.) (82)

37. Does a biblical text have only one literal sense? (82–83)

38. What is meant by the *dynamic aspect* of many texts? (83)

39. What is the proper relation of later "rereadings" of a text (giving a new meaning) to the meaning expressed by the human authors in their texts? (84)

40. How did the event of the resurrection of Jesus change the original meaning of certain Old Testament texts? (84)

41. What is a proper understanding of the *spiritual* sense? (85)

42. Discuss the relation between the spiritual and the literal sense. (85) What is the difference between an authentic spiritual sense and purely subjective interpretations? (86)

43. What is meant by the fuller sense? (87) Is it equivalent to the spiritual sense? (87)

44. What are the characteristics of Catholic exegesis, especially regarding "pre-understanding"? (88–89) And what are the dangers? (89)

45. What are some examples of "rereadings" in the Old Testament itself? (90–91)

46. What is meant by the expression, "Scripture reveals the meanings of events and...events reveal the meaning of Scripture"? (91–92) What are some chief examples? How did the event of the resurrection transform the previous understanding of scripture? (92–93)

47. What is meant by saying that even in the New Testament there is the absence of a sense of systematization and things are held in dynamic tension? (94)

48. The word *dialogue* is used on page 95 for the process of interpretation. What does this mean?

49. What factors entered into the process of the formation of the canon? (98)

50. What is the particular contribution of patristic exegesis? (99)

51. "All the members of the Church have a role in the interpretation of Scripture." (102) What role is assigned to bishops, what to the local church, what to individual Christians, what to

exegetes, what to the magisterium? (103–5) Note especially the section beginning on page 105: "Thus in the last resort…"

52. What are some of the principal guidelines for Catholic exegetes? (106–7)

53. What dynamic tension of values should be preserved in the teaching of scripture? (109)

54. What does exegesis contribute to systematic theology? (111–13)

55. What is to be said of the complex relationship between exegesis and moral theology? (113–14)

56. What are the respective roles of exegesis and speculative theology? (115–16)

57. Compare: "The text of the Bible has authority over the Christian Church at all times" (118) with the text of *Dei Verbum* given there. What difference do you notice?

58. *Actualization* means "contemporary application." What are the guidelines for authentic actualization? (117–21)

59. What is meant by *inculturation?* (121). Is it possible for the word of God to be both inserted in a particular culture and to transcend it? (122).

60. What two false solutions should be avoided? (123)

61. What are some of the highlights of this document concerning the relationship of biblical interpretation and the liturgy, *lectio divina*, pastoral ministry, ecumenism? (124–32)

62. What final appeal does the document make concerning diachronic and synchronic approaches? (132–34) About the role of exegesis as a *theological discipline?* (134)

Notes

2. The Bible Interprets the Bible

1. For further reading on the period from the Old Testament to Augustine and the canon, see Alan J. Hansen and Duane F. Watson, *A History of Biblical Interpretation,* vol. 1, *The Ancient Period* (Grand Rapids: Eerdmans, 2003).

2. The covenant with Abraham in Genesis 15 and 17 was unconditional, but it too pointed to the future in terms of land and descendants.

3. Sirach is especially interesting in that it quotes every book of the Bible except Daniel. It belongs to a period when the sacred authors were more interested in commenting on scripture than in creating the word of God afresh (as did the classical prophets). Ben Sira sometimes summarizes the Bible's teaching on a topic (e.g., 16:22–17:18 summarizes the theology of Genesis 1–2), and at other times uses a previous text as a point of departure for a moral lesson (e.g., 18:22 and Num 30:3). In so doing he anticipates some of the interpretative techniques the rabbis would use.

4. See Francis Martin, "Historical Criticism and New Testament Teaching on the Imitation of Christ," *Anthropotes* 6 (Dec. 1990), 265. On the more general question of New Testament exegesis, see R. N. Longenecker, *Biblical Exegesis in the Apostolic Period,* rev. ed. (Grand Rapids: Eerdmans, 1999).

5. *Mimesis* (Princeton: Princeton University Press, 1968), 73, 555. Quoted by Hans Frei, *The Eclipse of Biblical Narrative* (New Haven: Yale University Press, 1974), 28–29.

6. The theory of apparently random behaviors within a deterministic system, like the weather. See Ian Steward, *Does God Play Dice: The New Mathematics of Chaos* (Oxford: Oxford University Press, 1989).

7. That biblical events are open to future fulfillment explains why the church expects the gospel events—healings and miracles, for example—to be repeated in some fashion in the lives of individual Christians. It also explains why Christians take the images and stories and characters of the Apocalypse as prophetic of *our* times, often with bizarre and incredible applications. We may find those interpretations subjective and more the result of apocalyptic Rorschach than of sober scholarship, but the tendency is understandable in the light of the Bible's own tendency to apply the past texts and even events to the new and present situations. But it also grounds the necessity for some guidance in the ongoing application of texts, a role in which the church assumes the final responsibility.

8. Platonic contrasts appear in the letter to the Hebrews but still in a temporal, eschatological framework. The Gospel of John comes closest to Platonic thought when it tones down the strong eschatological thrust of the Synoptics for a more "vertical" presentation of Christ.

9. Doing good to enemies is partly foreshadowed by Proverbs 24:17 and 25:21 but as a preferred way of being avenged, whereas Matthew 5:41–48 affirms that God even blesses his enemies.

10. They were not completely arbitrary in this choice, for it is likely that Abijah was among the virgins in the king's harem awaiting to be called to the king's chamber.

11. Justin and Augustine argued for the superiority and the divine inspiration of the Septuagint over against the Hebrew. Although Pius XII in *Divino Afflante Spiritu* (1943) said that the original languages were the inspired ones, the New Testament uses the Septuagint, and the question of its inspiration and authority has been recently raised anew, e.g., by L. T. Johnson, *The Future of Catholic Biblical Scholarship: A Constructive Conversation* (Grand Rapids: Eerdmanns, 2002), 109–10.

12. Compare also the Hebrew with the LXX at Daniel 12:2 and Deuteronomy 33:2.

13. F. F. Bruce, *The Canon of Scripture* (Downers Grove, IL: InterVarsity Press, 1988), 76.

14. See Cecil Hargreaves, *A Translator's Freedom: Modern English Bibles and Their Language* (Biblical Seminar 22; Sheffield: JSOT, 1993).

15. *Biblical Exegesis in the Apostolic Period*, 2nd ed. (Grand Rapids: Eerdmans, 1999), 6–35. See also, W. R. Tate, *Biblical Interpretation: An Integrated Approach* (Peabody, MA: Hendrickson, 1997), 129–32.

16. *Mish Ber 1:3 on Deut 6:7.*

17. J. W. Doeve cites many examples in *Jewish Hermeneutics in the Synoptic Gospels and Acts* (Assen: van Gorcum, 1954), 66–75.

18. See also Romans 9:32–33, where Isaiah 8:14 and 28:16 are linked by the word *stone* and are interpreted as referring to the same reality. See further, Carol K. Stockhausen, *Moses' Veil and the Glory of the New Covenant: The Exegetical Substructure of II Cor. 3, 1–4:6, An Bib* 116 (Rome: Pontifical Biblical Institute, 1989), 26–27. On midrash in general see Jacob Neusner, *What Is Midrash?* (Philadelphia: Fortress, 1987).

19. I QpHab, VII, 1–5.

20. *On Abraham*, 28–30.

21. For an excellent comprehensive treatment of the history of Jewish interpretation, from biblical times to our day, see the essays in *The Jewish Study Bible* (New York: Oxford University Press, 2004), 1827–2194. And for the methods used in the Dead Sea Scrolls see Matthias Henze, ed., *Biblical Interpretation at Qumran* (Grand Rapids: Eerdmans, 2004).

22. Jacques Jomier, *The Bible and the Qur'an* (Fort Collins, CO: Ignatius Press; 2000; first published in 1964).

3. The Wealth of the Word

1. For a general treatment of the patristic period, see Manlio Simonetti, *Biblical Interpretation in the Early Church* (Edinburgh: T&T Clark, 1994); P. R. Ackroyd and C. F. Evans, *The Cambridge History of the Bible, vol. 1, From the Beginnings to Jerome* (Cambridge, UK: Cambridge University Press, 1963); R. M. Grant and D. Tracy, *A Short History of the Interpretation of the Bible,*

2nd ed. (Philadelphia: Fortress, 1989); J. W. Rogerson and W. G. Jeanrond, "Interpretation, History of," *ABD* iii. 424–43; R. L. Wilken, *The Spirit of Early Christian Thought: Seeking the Face of God* (New Haven: Yale University Press, 2003).

2. See the recent discussion by Geoffrey Mark Hahneman, *The Muratorian Fragment and the Development of the Canon* (Oxford Theological Monographs; Oxford: Clarendon, 1992), who follows A. C. Sundberg in the later dating. But the difficulties with the later date are just as serious, if not more so, as the objections raised against the earlier dating. See the review of Hahneman's work in *Catholic Biblical Quarterly* (hereafter *CBQ*) 56 (1994), 594–95.

3. *Church History* 3:25.

4. Text given in *Origins* 23 (Jan. 20, 1994), 541–55.

5. *Stromateis* (hereafter *Strom.*) 1.179 (3).

6. For a discussion of the issue see Henri De Lubac, *Medieval Exegesis I*, tr. Mark Sebanc (Grand Rapids: Eerdmans, 1998), 117–23.

7. *Strom.* II, 18, 94 (4). *Clement of Alexandria Stromateis Books One to Three; The Fathers of the Church: A New Translation*, tr. John Ferguson (Washington, DC: Catholic University of America Press, 1991), 85.

8. *Strom.* 1.15 (1).

9. Ibid. 6.7, 15.

10. *Strom.* III, chap. 7 end and chap. 15.

11. *Strom.* 6, 71–79. In Stoicism *apatheia* meant spiritual peace and well-being due to freedom from all passions. Although the fathers got the term *apatheia* from Stoic philosophy, they meant by it something distinctly Christian. It was not a state of unfeeling but a lack of compulsive thinking, a freedom from emotional complexes deriving from sinful disorders in the personality.

12. *Strom.* 7.57 (4).

13. See Ferguson, *Clement of Alexandria Stromateis*, 17.

14. Ibid.

15. *De Principiis,* IV, 19.

16. *Peri Archon* IV, iii, n. 3 (329, 331). De Lubac, *Exegesis* II, 391.

17. *Epistle of Barnabas,* 10, 9.

18. *Church History* 6, c. 3, nn. 10 and 12. De Lubac, *Exegesis* II, 264.

19. See *On Matthew,* Book 15, 3.

20. *Commentary on John* X, 172; *Commentary on Matthew* XIV, 11; XV, 30. Other references in Henri Clouzel, *Origen: The Life and Thought of the First Great Theologian* (San Francisco: Harper and Row, 1989), 73. Jerome would say the same: "We cannot understand Scripture without the help of the Holy Spirit who inspired it" (Epistle 120, q. 10, cited by De Lubac, *Exegesis* I, 362). For further understanding of Origen and his methods, see J. Danielou, *Origen* (New York: Sheed & Ward, 1955).

21. *De Principiis,* I, Praef. * (GCS, V, 14; *SC,* 252, 84–86), cited by I. de la Potterie, "Interpretation of Holy Scripture in the Spirit in Which It Was Written (*Dei Verbum* 12c), in *Vatican II Assessment and Perspectives* I, ed. René Latourelle (Mahwah, NJ: Paulist, 1988), 223.

22. *In Exod. hom.,* 4,5 (GCS, VI, 176–77); *SC* 16, 124–25); de la Potterie, "Interpretation," 225.

23. *Commentary on John,* I, 23.

24. M. Harl, *Origène: Philocalie 1–20: Sur les Ecritures, SC* 302 (Paris, 1983), 153; de la Potterie, "Interpretation," 227.

25. *In Cant.* I (PG XIII 86B).

26. This accounts for much misled modern reproach to Origen for despising the literal, historical sense. What moderns consider the literal sense of the parable of the prodigal son, for example, that is, Jesus' defense of his outreach to the marginalized and ultimately to the gentiles, Origen would consider the spiritual sense. See Crouzel, *Origen,* 62.

27. Crouzel, *Origen,* 63.

28. *On Genesis,* Homily V, tr. R. E. Hine, *Origen: Homilies on Genesis and Exodus* (Washington, DC: Catholic University of America Press, 1982), 120.

29. Origen's interpretation of this story shows the influence of Philo, whom Origen admired [*Commentary on Matthew* 15:3]. According to Philo, Lot's daughters were Counsel and Consent making the mind drunk with folly and producing illegitimate offspring. Philo, *On Genesis,* Homily IV, tr. Hine, 56.

30. *On Genesis,* Homily VI, tr. Hine, 121–22.

31. *On Genesis*, V, 120.

32. Tertullian, Origen, Hilary, Gregory the Great, and Augustine are only the most outstanding of the many witnesses who claim the forerunner and sanction of their allegorizing to be Saint Paul.

33. See *Commentary on John*, I, 39–40, and *De Principiis*, I, Praef.

34. See Ben F. Meyer, *Reality and Illusion in New Testament Scholarship* (Collegeville, MN: Liturgical Press, 1995), 180.

35. See Frances M. Young, *Biblical Exegesis and the Formation of Christian Culture* (Peabody, MA: Hendrickson, 1997), 182.

36. Ibid., 175

37. See J. N. D. Kelly, *Early Christian Doctrines*, 2nd ed. (New York: Harper & Row, 1960), 52–79.

38. *De poenit. hom.* 6,4.

39. *Praef. in Pss.*, ll. 146–62; CCG 6, pp. 7–8 (Leuven, Netherlands: Leuven University Press, 1980).

40. Suggested by Robert C. Hill in his introduction to *Saint John Chrysostom: Homilies on Genesis 1–17* (Washington, DC: Catholic University of America Press, 1986), 17–18.

41. *Divino Afflante Spiritu* AAS 35 (1943) 316; *Dei Verbum*, 13.

42. *Homily 2 on Genesis*; Hill, *Chrysostom*, 31; *Dei Verbum*, 11.

43. *Homily 44 on Genesis*.

44. *Homily 45 on Genesis*. The Elohist source exculpates Abraham on the basis of the fact that Sarah was indeed his half-sister, Genesis 20:12.

45. For a discussion of contemporary Orthodox theologians' understanding of *theoria*, see Grant R. Osborne, "The Many and the One: The Interface between Orthodox and Evangelical Protestant Hermeneutics," at *http://www.myriobiblos.gr/texts/english/osborne.html*.

46. See Margaret M. Mitchell, *The Heavenly Trumpet: John Chrysostom and the Art of Pauline Interpretation* (Louisville: John Knox Press, 2002).

47. *P.G.* 61:34. In the precritical phase of the development of theology, the science of God and the experience of God (theology and mysticism) were considered inseparable. For a survey of the patristic understanding of theology as an illumination of the intellect by faith energized by love, see Francis Martin, *The Feminist Question* (Grand Rapids: Eerdmans, 1994), 7–37.

48. *In Gal.,* 5, 19–21; *PL* 26, 445 A–B; de la Potterie, "Interpretation," 229.

49. *In Mc.,* 9, 1–7 (*CCL,* 78, 480, 87ff.); de la Potterie, "Interpretation," 229.

50. *In Gal.,* 4, 24 PL 26, 417A; de la Potterie, "Interpretation," 229.

51. *De Doctrina Christiana* (hereafter *De Doct. Chr.*), I, xxxvi, 40. Translations used here are from D. W. Robertson, Saint Augustine, *On Christian Doctrine* (New York: Liberal Arts Press, 1958).

52. *De Doct. Chr.* I, xxvi, 41.

53. Ibid.

54. Ibid., xxxvii, 41, and xxxix, 43. Augustine is characterized as Platonic here, but the text reflects 1 Corinthians 13, where the three virtues, especially charity, are said to be the end of knowledge and prophecy.

55. Ibid., xl, 44.

56. *De Doct. Chr.* II, xli, 62.

57. *De Doct. Chr.* III, xvii, 25; xxxiv, 49.

58. *De Doct. Chr.* II, xi, 16; xii, 17, 18; xvi, 24, 25; xviii, 28; xxx, 66; xl, 75.

59. *De Doct. Chr.* III, 1.

60. *De Doct. Chr.* II, vi, 7.

61. *De Doct. Chr.* III, ii, 2.

62. *De Doct. Chr.* II, vi, 8.

63. Ibid., viii, 13.

64. Ibid., viii, 12.

65. *On Genesis,* I, c. i, n. 1 (*PL* xxxiv, 247). My translation.

66. *De Doct. Chr.* III, x, 14.

67. Ibid., x, 15.

68. Ibid., xxii, 32.

69. *De Doct. Chr.* II, vi, 7.

70. *De Doct. Chr.* III, xii, 20.
71. Ibid., xxii, 32.

4. Climbing the Tower

1. For most of the material in this chapter I am indebted to the exhaustive four-volume work of Henri De Lubac, *Exégèse Médiévale* (Paris: Aubier, 1959), the first two volumes now having appeared in English as *Medieval Exegesis,* tr. Mark Sebanc (Grand Rapids: Eerdmans, 1998). In cases where the English translation was available, I cite simply as De Lubac; when quoting from the untranslated volumes, I indicate the French title, *Exégèse Médiévale.* I am also indebted to Beryl Smalley, *The Study of the Bible in the Middle Ages* (Notre Dame, IN: Notre Dame University Press, 1964). The latter is a general survey, the former focuses on the four senses developed in this chapter.

2. *Brevil, prol.,* Q., V, 201. De Lubac I, 27.
3. *In Boet. de Tr.,* q. 5, a. 4. De Lubac I, 27.
4. *Ep.* 64,m c. xxi (III, 135). De Lubac I, 75.
5. See the references in De Lubac I, 79–80.
6. *"In eo quod in Scripturis intelligis, caritas patet; in eo quod non intelligis, caritas latet."* Eugippius, *S. de laude caritatis, Thes.,* c. ccclii; *PL* LXII 1086AB. This and further references in De Lubac II, 141, n. 87.
7. *Tract. in Ioan.,* 8, 13 (*PL* 35, 1458, 1460).
8. *In Mc.* 9:1–70; *In Mt* II,13–35; *CCL* 77, 111, 953ff.
9. De Lubac II, 70–71.
10. *"Opera loquuntur...Facta, si intelligas, verba sunt,"* Augustine, *Serm.* 95, n. 3 (*PL* xxxviii, 582). De Lubac II, 86.
11. Augustine *Serm.* 2, n. 7 (*PL* xxxviii, 30–31). De Lubac II, 86.
12. *Coll.* 14, n. 8 (Pichery, *SC* 54, 290). De Lubac II, 87.
13. Saint Hilary, *Tr. myst.,* I, n. 1 (SC 19, 72). *Instr. psalm.* n. 5 (6). De Lubac II, 90.
14. Rupert, *PL* CLXX, 238A; Bede, *In Tob.,* XCI, 923 CD. De Lubac II, 97.

15. *In Marc.*, ii, 4 (xxi, 385). De Lubac, *Exégèse Médiévale* IV, 306.

16. Remigius of Auxerre, *In Gen.*, c. xliv (*PL* cxxxi, 120CD). De Lubac II, 224.

17. My translation. See De Lubac II, 101.

18. *In Cant.* III (202). *In Jer.* 18, n. 9. (*PG* XIII, 482AB).

19. *In Cant.* I (108). De Lubac II, 159.

20. De Lubac II, 138, summarizing a number of medieval authors.

21. Ambrose, *Ep.* 49, n. 3 (*PL* XVI, 1154 B). De Lubac II, 141.

22. Hans W. Frei, *The Eclipse of Biblical Narrative* (New Haven: Yale University Press, 1974), 153. "Figural interpretation" *(figura)* is a more Western term for typical interpretation *(typos),* which speaks of "type" (that which points forward) and "antitype" (that to which it points).

23. Bernard, *In Cant.*, s. 3, n.1; *PL* CLXXXIII, 794A; *De convers.*, c. iii, n. 4 *PL* CLXXXII, 836C. De Lubac II, 142.

24. God. d'Admont, *H. dom.* 24 (*PL* CLXXIV, 161A. De Lubac II, 142.

25. Cited by De Lubac II, 365, n. 100.

26. Bonaventure in particular favors the mystical understanding of the anagogical sense—that is, by contemplation one possesses the heavenly reality already now. *De reductione artium ad theologiam,* 5. De Lubac, *Exégèse Médiévale* IV, 267.

27. *In Gal.*, c. v, lect. 7. De Lubac, *Exégèse Médiévale* IV, 275.

28. *De annunt.*, s. 4 (Q., 9, 671). De Lubac II, 198. Of course today exegetes would not consider the text referring to the Virgin Mary in the literal sense.

29. *Collationes* XIV, c. 8 (*CSEL* 13/2 404f.).

30. References in De Lubac, *Exégèse Médiévale* IV, 266.

31. Atto of Vercelli (tenth century) *Exp. ep. S. Pauli (PL* cxxxiv *In I Cor.,* 367C, 372D; *In Gal.,* 531 A). De Lubac II, 223. Although he does not allegorize the teaching of Paul himself, he does say that Paul sets the example for allegorizing the Old Testament.

32. Rupert, *In Ap.*, VII, c. xii; *PL* CLXXIX, 1061 B; quoted by De Lubac I, 26.

33. Bede, *In Ex.* c. iii (*PL*, XCI, 294 D); quoted in De Lubac I, 27.

34. Aponius, *In Cant.*, III (52); William of St.-Thierry., *In Cant.* c. xxxviii; De Lubac I, 27.

35. *Coll.* 14, c. xi (Pichery, SC, 54, 197). De Lubac II, 204.

36. *In Ezek.* I, h. 7 (PL LXXVI, 844–48). De Lubac II, 204.

37. *Summa theol.*, tr. intr. q. 1, a 4, ad 2m. Cf. De Lubac, *Exégèse Médiévale* IV, 291.

38. *Rationale div. offic.*, proem. (Lyon 1672, 2); De Lubac *Exégèse Médiévale* IV, 307.

39. *Quaestiones in Heptateuchum*, ii, 90. *PL* 34, 629. Smalley, *Bible in Middle Ages*, 303.

40. *Summa Theol.* Ia–IIae, q. 102, a. 6 ad 4.

41. For references, see De Lubac, *Exégèse Médiévale* IV, 419. Erasmus would say the same. Cf. De Lubac, *Exégèse Médiévale* IV, 450.

42. *In Librum Iob Expositio* (Rome, 1562), 5. See Smalley, *Bible in Middle Ages*, 301.

43. *Quodl.* 7, q. 6, a. 14, ad 4m. De Lubac, *Exégèse Médiévale* IV, 276, n. 5.

44. Ibid. Cf. also *In Sent.*, prol., q. 1, a. 5.

45. *In 2 Sent.*, d. 12, q. 1, a. 2, ad 7m. De Lubac, *Exégèse Médiévale* IV, 276.

46. *Summa Theol.* I, q. 1, a. 10.

47. Ibid.; *De Potentia*, q. 4, a. 1. DeLubac, *Exégèse Médiévale* IV, 276. Hugh of St. Victor had said the same, namely that the word in its literal sense signifies a reality, which in turn signifies another reality (the allegorical sense). See the references in James Samuel Preus, *From Shadow to Promise: Old Testament Interpretation from Augustine to the Young Luther* (Cambridge, MA: Harvard University Press, 1969), 29–30.

48. *Summa Theol.* I, q. 1, a. 10. Scholars dispute whether Thomas fully agreed with Augustine that there is only one literal sense. One of the confusing texts is the following: "Since the literal sense is that which the author intends, and the author of sacred Scripture is God himself, who embraces everything at once with his

intellect, it is not improper, as Augustine says in book twelve of the *Confessions*, to say that even in the literal sense the same statement may have several meanings." (*De Potentia*, q. 4 a. 1. DeLubac 276.) But both in Augustine and Thomas it would seem that if we are speaking of the intention of the author who is God, then multiple meanings are possible, though these might not be seen by the human author, even when identifying an earlier type of a present fulfillment. For further discussion see Smalley, *Bible in Middle Ages*, 300, n. 3.

49. The *full* understanding of the literal sense is really available only to those in contact with the reality of which the text speaks, which assumes a stance of faith.

50. Erasmus will say the same: that while the literal sense is to be used for proofs, the allegorical is very helpful "to stir up the languishing, to console the dejected, to strengthen the vacillating...." Cf. references in De Lubac, *Exégèse Médiévale* IV, 452.

51. *Summa Theol.*, I, q. 1, a. 10.

52. See De Lubac, *Exégèse Médiévale* IV, 311.

53. *City of God*, Book 20, chap. 8 (*PL* xli, 670).

54. See DeLubac, *Exégèse Médiévale* IV, 364–67.

55. *Summa Theol.* Ia–IIae, q. 106, a. 4.

56. See Eric Voegelin, *The New Science of Politics* (Chicago: University of Chicago Press, 1952), 110–21, esp. 110–13) and *From Enlightenment to Revolution*, ed. John H. Hallowell (Durham, NC: Duke University Press, 1975), 3–13. Thanks to Dr. Glen Hughes for these references.

57. Quoted in De Lubac, *Exégèse Médiévale* IV, 389.

58. Francis Martin, *The Feminist Question* (Grand Rapids: Eerdmanns, 1994), 44–54.

59. See Henning Graf Reventlow, *The Authority of the Bible and the Rise of the Modern World* (Philadelphia: Fortress, 1985), 39–48.

60. *Opera Omnia*, 5, pp. 77–78.

61. For example, on the basis of the manuscript evidence available to him, in his first edition of the Greek New Testament in 1516 he eliminated the so-called Johannine comma of 1 John 5:7: "For there are three that bear witness in heaven, the Father, the Word, and the Holy Spirit; and these three are one." His judgment is followed today by the consensus of textual critics, but

Erasmus's omission brought such a storm of protest, and some additional textual evidence, that he restored it in later editions. *Adnot.* 1 John 5:5. Jaroslav Pelikan, *The Christian Tradition,* vol. 4 (Chicago: University of Chicago Press, 1984), 346.

62. *Opera Omnia,* 5, p. 13.

63. *Opera Omnia,* 3, pp. 1026, 1029, 1034.

64. *Opera Omnia,* 3, pp. 1029, 1034–35.

65. *Devotio moderna:* a school and trend of spirituality that originated in the Netherlands at the end of the fourteenth century and flourished in the fifteenth. It was characterized, among other things, by a distaste for speculation, a prayerful focus on the humanity of Christ, asceticism and interiority, retirement from the world and devotional reading of scripture, with a personalism that had less appreciation of the church and the hierarchy. The best example is Thomas à Kempis's classic work, *The Imitation of Christ.*

66. The controlling factor is the saving power of Christ. See Samuel Berger, *La Bible au seizième siècle* (Paris, 1879), 78.

67. Cf. De Lubac IV, 427–53. See also Albert Rabil Jr., *Erasmus and the New Testament* (Lanham, MD: University Press of America, 1993; rpt. of 1972 ed.).

68. On the recovery of typology and analogy via the event of the establishment of the canon, see Richard Swinburne, *Revelation: From Metaphor to Analogy* (Oxford: Clarendon Press, 1992).

5. The Path of Independence

1. See James Samuel Preus, *From Shadow to Promise: Old Testament Interpretation from Augustine to the Young Luther* (Cambridge, MA: Harvard University Press, 1969); A. Skevington Wood, *Captive to the Word: Martin Luther: Doctor of Sacred Scripture* (Grand Rapids: Eerdmans, 1969).

2. Luther did, however, engage the pre-Chalcedonian fathers and at least to that extent consulted tradition. He was at first, after all, an Augustinian monk. He also believed that the Holy Spirit was "necessary to understand all of Scripture as well

as every part of it." Paul Althaus, *The Theology of Martin Luther*, tr. R. Schultz (Philadelphia: Fortress, 1966), 77–78.

3. M. Luther, "Assertio omnium articulorum," *Werke*, vol. 7 (Weimar: Böhlau, 1883–), 96ff. Quoted in Hans Frei, *The Eclipse of Biblical Narrative* (New Haven: Yale University Press, 1974), 19. See also Althaus, *Theology*, 72.

4. Althaus, *Theology*, 81.

5. Ibid., 83.

6. Ibid., 85.

7. Ibid., 96.

8. Ibid., 97. For further discussion of interpretation in the Reformation period, see Richard A. Muller and John L. Thompson, eds., *Biblical Interpretation in the Era of the Reformation: Essays Presented to David C. Steinmetz in Honor of His Sixtieth Birthday* (Grand Rapids: Eerdmans, 1966).

9. On Calvin's hermeneutical method, see Alexandre Ganoczy and Stefan Scheld, *Die Hermeneutik Calvins: Geistgeschichtliche Voraussetzungen und Grundzüge* (Wiesbaden: Franz Steiner Verlag, 1983).

10. See, for example, his preface to the *Commentary on the Psalms*.

11. See Frei, *Eclipse*, 36.

12. François Wendel, *Calvin: The Origins and Development of His Religious Thought*, tr. Philip Mairet (New York: Harper & Row, 1950), 158–59.

13. Frei, *Eclipse*, 38–39.

14. See ibid., 251–54, 330, n. 1.

15. For a survey from the Renaissance to the nineteenth century, see John Sandys-Wunsch, *What Have They Done to the Bible?* (Collegeville, MN: Liturgical Press, 2005).

16. *Works*, 91; cited by Frei, *Eclipse*, 43.

17. *Works*, 61, quoted by Frei, *Eclipse*, 4.

18. Frei, *Eclipse*, 50.

19. As cited by Francis Martin, *The Feminist Question* (Grand Rapids: Eerdmanns, 1994), 58.

20. See Francis Martin, "Historical Criticism and New Testament Teaching on the Imitation of Christ," *Anthropotes* 6

(Dec. 1990), 273. In this section I draw substantially from this study.

21. For a thorough study of the crisis over the authority of the Bible in England and the development of Deism and its impact of biblical interpretation, see Henning Graf Reventlow, *The Authority of the Bible and the Rise of the Modern World* (Philadelphia: Fortress, 1985).

22. Frei, *Eclipse*, 52–54.

23. Ibid., 84–85, n. 45.

24. Ibid., 76.

25. Martin, "Historical Criticism," 276.

26. See Frei, *Eclipse*, 7, 84–85.

27. See his *Critique of Pure Reason*, tr. Norman K. Smith (New York: St. Martin's Press, 1929), 257.

28. *Constitution on the Church in the Modern World (Gaudium et Spes)*, 36.

29. Frei, *Eclipse*, 56.

30. Ibid., 110.

31. Ibid., 64.

32. Ibid., 122.

33. Ibid., 152.

34. *Abhandlung von freier Untersuchung des Kanons.*

35. *Eichhorns Urgeschichte*, pt. 1 (1790), p. xv. Quoted in Frei, *Eclipse*, 159.

36. Frei, *Eclipse*, 174.

37. For this section see ibid., 233–44.

38. See ibid., 271.

39. Ibid., 278.

40. Ibid., 255–66.

41. See Robert M. Grant, *A Short History of the Interpretation of the Bible* (New York: Macmillan, 1963), 155.

42. See Frei, *Eclipse*, 278.

43. Ibid., 280.

44. Hegel's hermeneutical theory is briefly described by Frei, *Eclipse*, 318.

45. *What Is Christianity?*, tr. T. B. Saunders (New York: Harper & Row, 1957; rpt. of 1901 ed.), 13–14.

46. Ibid., 278.

6. The Bible and the Church

1. *Christ and Renan: A Commentary on Ernest Renan's "The Life of Jesus,"* tr. M. Ward (New York: Sheed & Ward, 1928).

2. *Souvenirs d'enfance et de jeunesse* (Paris: Nelson, 1938), 133. Quoted by Robert M. Grant, *A Short History of the Interpretation of the Bible* (New York: Macmillan, 1963), 166.

3. *The Gospel and the Church,* 2 ed. (New York: 1909), 13. Cited by Grant, *History,* 168.

4. Ibid., 219; Grant, *History,* 168–69.

5. Father Athanasius Miller, secretary to the Biblical Commission, in the *Benedictinische Monatschrift* (1955, 49ff.), wrote, "In so far as matters are treated in these decrees, concerned neither directly nor indirectly with the truths of faith or morals, the research worker can obviously continue his investigations with complete freedom and make use of his conclusions, although always and in everything without prejudice to the teaching authority of the Church. It is today very difficult to imagine the situation in which Catholic scholars, for example, found themselves at the turn of the century....Today, when...many problems appear in an entirely new light, it is proper to smile at the 'constraint' and 'narrowness' that ruled at that time." Father A. Kleinhans, undersecretary of the commission, wrote in almost the same words in the *Antonianum* (1955, 64ff.). Father E. Vogt, rector of the Pontifical Biblical Institute, followed up these remarks in an article in *Biblica* (195, 565), applying the principle to the question of the identity of the biblical authors: "Among [the questions disputed at the time] especially are those which are concerned with literary criticism, that is, with authenticity or the identity of inspired authors. They were indeed made in defense of the faith, but today these questions have 'taken on a new aspect' since it is now more clearly seen that the inspiration of any biblical text is entirely safeguarded, whoever its human author may have been." See Jean Levie, *The Bible, Word of God in Words of Men* (New York: P. J. Kenedy, 1961), 187–89.

6. There was a parallel development in Protestant biblical studies following the work of Karl Barth.

7. Letter to Cardinal Suhard, Denzinger, 2302.

7. Hermeneutical Theory

1. Schleiermacher reacts against Friedrich A. Wolf, who held that each discipline has its own specifically different hermeneutics. Instead, Schleiermacher proposes a hermeneutics of understanding applicable to all hermeneutical fields. Thus he is credited with initiating a theory of general hermeneutics, that is, the hermeneutics of understanding. While it is true that he moved the discussion away from the world outside the text, as understood by earlier authors, he eventually became so psychologized by his interest in the processes of the author that he ended up outside the text as well.

2. *Hermeneutik,* ed. Heinz Kimmerle (Heidelberg: Winter Universitätsverlag, 1959 [Abh. Heidelberger Akad. Wissenschaften, Phil-hist. Kl., 1959]), 87. Quoted by Hans W. Frei, *The Eclipse of Biblical Narrative* (New Haven: Yale University Press, 1974), 294. Later interpreters will affirm this insight by speaking of the "effective history" of the text, which is available to the later interpreter, and either confirms the truth of the text or refutes its claims.

3. *Über die Religion* (1799); quoted by Robert M. Grant, *A Short History of the Interpretation of the Bible* (New York: Macmillan, 1963), 155.

4. "A Response to a Paper of Sandra Schneiders," *Proceedings of the Forty-Seventh Annual Meeting,* ed. Paul Crowley, Catholic Theological Society of America, 1992, 61–68. Schneiders's model of symbolic revelation is helpful in that it shows how the object revealed goes beyond the limits of specific propositions and therefore is always open to new understandings (and, as necessary, new propositions). The caution, however is that this model could be interpreted as authorizing an indifference regarding formulations, whether propositions or metaphors, so that one proposition or metaphor is as good as another, even if contradictory. In that case we would be back to nominalism. See the discussion by Francis Martin, *The Feminist Question* (Grand Rapids: Eerdmanns, 1994), 209–10.

5. See Richard E. Palmer, *Hermeneutics: Interpretation Theory in Schleiermacher, Dilthey, Heidegger, and Gadamer* (Evanston: Northwestern University Press, 1969), 98–123.

6. Quoted by ibid., 115.

7. Quoted by ibid., 116.

8. Palmer, *Hermeneutics*, 117.

9. There is some tension between the early and the later Heidegger on the relation of *Being* to *being-there*. On the one hand, Being is inextricably linked with being-there, that is, human being. On the other, Heidegger seems to indicate Being and being-there are independent, yet he won't let go of the principle that *Sein* is not available without *Dasein*.

10. Palmer, *Hermeneutics*, 131.

11. I owe the graphic and the sausage grinder image to my colleague, Dr. James Sauer.

12. *Introduction to Metaphysics*, 143; quoted by Palmer, *Hermeneutics*, 151.

13. See Palmer, *Hermeneutics*, 155.

14. See Bernadette O'Connor, *Martin Heidegger, Saint Thomas Aquinas, and the Forgottenness of Being.* Unpublished doctoral thesis at Duquesne University, 1982 (available from UMI Microfilms); Mario Enrique Sacchi, *The Apocalypse of Being: The Esoteric Gnosis of Martin Heidegger* (South Bend, IN: St. Augustine's Press, 2000).

15. *Introduction to Metaphysics*, 162; Palmer, *Hermeneutics*, 157.

16. *Being and Time* (Oxford: Blackwell, 1962), 21–24.

17. *Truth and Method* (New York: Seabury, 1975), xix.

18. Ibid.

19. A giant step has recently been undertaken in the publication of the series, *The Ancient Christian Commentary on Scripture* (Downers Grove, IL: InterVarsity Press, 2001–), which is a line-by-line commentary compiled from the early church fathers. Thomas Aquinas had done something similar in his *Catena Aurea,* but with the technology now available, this work promises to immeasurably enhance our understanding of the "effective history" of the texts.

20. See David W. Kling, *The Bible in History: How the Texts Have Shaped the Times* (New York: Oxford University Press, 2004).

21. Palmer, *Hermeneutics*, 165.

22. Sandra Schneiders offers the example of an investigator using a ruler as the method of research. If this is the only instrument I use, I will know reality only from the viewpoint of its physical extension, and I may even come to the conclusion that that's all there is to reality. *The Revelatory Text* (San Francisco: HarperSanFrancisco, 1991), 23–24.

23. Gadamer, *Truth and Method*, 258. For the whole discussion on prejudices as conditions of understanding, see 245–74.

24. Palmer, *Hermeneutics*, 217.

25. See J. Habermas, *Theory and Practice* (Boston: Beacon Press, 1973), esp. 16–19.

26. *Validity in Interpretation* (New Haven: Yale University Press, 1967).

27. *Interpretation Theory* (Fort Worth: Texas Christian University Press), 30.

28. Though he does not mention Ricoeur in his 1967 book, *Validity in Interpretation,* Hirsch obviously would disagree with him, as he does with Gadamer on this issue. One might be permitted to wonder whether the New Testament authors would have written anything if they knew there would be no control on the interpretations readers would give their works.

29. Ibid., 55.

30. Ibid., 79.

31. Structural analysis, as we will see later on, analyzes the text and its components with the intention of discovering beyond the surface structure, the deep structures underlying the text, the reservoir of formal possibilities that belong to literature as such.

32. Ricoeur, *Interpretation Theory,* 87–88.

33. Ibid., 92.

34. Ibid., 94.

8. Bernard Lonergan and Critical Realist Hermeneutics

1. (New York: Herder & Herder, 1972), 153–73. For this chapter see especially James B. Sauer, *Commentary on Lonergan's Method in Theology* (Ottawa: LWS, 2002); Sean E. McEvenue and Ben F. Meyer, *Lonergan's Hermeneutics: Its Development and Application* (Washington, DC: Catholic University of America Press, 1989); Sean McEvenue, *Interpretation and Bible: Essays on Truth in Literature* (Collegeville, MN: Liturgical Press, 1994); and Ben F. Meyer, *Reality and Illusion in New Testament Scholarship: A Primer in Critical Realist Hermeneutics* (Collegeville, MN: Liturgical Press, 1994). I am also indebted to my colleague, James Sauer, Professor of Philosophy at St. Mary's University and specialist in Lonergan, for his review of this chapter.

2. Meyer, *Reality and Illusion*, 8–21.

3. On the necessity of evidence, see E. D. Hirsch Jr., *Validity in Interpretation* (New Haven: Yale University Press, 1967), vii–xii, 180.

4. Meyer, *Reality and Illusion*, 30–39.

5. Ibid., 92.

6. Meyer has an entire chapter dedicated to the dispositions necessary to have "Access to the Understanding of the New Testament on Its Own Terms," ibid., 151–73.

7. Here Lonergan intersects with the tradition going back to Origen, Cassian, and Gregory the Great, that the more perfect the reader the better will he understand the text, since there will be a greater coherence between the revealing word (which calls to holiness) and the subject receiving it. See the section on Origen in chapter 3 and the paragraph on "Meaning and Personal Transformation" in chapter 4.

9. The World of the Text

1. On the various methods of biblical interpretation, see John H. Hayes, *Methods of Biblical Interpretation* (Nashville:

Abingdon, 2004), excerpted from the same author's *Dictionary of Biblical Interpretation* (Nashville: Abingdon, 1999).

2. See David Alan Black, *Rethinking New Testament Textual Criticism,* rev. ed. (Peabody, MA: Hendrickson, 2002); J. Harold Greenlee, *Introduction to New Testament Textual Criticism* (Peabody, MA: Hendrickson, 1995); Bruce M. Metzger and Bart D. Ehrman, *The Text of the New Testament: Its Transmission, Corruption, and Restoration,* 4th ed. (New York: Oxford University Press, 2005).

3. (New York: United Bible Societies, 1971).

4. See Mark Allan Powell, *What Is Narrative Criticism?* (Minneapolis: Fortress, 1990) with bibliographical notes. Also insights of John R. Donahue, in "Windows and Mirrors: The Setting of Mark's Gospel," *Catholic Biblical Quarterly* (hereafter *CBQ*) 57 (1995), 4–8.

5. David Rhoads, Joanna Dewey, and Donald M. Michie (Philadelphia: Fortress, 1982).

6. The mirror metaphor is not the invention of modern hermeneutical theorists. It is at least as old as Athanasius (d. 373), whose words were quoted by Pope Pius X in his 1911 encyclical *Divino Afflatu:* "The psalms seem to me like a mirror, in which the person using them can see himself and the stirrings of his own heart; he can recite them against the background of his own emotions" *AAS* 3, 633–35.

7. For a list and some examples of narrative patterns see Powell, *Narrative Criticism,* 32–34.

8. Meier-Sternberg in his monumental work, *The Poetics of Biblical Narrative* (Bloomington: Indiana University Press, 1987), 14–23, clarifies the distinctions between source-oriented and discourse-oriented inquiry and the limitations of each, and urges seeing the approaches as complementary.

9. See Werner H. Kelber, *The Oral and Written Gospel: The Hermeneutics of Speaking and Writing in the Synoptic Tradition, Mark, Paul, and Q* (Philadelphia: Fortress, 1983); George A. Kennedy, *New Testament Interpretation through Rhetorical Criticism* (Chapel Hill: University of North Carolina Press, 1984); William Kurz, "Narrative Approaches to Luke-Acts," *Biblica* 68 (1987), 197–200; Burton Mack, *Rhetoric and the New Testament*

(Minneapolis: Fortress, 1990); Burton L. Mack and Vernon K. Robbins, *Patterns of Persuasion in the Gospels* (Sonoma, CA: Polebridge Press, 1989); Stephen D. Moore, *Literary Criticism and the Gospels: The Theoretical Challenge* (New Haven: Yale University Press, 1989), 84–88; Vernon K. Robbins, *Jesus the Teacher: A Socio-Rhetorical Interpretation of Mark* (Philadelphia: Fortress, 1984); Phyllis Trible, *Rhetorical Criticism: Context, Method, and the Book of Jonah* (GBS, OT Series; Minneapolis: Fortress, 1994); Duane F. Watson and Alan J. Hauser, *Rhetorical Criticism of the Bible: A Comprehensive Bibliography with Notes on History and Method* (Biblical Interpretation Series 4; New York: Brill, 1994) and review in *CBQ* 57 (1995), 615–16; Wilhelm Wuellner, "Where Is Rhetorical Criticism Taking Us?" *CBQ* 49 (1957) 448–63.

10. Wuellner, "Rhetorical Criticism," 461.

11. Kennedy, *New Testament Interpretation.*

12. See "Rhetorical Criticism," 458–60.

13. (Philadelphia: Fortress, 1973).

14. See Ferdinand de Saussure, *Course in General Linguistics* (New York: McGraw-Hill, 1966).

15. Dan O. Via, editor's foreword in Patté, *Structural Exegesis for New Testament Critics* (Minneapolis: Fortress, 1990), viii.

16. Jean Calloud, *Structural Analysis of Narrative* (Philadelphia: Fortress, 1976), 9–10.

17. Patté, *Structural Exegesis,* 9–72.

18. Walter J. Ong, *Orality and Literacy: The Technologizing of the Word* (New York: Methuen, 1982; Routledge rpt., 1991), 162. For a further critique of structuralism see Terry Eagleton, *Literary Theory: An Introduction* (Minneapolis: University of Minnesota Press, 1983), 106–26; Wallace Martin, *Recent Theories of Narrative* (Ithaca: Cornell University Press, 1986), 102–6.

19. See Margaret Davies, "Poststructural Analysis," *ABD* V, 424–26; Stephen D. Moore, *Poststructuralism in the New Testament: Derrida and Foucault at the Foot of the Cross* (Philadelphia: Fortress, 1994) and review in *CBQ* 57 (1995) 407–8; A. K. M. Adam, *What Is Postmodern Biblical Criticism?* (Minneapolis: Fortress, 1995); Vincent B. Leitch, *Deconstructive Criticism: An Advanced Introduction* (New York: Columbia

University Press, 1983); Hugh J. Silverman and Don Ihde, eds., *Hermeneutics and Deconstruction* (Albany: State University of New York Press, 1985); D. Ingraffia, *Postmodern Theory and Biblical Theology* (New York: Cambridge University Press, 1995); D. Loy, ed., *Healing Deconstruction: Post-Modern Thought in Buddhism and Christianity* (Atlanta: Scholars Press, 1996).

20. Adam, *Post-Modern Biblical Criticism*, 27.

21. Leitch, *Deconstructive Criticism*, 254.

22. An example of a self-reversing contradiction: "I am absolutely certain that nothing is absolutely certain."

23. Paul Ricoeur, *Interpretation Theory: Discourse and the Surplus of Meaning* (Fort Worth: Texas Christian University Press, 1976), 6.

24. See Ong, *Orality*, 167–70; Ben F. Meyer, *Reality and Illusion in New Testament Scholarship: A Primer in Critical Realist Hermeneutics* (Collegeville, MN: Liturgical Press, 1994), 40–47.

25. For a scholarly critique of postmodernism and deconstruction, see Anthony C. Thiselton, *Interpreting God and the Postmodern Self: On Meaning, Manipulation and Promise* (Grand Rapids: Eerdmans, 1995).

26. See Stephen Moore's use of the method to interpret the Johannine story of the woman at the well, in *Poststructuralism and the New Testament*, 43–64.

27. (Amherst, NY: Prometheus Books, 2002), 192. See my review in *CBQ* 63 (2001), 160–61.

28. Traditional theology has distinguished language about God as *kataphatic*, referring to positive statements about God, what God *is* ("God is father," "God is all-knowing, all-powerful," and so on), and *apophatic*, referring to negative statements about God, what God is *not* ("God is immortal, unlimited, immense, immaterial").

10. The World behind the Text

1. See Joseph G. Prior, *The Historical Critical Method in Catholic Exegesis*, vol. 50 (Tesi Gregoriana, Serie Teologia, Rome: Gregorian University, 1999).

2. For a good overview, see Edgar V. McKnight, *What Is Form Criticism?* (Philadelphia: Fortress, 1969), rpt. 1997 by Wipf & Stock.

3. See J. Maxwell Miller, "Reading the Bible Historically: The Historian's Approach," in *To Each Its Own Meaning,* eds. Steven L. McKenzie and Stephen R. Haynes (Louisville: Westminster/John Knox, 1999), 17–34, with annotated bibliography.

4. Miller, "Reading the Bible," 18.

5. *From the Stone Age to Christianity* (Garden City, NY: Doubleday, 1957).

6. *A History of Israel* (Philadelphia: Westminster, 1981).

7. "Face to Face: Biblical Minimalists Meet Their Challengers," *Biblical Archeology Review* (hereafter *BAR*) 23 (1977), 26–42, 66.

8. Philip Davies, "What Separates a Minimalist from a Maximalist? Not Much," and William G. Dever, "Save Us from Postmodern Malarkey," *BAR* 26 (2000), 24–35, 68–69.

9. *The Mythic Past: Biblical Archaeology and the Myth of Israel* (New York: Basic Books, 1999).

10. Ibid., 239.

11. Dever has expanded his arguments in *What Did the Biblical Writers Know and When Did They Know It?: What Archaeology Can Tell Us about the Reality of Ancient Israel* (Grand Rapids: Eerdmans, 2001). And see Robert D. Miller's review of Thompson in *Catholic Biblical Quarterly* (hereafter *CBQ*) 62 (2000), 534–36. See also, James K. Hoffmeier and Alan Millard, eds., *The Future of Biblical Archaeology* (Grand Rapids: Eerdmans, 2004).

12. For an excellent survey of the major recent historical critics, see Mark A. Powell, *Jesus as a Figure in History: How Modern Historians View the Man from Galilee* (Louisville: Westminster John Knox, 1998).

13. In his portion of the study, *The Future of Catholic Biblical Scholarship: A Constructive Conversation* (Grand Rapids: Eerdmanns, 2002), Luke T. Johnson attacks the historical critics for missing the point of the sacred writings, for which the proper context for interpretation is not the academy but the

church. But at one point he seems to dismiss concern for the Bible's historical roots in a way that comes close to Bultmann's (121–23, 133–34).

14. For example, if Roman law permitted a woman to initiate divorce, a situation not foreseen by Jewish law, in which only the man could do so, would Jesus' prohibition of divorce extend to women? (See Mark 10:12).

15. *Jesus and the Victory of God* (Minneapolis: Fortress, 1996); *The Original Jesus* (Grand Rapids: Eerdmans, 1996).

16. E. P. Sanders has been accused of going too far in the criterion of coherence, making Jesus indistinguishable from his Jewish environment.

17. *The Lost Gospel: The Book of Q and Christian Origins* (San Francisco: HarperSanFrancisco, 1993); *A Myth of Innocence: Mark and Christian Origins* (Philadelphia: Fortress, 1998); *Who Wrote the New Testament? The Making of the Christian Myth* (San Francisco: HarperSanFrancisco, 1995).

18. *Sociology and the Jewish Movement* (New York: Crossroad, 1989).

19. *Jesus the Jew: A Historian's Reading of the Gospels* (London: Collins, 1973); *The Religion of Jesus the Jew* (Minneapolis: Fortress, 1993).

20. *Jesus the Magician* (New York: Harper & Row, 1978).

21. *Jesus the Sage: The Pilgrimage of Wisdom* (Minneapolis: Fortress, 1994).

22. *Cynics and Christian Origins* (Edinburgh: T&T Clark, 1992).

23. *The Historical Jesus: The Life of a Mediterranean Jewish Peasant* (San Francisco: HarperSanFrancisco, 1991).

24. *Meeting Jesus Again for the First Time: The Historical Jesus and the Heart of Contemporary Faith* (San Francisco: HarperSanFrancisco, 1994).

25. *Jesus and Judaism* (Philadelphia: Fortress, 1985); *The Historical Figure of Jesus* (London: Penguin, 1993).

26. *Jesus and the Language of the Kingdom: Symbol and Metaphor in New Testament Interpretation* (Philadelphia: Fortress, 1976).

27. *A Marginal Jew,* 2 vols. (New York: Doubleday, 1991, 1994).

28. N. T. Wright, *Jesus and the Victory of God* (Minneapolis: Fortress, 1996), 172.

29. N. T. Wright, *The Resurrection of the Son of God* (Minneapolis: Fortress, 2002).

30. It is precisely the multiplication of such divergent historical reconstructions that leads Luke T. Johnson to question the whole modern historical-critical enterprise. "There are on offer today more visions of 'the historical Jesus' and of 'early Christianity' than are compatible with the perception of history as a scientific discipline." *Catholic Biblical Scholarship,* 14–15; see also 133.

31. See Philip Jenkins, *Hidden Gospels: How the Search for Jesus Lost Its Way* (New York: Oxford University Press, 2002).

32. It may be even more surprising that there are scholars who profess to be Christian and yet deny the historicity of gospel narratives that witness to the foundational events of the faith. Such a one is Marcus Borg, who professes to be a Christian (his wife is an Episcopal priest) and yet denies that Jesus thought of himself as the Messiah (the title was given by the later church), that Jesus instituted the Eucharist, that there was a bodily resurrection or a virgin birth, or even that God intervenes in human affairs at all. These, he says, belong to "metaphorized history," the creation of the early church to symbolize the significance of the person and work of Jesus. See M. Borg and N. T. Wright, *The Meaning of Jesus* (San Francisco: HarperSanFrancisco, 1999), passim.

33. Those trapped in the Enlightenment's closed universe will also dismiss the stories of demonic possession and exorcisms as relics of a superstitious past, or as primitively understood states of insanity and the culturally limited ways of handling them, psychotherapy being the only professional way of dealing with such states today. However, renowned psychiatrist M. Scott Peck, of *The Road Less Traveled* (New York: Simon & Schuster, 1979) fame, from his experience of frustration with certain cases of obtuse resistance to truth and his observance of exorcisms, came to very different conclusions in his less well-known book, *People of the Lie* (New York: Simon & Schuster, 1983).

34. In Borg and Wright, *Meaning of Jesus,* 26–27.

35. *What Is Redaction Criticism?* (Philadelphia: Fortress, 1969), vi–vii.

36. See John H. Elliott, *What Is Social-Scientific Criticism?* (Guides to Biblical Scholarship, NT Series; Minneapolis: Fortress, 1993) and review in *CBQ* 57 (1995), 177–78. And John J. Pilch and Bruce J. Malina, *Biblical Social Values and Their Meaning: A Handbook* (Peabody, MA: Hendrickson, 1993). David G. Horrell, ed., *Social-Scientific Approaches to New Testament Interpretation* (Edinburgh: T&T Clark, 1999); Bruce Malina and Richard Rohrbaugh, *Social-Science Commentary on the Synoptic Gospels* (Minneapolis: Fortress, 1992) and *Social-Science Commentary on the Gospel of John* (Fortress, 1998); Bruce Malina, *The New Testament World: Insights from Cultural Anthropology*, 3rd ed. (Louisville: John Knox, 2001).

37. (Peabody, MA: Hendrickson, 1991).

38. A more recent example is Brian K. Blount, *Cultural Interpretation: Reorienting New Testament Criticism* (Minneapolis: Augsburg Fortress, 1995).

39. Erich Fromm, for example, in his popular *The Art of Loving* (New York: Harper, 1956) interprets the story of the fall in Genesis in a way that is more his psychological theory than exegesis. See also *Jung and the Interpretation of the Bible*, ed. David L. Miller (New York: Continuum, 1995), in which the authors do little more than redescribe psychological theory using biblical figures.

40. *The Interpretation of the Bible in the Church* (Boston: Pauline Books & Media, 1994), 79.

11. The World in Front of the Text

1. On reader-response criticism, see Terry Eagleton, *Literary Theory: An Introduction* (Minneapolis: University of Minnesota Press, 1983); R. M. Fowler, "Who Is 'the Reader' in Reader Response Criticism?" *Semeia* 31 (1985), 5–23; Elizabeth Freund, *The Return of the Reader: Reader-Response Criticism* (New York: Methuen, 1987); Roman Ingarden, *The Literary Work of Art: An Investigation of the Borderlines of Ontology, Logic, and Theory of*

Literature (Evanston: Northwestern University Press, 1973); Susan R. Suliman and Inge Crosman, eds., *The Reader in the Text: Essays on Audience and Interpretation* (Princeton: Princeton University Press, 1980); Jane P. Tompkins, ed., *Reader-Response Criticism* (Baltimore: Johns Hopkins University Press, 1980); Robert Fowler, *Let the Reader Understand: Reader-Response Criticism and the Gospel of Mark* (Minneapolis: Fortress, 1991; Stephen D. Moore, *Literary Criticism and the Gospels: The Theoretical Challenge* (New Haven: Yale University Press, 1989). Fernando F. Segovia and Mary Ann Tolbert, eds., *Reading from This Place*, vol. 2, *Social Location and Biblical Interpretation in Global Perspective* (Minneapolis: Augsburg Fortress, 1995).

2. Walter J. Ong, *Orality and Literacy: The Technologizing of the Word* (New York: Methuen, 1982; Routledge rpt., 1991), 176.

3. *Commentary on the Diatessaron*, 1, 18–19; SC 121, 52–53; second reading for office of readings, sixth Sunday in ordinary time.

4. Powell, *What Is Narrative Criticism?*, 16–18.

5. For a further study of this method, see Stanley E. Fish, "Interpreting the *Variorum*," in Tompkins, *Reader-Response*, 164–84.

6. Wolfgang Iser, *The Act of Reading: A Theory of Aesthetic Response* (Baltimore: John Hopkins University Press, 1978).

7. William H. Shepherd Jr., *The Narrative Function of the Holy Spirit as Character in Luke-Acts* (Atlanta: Scholars Press, 1994), 81. For examples of reader-response criticism applied to a gospel, see Robert M. Fowler, *Let the Reader Understand: Reader-Response Criticism and the Gospel of Mark* (Minneapolis: Fortress, 1991), and J. D. Kingsbury, "'The Reader' of Matthew's Gospel," *New Testament Studies* 34 (1988) 442–60.

8. On advocacy hermeneutics in favor of blacks, see Michael Joseph Brown, *Blackening of the Bible: The Aims of African American Biblical Scholarship* (Harrisburg, PA: Continuum, 2004).

9. The literature on feminist hermeneutics is immense. For an example of feminist hermeneutics, see the entire biblical commentary by Carol A. Newsom and Sharon H. Ringe, eds., *The*

Women's Bible Commentary (London: SPCK; Louisville: Westminster/John Knox, 1992) and review in *CBQ* 55 (1993), 600–602. And Elaine Mary Wainwright, *Towards a Feminist Critical Reading of the Gospel according to Matthew* (BZNW 60; Berlin/New York: de Gruyter, 1991), reviewed by Barbara Reid in *CBQ* 55 (1993), 620–22. The most comprehensive evaluation of Christian feminism and of feminist hermeneutics is found in Francis Martin, *The Feminist Question: Feminist Theology in the Light of Christian Tradition* (Grand Rapids: Eerdmans, 1994). See also A. C. Thistleton, *New Horizons in Hermeneutics. The Theory and Practice of Transforming Biblical Reading* (Grand Rapids: Zondervan, 1992), 450–51, 430–70.

10. A. C. Thiselton in his recent reprise of the hermeneutical questions criticizes the sociopragmatic systems of interpretation as reducing liberation to a power struggle where the oppressed fight with the oppressors' weapons. *New Horizons in Hermeneutics* (Grand Rapids: Zondervan, 1992).

11. There is a difference between affirming the infinite riches of the text, with the field of interpretations it sanctions, and the near agnosticism of some approaches that would sanction even contradictory interpretations, the pitfall of some postmoderns. See, for example, Brian K. Blount's assertion that "there is no single, final interpretation of a text." *Cultural Interpretation: Reorienting New Testament Criticism* (Minneapolis: Fortress, 1995), 183.

12. For example, in 1934, in the midst of the Depression, Minnesota passed a law that stayed mortgage foreclosures for a couple of years to try to keep homeowners in their homes, in literal violation of Article 1, "No state shall...pass any...law impairing the obligation of contracts." Those against the new law argued that it violated what the words meant to the framers in 1787, and besides if the price of housing fell dramatically the lender could lose a great deal of money. But the Court decided in favor of the law on rather vague grounds that the state had the power in view of the emergency created by the Depression.

13. Brown v. Allen, 344 U.S. 443, 540 (1953). For his assistance in formulating this section I am grateful to Michael Ariens, Professor of Constitutional Law at the St. Mary's University School of Law.

12. The World around the Text

1. See P. Ackroyd, "Original Text and Canonical Text," *Union Seminary Quarterly Review* 32 (1977) 166–73; J. Barton, *Reading the Old Testament: Method in Biblical Study* (Philadelphia: Fortress, 1984); W. Brueggemann, *The Creative Word: Canon as a Model for Biblical Education* (Philadelphia: Fortress, 1982); B. Childs, *The Book of Exodus: A Critical Theological Commentary* (Philadelphia: Fortress, 1974); *Introduction to the Old Testament as Scripture* (Philadelphia: Fortress, 1979); *The New Testament as Canon: An Introduction* (Philadelphia: Fortress, 1985); G. W. Coats and B. O. Long, eds., *Canon and Authority: Essays in Old Testament Religion and Theology* (Philadelphia: Fortress, 1977); H. Y. Gamble, "The Canon of the New Testament," in *The New Testament and Its Modern Interpreters,* ed. Eldon Jap Epp and George W. McCrae (Atlanta: Scholars Press, 1989); T. Hoffman, "Inspiration, Normativeness, Canonicity, and the Unique Sacred Character of the Bible," *Catholic Biblical Quarterly* (hereafter *CBQ*) 44 (1982) 447–69; T. Keegan, *Interpreting the Bible: A Popular Introduction to Biblical Hermeneutics* (Mahwah, NJ: Paulist Press, 1985), 131–44; E. Lemcio, "The Gospels and Canonical Criticism," *Biblical Theology Bulletin* 11 (1981), 114–22; Joseph Lienhard, *The Bible, the Church and Authority* (Collegeville, MN: Liturgical Press, 1995); Francis Martin, "The Biblical Canon and Church Life," in *Recovering the Sacred: Catholic Faith, Worship and Practice,* Proceedings of the Twelfth Convention of the Fellowship of Catholic Scholars, ed. Paul Williams (Pittston, PA: Northeast Books, 1990), 117–36; Bruce Metzger, *The Canon of the New Testament: Its Origin, Development and Significance* (Oxford: Clarendon Press, 1988 rpt.); J. A. Sanders, *Canon and Community* (Philadelphia: Fortress, 1984); "Canonical Context and Canonical Criticism," *Horizons in Biblical Theology* 2 (1980), 173–97; "Text and Canon: Concepts and Methods," *Journal of Biblical Literature* 98 (1979), 5–29; L. M. McDonald and J. A. Sanders, eds., *The Canon Debate* (Peabody, MA: Hendrickson, 2002).

2. See Grant R. Osborne, "The Many and the One: The Interface between Orthodox and Evangelical Protestant Hermeneutics," at http://www.myriobiblos.gr/texts/english/osborne.html.

3. See *Orality and Textuality in Early Christian Literature, Semeia* 65 (Atlanta: Scholars Press, 1995); William A. Graham, *Beyond the Written Word: Oral Aspects of Scripture in the History of Religion* (Cambridge, UK: Cambridge University Press, 1987, 2nd ed., 1993); Barbara A. Holdrege, *Veda and Torah: Transcending the Textuality of Scripture* (Albany: State University of New York Press, 1996); Susan Niditch, *Oral World and Written Word: Ancient Israelite Literature* (Louisville: Westminster/John Knox, 1996); Mary Carruthers, *The Book of Memory in Medieval Culture* (Cambridge, UK: Cambridge University Press, 1990).

4. Holdrege, *Veda and Torah,* 387.

5. See also Graham, *Written Word,* passim.

6. See John D. Harvey, *Listening to the Text: Oral Patterning in Paul's Letters* (Grand Rapids: Baker, 1998).

7. Walter J. Ong, *Orality and Literacy: The Technologizing of the Word* (New York: Routledge, 1982).

8. Ibid., 48.

9. Carruthers, *Book of Memory,* 74. Cicero died a half-century before Jesus was born; Quintillian, a Roman rhetorician, was a contemporary of the evangelists.

10. Allan Figueroa Deck has shown how Ong's description of oral culture applies to the Hispanic cultures of Latin America in *The Second Wave: Hispanic Ministry and the Evangelization of Cultures* (New York: Paulist Press, 1989), 43–44.

11. Ong, *Orality,* 55.

12. Ibid., 57–68.

13. *Memory and Manuscript: Oral Tradition and Written Transmission in Rabbinic Judaism and Early Christianity* (Copenhagen: Ejnar Munksgaard, 1964).

14. Orality persisted even after the invention of writing and printing. See the examples in Ong, *Orality,* 119.

15. Jack Goody, *The Domestication of the Savage Mind* (Cambridge, UK: Cambridge University Press, 1977), 37.

16. Ong, *Orality,* 178–79.

17. The Orthodox churches consider the Septuagint to be the inspired word of God, the differences from the Hebrew text being due to divine inspiration. F. F. Bruce, *The Canon of Scripture* (Downers Grove, IL: InterVarsity Press, 1988), 82.

18. "By the close of the second century...we can see the outlines of what may be described as the nucleus of the New Testament. Although the fringes of the emerging canon remained unsettled for generations, a high degree of unanimity concerning the greater part of the New Testament was attained among the very diverse and scattered congregations of believers not only throughout the Mediterranean world but also over an area extending from Britain to Mesopotamia." Metzger, *Canon of the New Testament*, 74. See also Gamble, "Canon of the New Testament," 201–43; Martin, *Feminist Question*, 118.

19. Brevard Childs, *Introduction to the Old Testament as Scripture* (Philadelphia: Fortress, 1979). See now his *Biblical Theology of the Old and New Testaments* (Minneapolis: Fortress, 1993), and the lengthy review of his work by M. O'Connor, *RSR* 21 (April 1995), 91–96. Instead of canonical criticism, the term "canon-contextual" criticism has been used. Childs is faulted by O'Connor for ignoring the role of the liturgy in the shaping and interpretation of the canon.

20. I, A, 4, 6.

21. Sanders, *Canon and Community,* passim.

22. Quoted in Joseph Jensen, OSB, "Inclusive Language in the Bible," *America* 171 (Nov. 5, 1994), 16.

23. Jensen, "Inclusive Language," 16.

24. Is the unity of the canon merely external (because the church said so), or is it an internal unity? The latter would have to deal with the great diversity in the Bible. Sanders finds in the Old Testament a unity in its monotheizing thrust and its bias in favor of the weak and dispossessed (*Canon and Community,* 51–56). The Christian canon finds its unity in the paschal mystery, Christ. The unity decided externally was based on a judgment of internal unity.

25. "The canon of the Bible is, among other things, an oppressive ideological institution, one that *prevents* [italics his] people from reading these diverse and ambiguous books or that so

controls the reading of these texts that people are in effect blinded and crippled by the canonical constraints." George Aichele, *The Control of Biblical Meaning: Canon as Semiotic Mechanism* (Harrisburg, PA: Trinity Press International, 2001), 226.

26. This ending of 1–2 Chronicles (36:22–23) is identical with beginning of Ezra 1:1–3a. Ezra-Nehemiah is the second part of the chronicler's work, following the author's historical sequence from the kings to the postexilic restoration. But later Ezra-Nehemiah was moved ahead of 1–2 Chronicles in order to sequence the books of Samuel and Kings. The result was that Chronicles appeared as a meditative reprise of the story of the Kings, with the exile. Since Chronicles would then have ended in verse 21 with the negative note about the land lying waste for seventy years, the beginning of Ezra was repeated as a positive conclusion to 1–2 Chronicles. In any case, the result is that the Hebrew Bible ends with a focus on the temple and the priesthood.

27. Under the Romans the priests and the temple authorities enjoyed a subordinate authority over the Jewish people. Is it any surprise that Jesus' claim to be the Messiah would threaten their authority and that his cleansing of the temple would lead them to seek his death?

28. J. W. Miller, *How the Bible Came to Be: Exploring the Narrative and Message* (Mahwah, NJ: Paulist Press, 2004).

13. The Spiritual Sense of Scripture

1. *IBC*, II.B.2.b.

2. Ignace de la Potterie, "Interpretation of Scripture in the Spirit in Which It Was Written," in René Latourelle, ed., *Vatican II Assessment and Perspective Twenty-Five Years Later*, vol. 1 (Mahwah NJ: Paulist Press, 1988), 242.

3. *The Jewish People and Their Scriptures in the Christian Bible*, 21. They quote Ambrose Autpert: "Not only fulfilled, but also transcended."

4. Frances M. Young, *Biblical Exegesis and the Formation of Christian Culture* (Peabody, MA: Hendrickson, 2001, rpt. of 1997 ed.), 153, 196, and passim.

5. *Philadelphians,* 8. Young, *Biblical Exegesis,* 16.

6. I employed the thematic method in *The Holy Spirit: Growth of a Biblical Tradition* (Peabody, MA: Hendrickson, 1976, rpt. 1993 and Eugene, OR: Wipf and Stock, 2006).

7. *IBC* II.B.3.a.

8. *IBC* II.B.3.b

9. *The Sensus Plenior of Sacred Scripture* (Baltimore: St. Mary's University, 1955).

10. "The Problems of the *Sensus Plenior,*" *Ephmerides Theologicae Lovanienses* 43 (1967), 460–69; "Hermeneutics," *New Jerome Biblical Commentary* (Englewood Cliffs, NJ: Prentice-Hall, 1990), 1157.

11. Recently Thomas Brodie has suggested that the narrative sequence in Luke (or "Proto-Luke") corresponds exactly to order and the content of the Elijah-Elisha narratives in the Pentateuch: *The Birthing of the New Testament: The Intertextual Development of the New Testament Writings* (Sheffield, UK: Sheffield Phoenix Press, 2004).

A Suggested Method of Study

The following method may be used for personal study or as an assignment in hermeneutics. Selections are limited to the Gospels of Matthew or Luke in order to facilitate study of source and redaction criticism, on the generally held assumption that these Gospels are dependent on Mark plus their own independent sources.

1. Select a passage from Matthew or Luke.

2. Using commentaries, articles, and other research tools, examine the text successively from the following viewpoints.

3. The World of the Text
   (If the readers or students know Greek and have been sufficiently introduced to textual criticism, they should first do the textual critical investigation.)
   a. Narrative criticism
   b. Rhetorical criticism
   c. Structural criticism

4. The World behind the Text
   a. Historical criticism of the text: Form Criticism
   b. Historical criticism of the events
   c. Redaction criticism
   d. Sociocultural Criticism

5. The World in Front of the Text
   a. Reader-response criticism
   b. Advocacy criticism: Select some cause or concern that might find support in this text.

    c. Pastoral application: Select some pastoral situation in which you might use this text (for example, a CCD or confirmation class, a high school religion class, an adult faith-sharing group, a prison ministry, hospital ministry, a homily for a parish Sunday liturgy, a children's liturgy, a youth group, a young adult group, a retreat, and so on) and explain how you would use the text in a way that would be meaningful to your audience.

6. The World around the Text
   (Remember that canonical criticism works with the text in its final form.)
       a. In what way does the rest of the individual work (Matthew or Luke) affect the meaning of this passage? (For example, by way of confirmation or tension, contextualization, balancing)
       b. In what way does the rest of the New Testament affect the meaning of this passage? Any tension noticeable? Or confirmation? Contextualization?
       c. What is the significance of the placement of this Gospel among the first books of the New Testament?